POLITICS AND SOCIETY IN WALES

The Information Age

TECHNOLOGY, LEARNING AND EXCLUSION IN WALES

By

NEIL SELWYN and STEPHEN GORARD

*Published on behalf of the Social Science Committee
of the Board of Celtic Studies of the University of Wales*

UNIVERSITY OF WALES PRESS
CARDIFF
2002

© Neil Selwyn and Stephen Gorard, 2002

British Library Cataloguing-in-Publication Data.
A catalogue record for this book is available from the British Library.

ISBN 0–7083–1708–1

The rights of Neil Selwyn and Stephen Gorard to be identified as joint authors of this work have been asserted by them in accordance with the Copyright, Designs and Patents Act 1988.

Typeset at University of Wales Press
Printed in Great Britain by Bookcraft Ltd, Midsomer Norton

Series Editor's Foreword

In the last fifty years or so the inhabitants of the advanced industrialized, or post-industrial, societies have gradually become more disillusioned with technology. Their belief that technological change was synonymous with human progress had been nurtured in the later stages of the nineteenth century and the first half of the twentieth century. The nuclear bombs that were dropped on Hiroshima and Nagasaki did a great deal to dent this faith but the idea persisted that, when it was put to *good* use, technology could solve a great many of our most intractable problems. Even thirty years ago, schoolchildren studying A-level geography were told that nuclear power would soon make the production of electricity so cheap that it would not be worth sending bills to electricity consumers. This makes A-level geography teachers sound a little foolish but this book shows that a similar degree of optimism was in evidence when commentators and policy-makers first began to contemplate the revolution in information and communication technology. It seems we have still not lost our faith in the magical effects of the technological fix. *The Information Age* shows that we simultaneously overestimate the reach of technological solutions and underestimate the complexity and intractability of the social problems we imagine new technology can solve.

This is the second volume in the Politics and Society in Wales Series. The first volume in the series, *New Governance – New Democracy?*, focused on emerging evidence of the shape of politics and government in post-devolution Wales. Like the first volume in the series, *The Information Age* is informed by a great deal of original research and has immediate relevance to debates about policy and policy-making. *The Information Age* also recalls the volume on devolution in that it is concerned with an extremely important change in the context within which public and private life in Wales is carried on, and it makes an early intervention in respect of a story which is far from finished. The two volumes are also similar in the sense that they grapple with a topic within which it is not always clear how much of the initiative for making change really lies with the people of Wales. It is particularly clear in the case of the relationship between information and communication technology (ICT) and education and training that many of the initiatives that affect Wales have not originated in Wales and, in any case, are better understood not as initiatives but as reactions, and sometimes belated reactions, to global events.

The whole world has now been made aware that the information age presents a new series of challenges. When they think about these issues, one question is often at the forefront of people's minds: how will their country be able to respond to the new opportunity to compete that the information age represents? A few small countries – Singapore maybe, Finland definitely – have had rather more cause to believe in this talk of opportunity, and to see the information age as a time when the scales can tip in favour of a small country. Yet when the inhabitants of other small countries (and some that are not so small) try to analyse what the information age may mean for them, they are apt to feel that they are at the mercy of forces which are far beyond their control and sometimes beyond their comprehension. They fear they will simply never have the resources or expertise that will allow them to take advantage of any of the new opportunities they are told are on offer.

The challenges that are described in this book are being faced by people across the world; indeed it is one of the characteristics of the information age that the degree of common experience between people from different countries is massively enlarged. In respect of education and training, for example, ICT further reduces people's dependency on local provision. This should not lead us to the conclusion that ICT is necessarily an equalizing force. The authors of *The Information Age* are deeply concerned about the *adverse* effects of ICT on social inequalities, especially those inequalities that persist within a society, and this is why their book bears the subtitle *Technology, Learning and Exclusion in Wales*. Neil Selwyn and Stephen Gorard remind us that great hopes have been expressed about the levelling effects of ICT (just as similar hopes have been invested in other technologies in the past). In particular, hopes have been expressed about the potential for ICT to address problems of social exclusion. The idea that the information age will be an inclusive one has certainly been a feature of the rhetoric of many governments. If, on the basis of their research, Selwyn and Gorard are sceptical about the scale and effectiveness of government responses to the challenge of the information age, they are deeply pessimistic about the chances of ICT leading to anything other then the reinforcement of existing patterns of inequalities.

Social divisions and inequalities were discussed in the first volume in the Politics and Society in Wales Series, but *The Information Age* begins a process of social scientific analysis and description of Welsh society that will be elaborated in later volumes. *The Information Age* begins this task by showing us a society which is characterized by inequality in prosperity and well-being. It shows us that Wales is not the sort of society in which all citizens can look forward to the information age with the same measure of hope and expectation. For all the dramatic changes that have taken place in Wales – the demise of traditional industries, the import of foreign investment, the feminization of the workforce, and devolution – a great deal remains to be done, in particular, in education and training.

For many people anxiety about education and training in Wales is underpinned by a desire to lift the low levels of productivity and prosperity which are signalled by stubbornly low levels of GDP per head. Selwyn and Gorard want us to remember that there is more to education and training than output per head and that the information age is not reducible to the 'digital economy'. It is a big mistake, and possibly counter-productive even in narrow economic terms, to think of education and training simply in terms of their economic pay-off. When it comes to the social changes that are needed to influence attitudes to learning which are not reducible to the calculation of economic benefit, it is possible that Wales has even regressed.

In *The Information Age* we learn that, in some important respects, the picture is still a depressing one. There are a few positive signs, but the authors are fully justified in making informed and constructive criticism the heart of their argument. It is not surprising that an appraisal of Welsh society involves constructive criticism of public policies and indeed public bodies. There are hard lessons to be learned here, especially about the limits of public policy. However hard they might be to attend to, these lessons have to be understood.

Ralph Fevre
Cardiff, November 2001

Contents

Figures and Tables

Preface

Newly devolved Wales is facing the challenge of developing an appropriate strategy for using information and communications technology (ICT) in this information age. As a small country, linked to a much larger neighbour within a globalized economy, some key questions come to the fore, such as:

• What does it mean for a small country to have a separate ICT policy?
• How can ICT be used purposefully to overcome the barriers of communication, time and space?
• How can ICT be used more purposefully to increase social inclusion and economic competitiveness in countries such as Wales?

The book examines such questions through a consideration of ICT in society, politics and economy, and in an extended study of its role in promoting knowledge and social inclusion. Crucially, and in light of research conducted by the authors in Wales, the book reveals some of the potential shortcomings of relying on technology alone to promote such knowledge and social inclusion.

Setting out to examine the information age is a potentially boundless task and in doing so we have attempted to strike a balance between discussing the future issues that countries such as Wales are having to face up to over the next decade, and taking a careful look at the realities of the information age for present-day Wales. As we argue throughout the book, the tendency to look only forward to what *may* happen as opposed to looking at what *is* actually happening is an underlying weakness of many contemporary discussions of technology and society. We have overtly set out to avoid this undesirable perspective by balancing our discussion of the many issues that the information age throws up with an empirical investigation of how ICT is beginning to be implemented in Wales in the public-policy setting of education and training. This focus on the rhetoric *and* reality of Wales in an information age allows us, we feel, to reach a more accurate and considered picture of what has quickly become an emotional and hyperbolic area of debate.

From this perspective the first section of this book takes a look at the wider issues entailed by the information age from the perspective of Wales, the UK as a whole and at a global level. Chapters 1–4, therefore, examine the problems and opportunities facing Wales in devising an appropriate strategy for using information and communications technology. They present alternative views of the relationship between society and technology, in a variety of public-policy settings.

The second part of the book then focuses on education and training as one of these public-policy areas, and it does so both because ICT policy is more mature in this area (and we can therefore assess its actual impact) and because in discussing education we need also to discuss many other areas of related policy, including the economy and social inclusion. Chapter 5 sets the scene for this extended case study by outlining the key issues for lifelong learning in Wales. Chapter 6 examines recent ICT-based initiatives for both school and post-compulsory phases in more detail. In particular, chapter 6 explains how the 'virtual education' movement is intended to improve participation in lifelong learning, benefiting Wales economically and combating social exclusion. Chapter 7 contains a brief account of our empirical sources and analytic techniques for the primary evidence presented in the remainder of the book.

Chapter 8 then goes on to report the findings of a large-scale study of patterns of participation in education and training. It shows how significant the problem is that virtual education schemes are setting out to tackle. A very large proportion of the population of Wales do not participate in education or training of any sort after leaving school, and this pattern is determined by long-term background factors and past experiences leading to relatively stable 'learner identities'. Chapter 9 presents an account of the setting-up of bodies, such as the University for Industry (Wales) and the Wales Digital College, intending to overcome these habits of non-participation by breaking down barriers such as travel, time and cost. The account is presented in the words of the key actors in this task. Chapter 10 presents evidence of the early take-up of these opportunities, and the quality of the learning experiences provided. Chapter 11 presents the stories of individual learners in a variety of ICT-related settings, including on-line tuition, drop-in centres and cyber-cafés. Chapter 12 draws together the conclusions from all three sections of the book, and presents some recommendations for the future of Wales in an information age.

The research described here was supported by the Spencer Foundation of the USA (SG#199900305) and by the Economic and Social Research Council (L123251041). We would like to thank all friends, colleagues and respondents who have helped with the study, including Ralph Fevre and John Furlong as well as Patrick White for his locating of numerous sources of information. Particular thanks are due to Gareth Rees who managed the study described in chapter 8 and Sara Williams who worked with us for a year, collecting and analysing information and sources of data as well as carrying out many of the interviews for the research described in chapter 11.

We would like to thank everyone who took part in the interviews for our study, and all at the Wales Digital College for their co-operation. It is taken as our starting assumption that everyone working on an ICT strategy for Wales is doing so with the best of intentions, and to the best of their ability. All case studies used herein are exemplars only, and are generally taken from the most successful or most prominent activities in this area. Any criticisms are made with the intention of seeking improvement and suggesting ways in which social, economic and educational problems do, and more crucially do not, have purely technological solutions.

List of Abbreviations

AM	Assembly Member
BBC	British Broadcasting Corporation
BT	British Telecom
CLAIT	Computer Literacy and Information Technology
DfEE	Department for Education and Employment (now DfES)
DfES	Department for Education and Skills
DTI	Department of Trade and Industry
DTV	digital television
ESRC	Economic and Social Research Council
ETAG	Education and Training Action Group
EU	European Union
FE	further education
FEU	Further Education Unit
GCSE	General Certificate of Secondary Education
GDP	gross domestic product
HE	higher education
HEI	higher education institution
HEFCW	Higher Education Funding Council Wales
ICT	Information and Communications Technology
IITF	Information Infrastructure Task Force (US)
ISDN	Integrated Services Digital Network
IT	information technology
ITEC	Information Technology and Enterprise Centre
LEA	local education authority
LIC	Library and Information Commission
MSC	Multimedia Super Corridor (Malaysia)
NASA	National Aeronautics and Space Administration (US)
NGfL	National Grid for Learning
NHS	National Health Service
NIACE	National Institute for Adult and Continuing Education
NII	National Information Infrastructure (US)
NOF	New Opportunities Fund
NVQ	National Vocational Qualification
OECD	Organisation for Economic Co-operation and Development
OHMCI	Office of Her Majesty's' Chief Inspector for schools
OU	Open University
PC	personal computer
RSA	Royal Society of Arts
S4C	Sianel Pedwar Cymru (the Welsh Channel 4)
SME	small and medium-sized enterprises
TES	*Times Educational Supplement*
UfI	University for Industry
WDA	Welsh Development Agency
WDC	Wales Digital College
WEA	Workers' Educational Association
WIS	Wales Information Society
WWW	World-wide Web
YMCA	Young Mens' Christian Association
YTS	Youth Training Scheme

1

Thinking about Wales in an Information Age

Machines were invented
To cope, but they also were limited
By our expectations. Men stared
With a sort of growing resentment
At a life that was ubiquitous and
Unseizable.
(R. S. Thomas, 'Remedies', 1972)

A belief in the apparently limitless potential of technology – curtailed only by the mindset of those who use it – is as pertinent to the Wales of today as it was in the post-war Wales of R. S. Thomas. Of course, the fortunes of Wales have been long intertwined with technology. From Trevithick to Marconi, the development and exploitation of technology has been at the core of Welsh economic and social life. Yet, over the last decades of the twentieth century and during the first years of the twenty-first, this national relationship with technology has assumed a heightened significance in the form of new information and communication technologies. We are now, according to many, living in a world of e-commerce and e-government, cyberspace and cyborgs. The worlds of business and industry are driven by 'clicks and mortar' institutions and 'dot.com millionaires', whilst concerns over 'digital divides' look set to dominate the social agendas of countries, large and small, around the world. The National Assembly for Wales was quick to set out its aim to produce a *'betterwales.com'* and *'Cymru Ar-lein'*. We are frequently reminded that Wales is experiencing a twenty-first-century 'information revolution' every bit as significant as the industrial revolution two centuries before. For many the present decade is seen as *the* pivotal period in the ongoing (re)construction of countries such as Wales as confident and competitive 'e-nations'.

Such confidence is rooted in a series of rapid technological developments over the last fifty years. The progression from the mainframe computers of the 1950s to the emergence of the micro-computers of the 1970s led to much excitement over the 'micro-electronics revolution' and its emphasis on the miniaturization and increased processing capacities of new micro-chip-based information technologies. Similarly, the rise of tele-communications networks and the extension of 'wireless' communications into worldwide digital networks prompted visions of a 'global village' and the compression of distance and time in information storage and com-munications. Latterly, from the 1990s onwards, the widespread emergence of multimedia applications and the Internet has heralded a new tech-nological climate, where the convergence of information processing and telecommunications technologies into 'information and communications technology' has prompted many commentators to announce the final dawning of the information age.

Yet beyond the enthusiastic proclamations of futurologists, the some-times superficial interest of politicians and, of course, those who stand to gain financially, what *does* the concept of the information age actually mean for countries such as Wales? More importantly, how are the perceived demands of the information age beginning to impact on Wales and those who live there? In some areas of Wales unemployment has remained at above 25 per cent for the last two decades, and around a third of the population has not engaged in any form of education or training since leaving school. Facts such as these put popular media concerns over the fluctuating prices of 'dot.com' shares and new generations of mobile telecommunications into stark perspective. As with much social change, it is often easy to be seduced by the rhetoric of the information age debate, whilst ignoring the realities it tends to obscure.

Thus, in setting out we would do well to start with a note of caution, rather than get swept along on a tide of technophilia. We must not lose sight of the more fundamental questions that need to be asked of the apparent restructuring of society around technology, communications and information. Indeed, for many in Wales at the moment, the only questions being asked of the information age are framed within the overall inevit-ability of impending changes and the associated imperative to seize its bountiful opportunities. As these two breathless examples demonstrate, Wales in an information age is, for some, only a matter of 'when' not 'how' or 'why':

> The on-line, digital world offers huge and highly legitimate opportunities. You don't need to spend a fortune to take advantage. With [Wales's] geography and cultural mix if we haven't already started, it is the thing that we should do next. (Finch, 1998: 17)

> The information revolution already affects the way we live, work and play in Wales. It will continue to do so. That is inevitable. (Rowe-Beddoe, 1999: 3)

From one perspective such responses are entirely understandable given the fast-changing, technology-dominated era that we are living in. For some, a love affair with new information and communication technologies has been inevitable, given the air of blue-skies optimism that has accompanied information technology since its inception. As soon as mainframe computers began to be used outside the research laboratories and military applications, and were introduced into the public domain, an ensuing 'megahype' was quickly propagated by 'data merchants' with an intrinsic interest in selling information technology to society (Roszak, 1995). Indeed, the computer has been long heralded as the epitome of 'progress', following on from a long-held belief in technologically induced progress which can be traced back to the Enlightenment tradition (Marx, 1987). Now, the rapid technical development of information and communication technologies leaves many people convinced of their centrality to society's lurch into the twenty-first century. Thus, society's trust in ICT continues to be couched in very modernist terms. As Kitchen (1998: 57) concludes: 'The basic tenet is that we will use technology to progress and that potentialities will be realised simply because they are possible.'

QUESTIONING THE 'TECHNICAL FIX'

Much of what has been written and said about ICT therefore adheres to a viewpoint where virtually all of society's problems, be they economic, political, social or ethical, are subject to a 'technical fix' (Volti, 1992). 'Seizing the assumed promise of the "micro-electronics revolution" we are proffered a technological paradise against which our apprehensions and fears seem absurd. No matter how entrenched and worrisome, IT, adroitly managed and rapidly accepted, is the solution' (Robins and Webster, 1989: 30). Societal trust in the technological fix has been well established (Weinberg, 1966), in fields ranging from medicine to the environment, and has increased considerably since the advent of computerized technology. Indeed, as Postman (1992) contends, the overriding 'message' of new technologies is that the most serious problems that confront society require technical solutions through fast access to information that is otherwise unavailable.

Questioning the value and worth of ICT has been generally frowned upon. For example, at the beginning of the 1970s, the computer scientist Joseph Weizenbaum published a short piece in the academic journal *Science* in which he questioned the tendency of computer scientists to ignore the 'side-effects' of technology (Weizenbaum, 1972a). Response to his socially focused perspective was swift and damning:

Computers are having a substantial impact on society generally, and not on a tiny, affluent fraction of society, as Weizenbaum would have us believe. There is considerable evidence of this from many quarters (health care, education, banking and so forth). It is also clear that this impact is growing and is becoming increasingly uniform in all walks of life. As far as society as a whole is concerned, the primary effects of computer technology are more important than their side effects. It is only the more philosophically inclined who find the potential side effects more important ... It takes a rare person to spend more than a few hours pondering the philosophical implications of that proposition. (Coles, 1972: 561)

The tone of such responses to a more questioning stance on technology continues to be as dismissive as in the example above; implying a lack of understanding or misconception of technology on the part of the dissenters. However, as Weizenbaum (1972b) retorted at the time, it is possible that such criticism merely 'documents the tragedy' to which he was attempting to call attention – a deep-rooted lack of self-analysis among the ICT community and irreversible faith in technological 'progress'.

Given this 'orthodoxy of optimism', many commentators when approaching the role of ICT in society ultimately conform to one of the two dominant paradigms that beset discussions about technology: either technological or social determinism. On the one hand many political and academic commentators see ICTs as an inevitable consequence of technological development and change, adhering to an overtly *technological determinist* view of technology and society. As Woolgar (1996: 88) details, technological determinism is 'the belief that new technology emerges as an extrapolation of previous technologies, with the characteristics of a technology hav[ing] a direct impact on social arrangements'. This view sees technology as guiding and shaping society with its own logic, as an influence autonomous to social forces. Thus, technology is seen as a driving force of society: as technology changes so society follows. Although it is difficult to find anyone actively aligning themselves with technological determinism such discourse has been central in post-war thinking about technology in the Western world from Herbert Marcuse to Marshall McLuhan. As we will soon see, a form of technological determinism has also been prominent in much post-industrial discourse and thinking about the information age.

Indeed, a brief reconsideration of some of the rhetoric discussed earlier reveals a technologically determinist influence in the discourse surrounding Wales in an information age. For example, technology can be presented unproblematically as having a transformatory effect on the Welsh economy. In this way ICTs will revolutionize how workers are (re)trained, and improve productivity and competitiveness; the Internet will have a transforming impact on the nature of Welsh business and trading. The repeated theme behind such proclamations could not be clearer: information and communications technology is a natural yet transformatory stage in the progression of Welsh business and industry. This fits neatly into the traditional technological determinist view of such change as inevitable, with necessary 'impacts' upon society, thus making it an effective vehicle for achieving organizational 'progress' (Williams and Edge, 1996).

This determinist language is also apparent in the common anthropomorphism of ICT. A timely example of this is the Internet, which is after all an inanimate instrument, when it is given animate capabilities and therefore assigned an agency beyond its means. Thus, to give one example, the Internet and other telecommunications technology are often popularly portrayed as being capable of 'bringing remote Internet users into Wales'. But does the Internet as an inanimate technology really have the capability of 'bringing' the 'experience' of Wales to people around the world, or is this a means of obscuring the real actors – in this case the telecommunications industry? Expanding this line of argument, the anthropomorphism of assigning agency to technologies such as the Internet primarily serves to obscure the vested interests that underlie the successful (and profitable) implementation of the technology.

A similarly pervasive societal discourse is that of ICT as 'just a tool', a more or less neutral means to an economic, political or social end. This opposite view of the determinist relationship between society and technology asserts that it is society that shapes and influences technology. Thus *social determinism* posits that technology is a neutral instrument that can be moulded and used for various purposes. In this approach, technologies merely appear in response to society's demands and the interests of the market; what society wants society will get. As Wise (1997) asserts, from such a social determinist view technology is contingent on interpretation and interpretative frameworks. The properties of objects are not inherent in the objects themselves but conferred on objects by social consensus and definition. Thus society shapes technology (as opposed to the technological deterministic view of technology shaping society).

This belief is strongly reflected in the overt presentation of ICT as 'just a tool'. For example, ICTs are currently portrayed as appearing in response to the educational needs and demands of teachers and learners. Christopher Evans's famous vision of the 'Mighty Micro' at the end of the 1970s saw billions of pocket teaching-computers sweeping through education in response to consumer demand. Today educationalists are also keen to position the Internet firmly as a market response to real educational demands. Education can now have what it is 'keen to embrace'. Yet one can argue that the social determinist treatment of ICT is equally as constricting as the technological determinist discourse. As Bromley (1997: 54) asserts, to view ICT in purely instrumentalist terms is to overestimate its flexibility and neutrality:

> Recognising the significance of the context of use, the responsiveness of technologies to social dynamics, is a useful insight, but technologies are not infinitely malleable; they cannot be put to absolutely any end at will, and certainly not with equal ease.

Similarly, as Winner (1980) argues, although social determinism acts as an antidote to 'naïve' technological determinism it is itself flawed in assuming that the technologies themselves are of little importance. In short, social determinism fails to recognize that technological artefacts are imbued with politics in their own right. To view new ICTs as neutral tools arising from societal demand may be to misread the social and cultural significance of the technology itself.

This history of 'misreading' technology and society acts as a warning at the start of this book. There is clearly a pressing need to step beyond the limitations of previous analyses of ICT if we are to gain a deeper understanding of countries like Wales in an information age. We need to be aware of the social, cultural, political, economic and technological aspects of ICT – the 'soft' as well as the 'hard' concerns. Echoing Qvortrup's (1984: 7) argument that such questions 'cannot be properly understood if we persist in treating technology and society as two independent entities', this book strives to move beyond the view that technology is distinct from society in either its cause or its effect. Instead, in this book we make a conscious effort to move away from positions of either 'technophilia' or 'techno-neutralism' towards a perspective that avoids drawing a clear technology/society distinction, and focuses on the social contexts where technologies and policies are developed, and the ones where they are used. Such a 'questioning' approach is not to be wilfully obtrusive, but to attempt to ask our questions from a more objective social-scientific perspective.

Having sketched out a theoretical position, we must finally move on to explore the rather nebulous concept at the heart of this book – the much talked about but less often defined 'information age'.

DEFINING THE INFORMATION AGE

From the 1970s onwards, society's love affair with the 'computer revolution' has evolved steadily; firstly into a wider notion of an 'information revolution' which has then been gradually refined into present notions of an 'information society' and 'information age'. Although this semantic refinement clearly signals that such concepts are not purely concerned with technology, what does the shift in focus away from technology *per se* to these wider notions actually refer to? In other words, what factors are being referred to within the 'information age' label?

At the most visible level of political slogan and soundbite, the notion of the information age appears relatively straightforward. As the Blair administration stated a year after the Labour Party's election to government in 1997:

> Information is the key to the modern age. The new age of information offers possibilities for the future limited only by the boundaries of our imaginations. The potential of the new electronic networks is breathtaking – the prospect of change as widespread and fundamental as the agricultural and industrial revolutions of earlier eras. (Blair, foreword to Central Office of Information, 1998)

Such definitions are deliberately vague, yet with a *gravitas* that almost precludes any further questioning of what the information age is, above and beyond that it refers to a 'widespread' and 'fundamental' change based on electronic networking and other such technological change. In this way the notion of the information age functions mainly as a rallying call for action and intervention in the face of fundamental but indeterminate societal change. As Miles (1996: 51) concludes:

> The future is therefore indeterminate in many ways. Policies to influence future directions need to recognise that ICTs allow for new rules of the game in all areas of economic activity and that organisations of all types need to innovate and redefine their objectives in this context. Not all developments will involve the new technologies, but often they will be central. Standing still is rarely an option. Although beleaguered services and individuals may resent being told about the need to adapt, a sea change is taking place – hence the importance of elucidating and understanding competing views of the information society.

So, for many politicians and commentators, this notion of the information age is so straightforward that its definition can be treated as implicit and already understood by all. Considerable surprise was expressed at the Welsh Development Agency's finding in 1996 that only 12 per cent of the Welsh population 'fully understood' what the information age was; with the vast majority of respondents only able to make vague references to computers, information technology or the Internet. Yet, rather than revealing the ignorance of the Welsh population as was claimed at the time, perhaps this finding merely underlines the complexity of the issues that the concept of the information age refers to. Moreover, it could be seen to point to the foolhardiness of attempting to define the information age away in a couple of bland sentences or soundbites. So, rather than happily adhere to such 'non-definitions' as offered above, the remainder of this chapter will attempt to 'unpack' more carefully the many issues underlying the discourse of the information age and information society and, therefore, set out the broad context for this book.

EMERGENCE OF THE INFORMATION AGE DISCOURSE: FROM DANIEL BELL TO MANUEL CASTELLS

As with many widely used and abused concepts, the idea of the 'information society' originated from diverse sources, most notably social and economic forecasting, governmental policy formation and even speculative 'futurology'. Indeed, the concept of the 'information society' first came to the attention of many through the work of futurologists such as Alvin Toffler, Tom Stonier and others. Thus, throughout the Cold War-fixated and economic-crisis-ridden 1970s and 1980s various optimistic visions of technology-led new eras became best-sellers – a trend repeated by a similar rash of writings in the Internet-obsessed 1990s. Whilst it is easy to dismiss such accounts of these new technology-based societies as fanciful and popularist, work such as Alvin Toffler's *The Third Wave* certainly introduced many of the key aspects of the information age discourse to a wider audience. For example, via his discussion of 'techno-rebels' and 'telecommuters', the rise of the 'prosumer' and the 'crack-up of the nation', Toffler highlighted many issues currently seen as being at the heart of the contemporary information age debate. Similarly, Christopher Evans's *The Mighty Micro* did much in the UK to bring public attention to the 'computer revolution' and the perceived shift 'from the amplification and emancipation of the power of muscles to the amplification and emancipation of the power of the brain' (Evans, 1979: 13). Supported by other authors such as Naisbett, Stonier and Martin the beginning of the Thatcher/Reagan era in the West was therefore awash with visions of more affluent, prosperous and flexible information-led societies. These were soon reinforced by a range of highly influential social forecasts from the USA and Europe, such as those of Masuda (1981) and Nora and Minc (1980).

A decade later this was repackaged in books by authors such as Ester Dyson, Bill Gates and Nicholas Negroponte, with Negroponte even arguing for the shift into a highly networked and intensely individualized 'post-information age'. The Microsoft supremo and occasional futurologist Bill Gates (1995: 284) perhaps summed up these information age visions most succinctly when he argued that ICT will

> enhance our leisure time and enrich our culture by expanding the distribution of information. It will help relieve pressures on urban areas by enabling people to work from home or remote-site offices. It will relieve pressures on natural resources because increasing numbers of products will take the form of bits rather than manufactured goods. It will give us more control over our lives, enabling us to tailor our experiences and the products we use to our interests. Citizens of the Information Society will enjoy new opportunities for productivity, learning and entertainment. Countries that move boldly and in concert with each other will enjoy economic rewards. Whole new markets will emerge and a myriad new opportunities for employment will be created.

Recently, such popularist visions have been both empirically examined and theoretically transformed in the writings of Manuel Castells who, throughout the 1980s and 1990s, developed his concept of the 'Network Society'; culminating in his three-volume *Information Age* series (Castells, 1996, 1997, 1998). For Castells, one of the key features of the information society is the 'networking logic of its basic structure' (1996: 21), brought about by developments in IT, the restructuring of capitalism and statism in the 1980s, as well as the rise of cultural-social movements such as feminism and ecologism. Thus, for Castells:

> dominant functions and processes in the information age are increasingly organised around networks. Networks constitute the new social morphology of our societies and the diffusion of networking logic substantially modifies the operation and outcomes in the processes of production, experience, power and culture. While the networking form of social organisation has existed in other times and spaces, the new information technology paradigm provides the basis for its pervasive expansion throughout the entire social structure. (1996: 469)

According to Castells, the Network Society is evident in contemporary patterns of economic activity depending ultimately on the dynamics of the global economy, the 'network enterprise' of modern multinational corporations, the networking of labour in the form of 'flexi-workers' as well as 'global' social movements such as the recent anti-capitalist campaigns in Seattle, London and Sydney. Like other authors, Castells also points towards the redefinition of time and space – arguing that the network society is organized around 'timeless time' and an emphasis on the 'space of flows' (i.e. the movement of information or money) rather than the space of places (i.e. their original location). However, despite the general nature of this analysis Castells is careful to stress the non-homogeneity of the information age, with different societies displaying different reactions to global processes:

> The implicit logic of the Network Society appears to end history, by enclosing it into the circularity of recurrent patterns of flows. Yet, as with any other social form, in fact it opens up a new realm of contradiction and conflict, as people around the world refuse to become shadows of global flows and project their dreams, and sometimes their nightmares, into the light of new history making. (Castells, 1999: 410)

Many, if not all, of these accounts can be traced back to the emergence, during the late 1960s and early 1970s, of the notion of post-industrialization, as popularized by authors such as Alain Touraine (1969) and Daniel Bell (1973). Here Bell, Touraine and others, mapped society's shift from an agrarian to an industrial basis, with a subsequent economic shift from land to manufacturing, followed by a modern-day shift from an industrial to a post-industrial society. In this, provision of services, the rise of professional, scientific and technical groups and, most importantly, information technology were seen as being new 'axial principles'. So, for Post-Industrialists, as in all the accounts that we have just discussed, the information age can be characterized as involving the commodification of information and growth of telecommunications technology and the resulting new social framework. This, in turn, has fundamental implications for 'the way economic and social exchanges are conducted, the way knowledge is created and retrieved, and the character of work and occupations' (D. Bell, 1973: 14).

APPROACHING THE INFORMATION AGE AS PROBLEMATIC

Within all the foregoing accounts of the information age, economic, social and cultural changes are seen as being driven by, or at least shaped around, the ongoing development of information and communications technology. As D. Bell (1980) continues, in the post-industrial information society, tele-communications and computers are therefore 'decisive for the way economic and social exchanges are conducted, the way knowledge is created and retrieved, and the character of work and organisations in which men are engaged'. Indeed, the notion of the computer acting as the catalyst of the information revolution just as the steam engine acted as the catalyst of the industrial revolution is regularly used by proponents of the information age thesis. Yet even at this early stage of our analysis the centrality of technological 'progress' in such discourse should warn us again of the technological determinism implicit in many of these accounts of the information age. As Robins and Webster (1999: 89) contend, 'in this cocktail of scientific aspiration and commercial hype, there are a number of implicit but significant assumptions' that need to be challenged within any analysis of a country like Wales in an information age. In particular, to what extent does the information age mark a *new* historical era of freedom and abundance as opposed to the constraints and scarcity of previous eras? Is the shift from industrial to post-industrial societies as marked as we are being led to believe and, most importantly, are such changes as socially beneficial as we are being told? In other words, to what extent is the information age a fundamental transformation or merely 'more of the same'?

In positing such questions, we must be careful not to reject the value of such accounts of the information age outright. Despite the problems that there may be with the accounts of Bell, Toffler and Castells, all of their work is based on significant changes in contemporary society and, as such, outlines major areas of concern for any social scientist. Thus, as Lyon (1996) reasons, it makes sense at least to treat the notion of the information age as 'problematic', i.e. as a useful means of highlighting clusters of issues for present investigation rather than a foolproof blueprint for the future of Wales. We can use the idea of an information age to point us towards salient areas of questioning. We have identified four broad strands of the information age debate with which to conclude this introductory discussion: the economic, political, cultural and social aspects of the information age.

One of the most widely discussed areas of the economic change entailed in the information age is the apparent restructuring of paid work and official organized production and services. For example, ICT has been seen by many as assisting the expansion of the service sector with an associated shift in patterns of employment – away from the traditional 'nine to five, job for life' towards the individualization of working patterns and the rise of 'flexi-workers' and careership. In particular, much has been made of the rise of 'information' (and latterly 'knowledge') workers and the associated growth of the information sector. Economic and educational policies relating to the information age have often been justified by notions such as '60 per cent of all new jobs requiring advanced ICT skills' (US Department of Commerce, 1998). Moreover, as well as the rising importance of the information sector, there is also seen to be the increased 'informization' of all work – be it in the primary, secondary or tertiary sectors of production. Castells (1999) talks of 'information agriculture' and 'informational manufacturing' where such industries are relying, more than ever, on using technology to process information and knowledge. The message is clear: an information age economy requires an information-skilled workforce in order to succeed.

The information age is characterized for many authors by the rising importance of information and knowledge as key sources of power and competitiveness for individual countries and the increasingly powerful transnational corporations in the 'global knowledge economy'. Of course, as Castells (1996) reasons, an 'information society' has been prevalent since medieval Europe's cultural structuring around Scholasticism. However, the present information age discourse refers specifically to a notion of 'informational society'; in other words, 'a specific form of social organisation in which information generation, processing and transmission become the fundamental sources of productivity and power, because of new technological conditions emerging in this historical period' (Castells, 1996: 21).

From Castells's perspective of the Network Society, it is the global transmission of information that is at the heart of countries' prosperity and competitiveness in the information age. Indeed, although economic activity is apparently concentrated at a regional or even local level, its fate ultimately depends on global consequences:

> Most economic activity in the world, and most employment are not only national but regional or local. But, except for subsistence economies, the fate of these activities, and of their jobs, depends ultimately on the dynamics of the global economy, to which they are connected through networks and markets. Indeed, if labour tends to be local, capital is by and large globalised – not a small detail in a capitalist economy. This globalisation has developed as a fully fledged system in only the last two decades, on the basis of information/ communications technologies that were not previously available. (Castells, 1999: 400)

Despite the tendency for many commentators to focus on the economic aspects of the information age, some have also recognized political implications. For example, to continue the global economic theme previously discussed, the national sovereignty of individual countries in the light of large transnational corporations is increasingly questionable; especially in terms of influencing or setting economic agendas. The potential clash between governmental and non-government actors is also reflected in the perceived blurring of boundaries between public and private activities that information and communications technology is seen to bring about. For example, the private provision of Internet-based education or health-care services looks set to grow, with 'traditional' public education provision now only one of many sources available to parents and learners. The ICT-based provision of public services is seen as vital to the continuation of governmental public welfare programmes.

On the other hand, some commentators see ICTs as leading to *new* forms of politics and political participation – as illustrated in ongoing debates over the emergence of 'cyber-democracy' and 'e-government'. In theory, it is argued, the instantaneous and interactive nature of ICT can lead to a more responsive and participatory form of politics – effectively allowing citizens new levels of contact and interaction with politicians and governmental bodies. Indeed, the notion of a democratic political community has been adopted with vigour by both politicians and technological enthusiasts – keen on recreating an electronic *agora* harking back to classical notions of the Greek democratic state (Rheingold, 1994). Similarly, Castells (1999) points to the media becoming the essential 'space of politics' in the information age.

Finally, although often underplayed, some social aspects of the information age are also beginning to be seen as important by politicians and commentators. In particular, issues of inequalities of access to both technology and information have prompted concern about emerging 'digital divides' both between countries and across particular social groups. Concerns about information inequalities between developed and developing nations have been augmented by issues of inequalities in terms of gender, race, ethnicity, age and socio-economic status. As Castells (1999: 403) concludes, 'The information age does not have to be the age of stepped-up inequality, polarisation and social exclusion. But for the moment it is.'

Questions concerning who is 'connected' to information and technology have come to prominence over the last five years and formed a third, but so far relatively undeveloped, element to the information age agenda; especially in industrialized 'technology-advanced' countries such as the USA and UK. It is this theme that forms the basis for the extended study in the later parts of this book.

KEY QUESTIONS

All these points lead us neatly into framing the key questions that should be asked of the information age. As we have seen, perhaps only by questioning the very notion of the information age can we begin to uncover the economic, political, cultural and social issues that underpin the fortunes of Wales at the beginning of the twenty-first century. Through rejecting an account based on simple faith in technological progress inevitably shaping societies, more questions than answers come to the fore. For example, to what extent are Wales's economic fortunes dependent on the 'information sector'? What actual demand is there for 'information workers' and what do such jobs actually entail? What is the purpose, function and content of 'information work'? Are ICTs leading to the expansion and extension of public services to all social groups? Are ICTs contributing to a democratization or marginalization of public participation in political processes? What effect is technology-based economic activity having on the sovereignty of both local and national governments? How is access to technology patterned according to individual factors such as age, gender, class, geography (both in terms of distance and terrain) and ethnicity, and, most importantly, how are different social groups then able to make use of this access?

Most crucially, we need to examine the revolutionary nature of the information age: how 'new' and 'different' are these changes?

> To what extent does ICT usher us into a new kind of society? And at this point a further query is highlighted: what is the social *meaning* of the 'information society'? Is it better understood as a kind of 'myth' or 'utopia' than the social 'forecast' it is more frequently taken to be? (Lyon, 1996: 67)

With this in mind, the next chapter explores the challenges of the information age from a more specifically Welsh perspective. What relevance do all the debates, discussions and theorization highlighted in this chapter have for a recently devolved 'stateless' nation in the north-west corner of Europe?

2

Information Age Issues for Wales

INTRODUCTION

The sheer scope of the foregoing descriptions of the information age makes for alarming reading when considering the position of Wales in the emerging global information order. With many commentators conceding that the efforts of even economically powerful countries such as the USA can have only limited influence on the relentless march of global capital flows, what hope can there be for smaller nations in shaping their own destinies in the information age? Yet, approaching the information age as problematic has moved us away from viewing the information age in purely global economic terms as if the social, cultural and political aspects of life have suddenly ceased to exist. We should be reminded of the continued importance of individual nations in, if not shaping their own destiny, then at least creating their own luck with regard to policy formation in the information age. After all, the increasing importance of global issues can be seen as heightening the importance of the remaining local factors in mediating the decidedly non-homogeneous impact of ICTs on society. It is from this perspective that we outline information age issues for Wales in this chapter.

Certainly, we are not alone in adopting this viewpoint. A bullish belief in the ability of Wales to stand alone in the information age has been much in evidence among Welsh policy-makers and the wider business community, at least in recognizing the present opportunities to shape actively rather than acquiesce passively in the 'information revolution':

> The nature of [the information revolution], and the extent to which we benefit both economically and socially from the new possibilities rather than being simply led by them is a vital issue – in other words will information and communication technologies become our servant or our master? The answer lies within our control here in Wales. (Rowe-Beddoe, 1999: 3)

> The resilience of the Welsh people should never be underestimated. We led the first industrial revolution and we can do it again. (Morgan, 2001: 6)

Such sentiment is laudable, but reveals little about the specific questions that the information age throws up for Wales – let alone what the possible answers may be. So what are the specific issues underlying such 'fighting talk'? This chapter contextualizes information age issues from a local Welsh perspective and maps out Wales's distinctive elements and the corresponding issues that ICT is seen as raising, in particular Welsh geography, national and cultural identity, sense of community, language and economy.

ISSUES OF GEOGRAPHY

Although it may appear perverse to commence our analysis of information age issues with the decidedly non-technological area of geography, Wales is a country strongly defined by its space and terrain. Indeed, one of the fundamental reasons why we should be concerned with *Wales* in an information age as opposed to the United Kingdom (or even Europe), centres on the unique geography of Wales.

Although Wales covers only one-twelfth of the United Kingdom by land area, it is a country of stark contrast between the predominantly rural areas of mid-Wales, the north-west and west on the one hand and the industrialized north- and south-east which contains the bulk of the population (Welsh Office, 1999). A broad mountainous spine runs up the country from the Brecon Beacons in the south to Snowdonia in the north, with about a quarter of the land being over 300 metres above sea level. Outside the largest urban areas of Newport, Cardiff and Swansea in the south and Wrexham in the north-east, much of Wales is picturesque yet remote. Some 20 per cent of the land area is covered by the three National Parks of Snowdonia, Brecon Beacons and the Pembrokeshire Coast alongside several other areas of outstanding natural beauty such as the Gower peninsula and Anglesey Heritage Coast. A total of 77.9 per cent of Wales is given over to agriculture, the highest proportion in the European Union. Moreover, although Wales is also much smaller in area than England, its population density is minimal by comparison; currently standing at an average density of 141 people per square kilometre – only about half the UK average. The least densely populated local authority in England is Northumberland and even that is three times as densely populated as Powys in Wales. The most densely populated local authority in England, Kensington, is over twelve times as dense as Cardiff and the Vale of Glamorgan. This low population density, the isolation of the more densely populated areas north and south, and the difficult terrain to traverse in between are reinforced by a lack of transport infrastructure in most areas.

The geographic constraints of Wales have therefore prompted many to seize upon information and communications technology as potentially transforming the country beyond its current physical limitations (and presumably more cheaply than actually building roads and rail lines running north to south for example). In particular, the argument of ICT rendering geography irrelevant has a particular resonance in a country as disparate as Wales. In overcoming geographical barriers of proximity and distance, the Internet has been seen as especially relevant to the rural areas of Wales, potentially overcoming and revitalizing the country's traditionally limited geographic and physical infrastructure:

> Such infrastructure is thus seen as a hindrance to, even the cause of, the fragmented culture that is Wales. But whereas newspaper distribution follows road and rail routes (and the vast majority of newspapers consumed in Wales are produced in England), with the Internet such physical links become irrelevant. (Mackay and Powell, 1997: 204)

From an international perspective, telecommunications technology can also be seen as having the potential to convert Wales from being a peripheral nation to one at the heart of both the United Kingdom and Europe. Again, drawing on the 'decentralizing' rhetoric of ICT, Osmond reasons that through new information technologies distance will no longer be a drawback for a small territory on the north-west corner of the European Union:

> One undoubted beneficial consequence of the Information Society for Wales is its potential for abolishing differences between centre and periphery. The so-called information superhighway is the global infrastructure in which distance is no drawback to economic performance . . . This has great implications for a territory like Wales, which in the past has often been regarded as peripheral to mainstream British and European developments. (Osmond, 1999: 5)

Such arguments are powerful and, as we shall see, have already proved persuasive in stimulating public and private activity in Wales. Yet, to subscribe fully to this 'death of geography' thesis is to overlook the remaining potential importance of the local in the information age. Indeed, the unique geography of Wales is recognized by many commentators as providing a fundamental challenge, as well as an opportunity, to the transformation of Wales into an ICT-based nation.

First and foremost is the problem of constructing a high-quality nationwide ICT infrastructure. Despite the National Assembly for Wales's (2000: 14) claim that 'we have more than 500,000 km of optical fibres installed in

Wales on which to build a first-class broadband telecommunications infrastructure', the geography of Wales is recognized as providing a significant barrier to the *full* 'wiring up' of the country. With the laying of telecommunications cabling in the south-east corner of Wales not having progressed much further north than Pontypridd, and the mountainous terrain of parts of the rest of the country making even digital transmissions difficult, the idea of a 'first-class broadband telecommunications infrastructure' for the whole country appears optimistic. As Courtney and Gibson (1999) contend, it is rural Wales which looks set to lose out here. Although most of rural Wales is served by digital telephone exchanges they do not support the basic data networking services such as Integrated Services Digital Network (ISDN) seen as providing the backbone of modern telecommunications services. Moreover, even when rural customers do enjoy full digital connections the distance between the individual user and the digital telephone exchange remains a crucial mediating factor in determining the quality of connection which degrades with distance – a very real problem for much of dispersed rural Wales.

Similar discrepancies occur with regard to the coverage of mobile wireless communication in Wales, with the mountainous terrain and widely dispersed population leaving large parts of Wales uneconomic for mobile network companies to service. In particular, rural parts of mid, west and north Wales have consistently endured relatively poor levels of coverage. As these areas catch up, the cutting-edge technology will have changed again. Thus, for many residents in Wales access to quality connections to telecommunications networks remains an 'accident of location' rather than choice (Courtney and Gibson, 1999), leaving the issue of geography and rural isolation as important to Wales in the information age as it has ever been: 'The A55 is likely to lead to nowhere on the "information superhighway" and most of rural Wales is unlikely to be cabled up. The reason – the cost of cabling rural consumers is prohibitive' (Williams, 1996: 27).

The first fundamental issue for Wales in an information age is thus an age-old one: harnessing and overcoming the land. Can Wales overcome traditional geographical constraints via ICT or are, as Osmond (1999: 7) admits, 'the old patterns associated with rail and road communications in danger of re-asserting themselves' yet again?

ISSUES OF NATIONAL AND CULTURAL IDENTITY

If the use of ICT looks set to be greatly affected by (and potentially have a great effect on) the geography of Wales then the same can also be said of the sense of Welsh cultural and national identity. Wales has enjoyed a limited cultural resurgence over the last ten years, apparent in the rising worldwide profile of Welsh popular culture in the media and arts. The legacy of the (albeit London and Cardiff media-manufactured) 'Cool Cymru' image during the late 1990s still endures – fanned by cultural confidence and the success of Welsh performing arts. The present-day images of internationally successful Welsh bands such as the Manic Street Preachers and the Super Furry Animals as well as Hollywood stars such as Catherine Zeta Jones and Anthony Hopkins sit in stark contrast to the preceding decades. Wales was seen by some to be culturally bereft of a coherent national identity beyond images of daffodils, a national rugby team, and the grim realities of work in the coal and steel industries. As Williams reflected just before the rise of 'Cool Cymru' in mainstream UK culture:

> There are no distinctive images which come readily to mind to represent Wales today – except of course the icons and symbols of the past. If there is to be a present in Wales then cultural producers must increasingly address the meaning of 'Welshness' in its own terms, rather than seeking an artificial model for others. (Williams, 1997: 10)

New technologies such as the Internet are viewed in some quarters as ideal vehicles for promoting this 'new Wales' to a global audience – and indeed reinventing Wales as a country via a process of national 'Cyber-boosterism' (Brunn and Cottle, 1997). For Welsh commentators such as Parsons (2000) information and communication technologies such as the Internet therefore have the potential for Wales to extend a parochial sense of 'Cool Cymru' into a global 'Cyber Cymru':

> Perhaps we should begin to think about Wales and Welshness differently; as both a physical place, and an imagined, shared 'global' experience. The dragon may occupy two realms as well as possess two tongues: Real-Wales and what we might term Cyber-Cymru. And, from a public policy perspective, it might well be that investing in Cyber-Cymru or a Cyber-Gwladfa could have considerable benefits for the positioning and 'marketing' of the country in the new millennium. (Parsons, 2000: 3)

New information and communications technologies are optimistically seen by some as offering the opportunity to 'reinvent' Wales as a nation and to project a coherent message to the rest of the world. Free from the physical marginalization of being on the edge of Europe, so the argument goes, within the borderless domain of cyberspace the Welsh 'brand' can sit side by side with that of larger countries such as the USA and compete for tourism, trade and international attention on an equal footing.

Yet, just as Wales appears to be succeeding in 'addressing the meaning of Welshness in its own terms', the new culturally defining technologies are seen by some to be moving the goalposts again. Despite the potential of using ICTs as a means through which to transmit the image of 'new Wales' to the *outside* world, more pessimistic commentators are instead pointing towards the danger of ICTs providing an insidious route *inside* Welsh culture to eroding 'outside' influences. The very opening up of Wales to the world via ICT is also seen as opening Wales up to a new 'media imperialism' of such technologies:

> It is the issue of content on these new delivery systems which will populate the sky that should concern us in Wales most . . . we have good cause to fear that the content being fed into this insatiable 'exotic animal' will be mainly American. (Beynon, 1996: 48)

The internal reinvention of 'Cool Cymru' during the late 1990s was, in no small part, assisted by the coherent and consistent messages emanating from the 'traditional' Welsh media of newspapers, television and radio. However, as Mackay and Powell (1996) warn, new information and telecommunications technologies now present a fragmented threat to a hitherto consolidated media sector in Wales presenting a united Welsh identity – at precisely the time that a newly devolved nation may be striving to maintain a coherent image:

> It may be that the outcome is good for minorities (and minority interests) in Wales, but does not assist the media in their construction of a Welsh nation. In other words, the emerging media perhaps reflect the hybrid nature of Wales, rather than the monolithic nation with somewhat fixed attributes which the media in Wales have hitherto been so prominent in promoting. (p.32)

For those taking this argument to its logical conclusion, therefore, ICT threatens to compromise the progress that Wales has made over the last ten years by rewriting the rules of national and cultural identity and resulting in a potential 'death' of Wales as a nation:

> Changes in our concept of space and geography are challenging the very basis of the construction of national identities in the modern world. The information revolution threatens to kick away the chair of national identity just at the time when many people in Wales are preparing to sit upon it. (Williams, 1996: 29)

ISSUES OF COMMUNITY

Similar arguments arise with reference to the effect of ICT on notions of community in Wales. It is contended that Wales has been founded historically upon a solid sense of community, but that Wales as a 'community of communities' is now under threat. If the notion of physical community can be argued to be floundering in Wales then the Internet is enthusiastically seen by some as an opportunity to re-establish Welsh communities on a grander and more flexible scale. Using the on-line activities of North American Welsh individuals as an example, Wayne Parsons argues that the Internet is an ideal 'place' for the Welsh to establish communities – seeing that Wales 'has long existed less as a distinct nation-state so much as a state-of-mind' (Parsons, 2000: 11). Indeed, the Internet appears to be proving valuable in providing those living in Wales, ex-patriates and those claiming a Welsh heritage with a medium through which to communicate and interact with each other. From the *Gwefan Cymraeg Efrog Newydd*/New York Welsh Homepage to *Y Gymdeithas Gymreig*/Sydney Homepage there is certainly a vibrant and visible 'international' Welsh presence on the worldwide web. On this basis alone, many would therefore agree with Parsons that the Internet could well be the new site for global Welsh community-building in the twenty-first century.

Such enthusiasm for the construction of Welsh on-line communities resonates with widely held views of information and telecommunications technology as inevitably leading to 'virtual communities' – both re-igniting existing local communities and creating new (dispersed) communities. Indeed, there has long been an excitement amongst technologists surrounding computer-mediated communication and its potential for altering and creating new forms of social relations – based on the libertarian notion of the Internet allowing each user an equal voice, or at least an equal right to speak (Foster, 1996):

> Communications networks offer the prospect of greater opportunities for seeking advice, challenging orthodoxy, meeting new minds and constructing one's sense of self. Entirely new notions of social action, based not upon proximity and shared physical experience but rather on remote networks of common perceptions, may begin to emerge and challenge existing social structures. (Loader, 1998: 10)

In the eyes of many enthusiasts, on-line communication is a powerful medium for specialist but disparate groups of like-minded individuals to form democratic virtual communities, providing mutual support, advice and identity (e.g. Gates, 1995; Rheingold, 1993). According to Rheingold, virtual communities can be defined as 'the social aggregations that emerge from the Net when enough people carry on those public discussions long enough, with sufficient human feeling, to form webs of personal relationships in cyberspace' (1993: 5). There is considerable excitement amongst Welsh ICT users over the importance of these burgeoning Welsh on-line communities and the use of the Internet to revitalize a virtual sense of belonging amongst Welsh people, extinct in Wales itself in some respects, and even where the individuals are widely scattered.

Of course, it can be argued that such utopian views of computer-mediated communications leading to a reinvention of Welsh 'community' belie the reality of many such on-line groups. There is disagreement over the nature and value of on-line collectivities. As Holmes (1997: 16) contests, 'community is not something to be constructed through a piece of technology.' In this way the actual value of the Internet in establishing 'virtual' Welsh communities can be strongly challenged. Postman (1993) contends that on-line 'communities' should not be classed as such as they lack the crucial element of a common obligation between members, thus devaluing the nature of community debate or action. Following this line of argument it could be contested that on-line collectives will only ever be disconnected talking-shops devoid of any real shared impetus. As S. G. Jones (1997: 30) contends, 'the Internet allows us to shout more loudly, but whether our fellows listen is questionable, and whether our words make a difference is even more in doubt.'

Thus, an alternative perspective on ICT and a coherent sense of Welsh community takes the view that engaging in Welsh cyber-communities may even cause damage, through trivialization, to the physical communities it seeks to augment or even replace. As Beynon (1996) argues, ICT threatens to erode the traditional patterns of life, mutual support systems and renewed existence of the Welsh language in Wales – potentially leading to a new *argyfwng gwacter ystyr* or crisis of meaninglessness. In this way ICT might divide rather than unite the Welsh people:

> There are also questions about the impact of the new technology on cultural identity. For some, cabling the valleys and wiring hills of Wales will unite people in a new electronic community. This is a little fanciful. Rather the technology is building new kinds of communities . . . It is the era of 'niche' markets whereby people are brought together according to their particular interests and/or activities. Thus a pigeon fancier in Llanelli can be united with other pigeon enthusiasts throughout the world by the means of the new technology. The result could be a more segmented Wales. (Williams, 1996: 29)

ISSUES OF LANGUAGE

Many of these debates over a sense of Welsh identity and culture are epitomized in the ongoing political and cultural revival of the Welsh language. Seen as one of the oldest existing languages in Europe, the resurgence of the Welsh language over the last thirty years has been a prominent feature of life in Wales. These were book-ended by two Acts of Parliament. The Welsh Language Act of 1967 made limited provision for the Welsh language to be used in the courts and in public administration. The subsequent Welsh Language Act of 1993 provided for Welsh to be treated on the basis of equality with English and established a statutory Welsh Language Board to promote the language and facilitate its use.

Officially, therefore, Wales is a bilingual nation, and all major public and private organizations have a Welsh language policy as a result of the 1993 Act. Such developments can be seen as protective measures because only a tiny fraction of the population actually use Welsh, since even those who speak Welsh can also speak English. A consistent minority of around 20 per cent of the population have claimed to be able to speak 'some' Welsh in the last three censuses since 1971, constituting around 500,000 people in real terms. A Welsh Office (1995a) survey found that 13.4 per cent of the population of Wales claimed to be fluent in Welsh, while 66.1 per cent claimed no knowledge of Welsh at all. Another survey suggests that fewer than 2 per cent of households in industrial south Wales speak Welsh at home (Gorard et al., 1997a), while in practice very few companies use Welsh as their language of choice in the business world (Future Skills Wales, 1998). In general, the less developed rural parts of north and west Wales have a majority of bilingual residents, while the eastern counties and coastal cities have a majority of English monoglots (see table 2.1). Of course, the majority of Welsh-speakers also live in these predominantly English-speaking areas, such as Cardiff, because that is where the majority of everyone lives. In general, these Welsh-speakers are from families with higher educational, and more prestigious occupational, backgrounds than their English-speaking counterparts (Giggs and Pattie, 1994).

Because of these discrepancies and its continued precarious nature as a national language, considerable political effort and resources have been devoted to stimulating the Welsh language. For example, effort has been put into stimulating the Welsh language through education. The compulsory teaching of Welsh in all schools (as either a first or second language) as well as the establishment of Welsh-speaking *ysgolion Cymraeg* has led to increases in the proportion of schoolchildren who can speak some Welsh over the last two decades (although these appear to have been matched by equivalent decreases among older age groups). Similarly, a

Table 2.1 Welsh-speaking population as percentage of those aged three+
1931–1991

	1931	1951	1961	1971	1981	1991
Clwyd	41.3	30.2	27.3	21.4	18.7	18.2
Dyfed	69.1	63.3	60.1	52.5	46.3	43.7
Gwent	4.7	2.8	2.9	1.9	2.5	2.4
Gwynedd	82.5	74.2	71.4	64.7	61.2	61.0
Mid Glamorgan	37.1	22.8	18.5	10.4	8.4	8.5
Powys	34.6	29.6	27.8	23.7	20.2	20.9
South Glamorgan	6.1	4.7	5.2	5.0	5.8	6.5
West Glamorgan	40.5	31.6	27.6	20.3	16.4	15.0
WALES	**36.8**	**28.9**	**26.0**	**20.8**	**18.9**	**18.7**

Source: V-Wales, 2001.

rising demand for Welsh classes at all levels in Wales has been reported, with nearly 24,000 adults attending Welsh classes in 1999 (Welsh Language Board, 2001), although to what extent these figures genuinely represent an increase over time is debatable (see Gorard et al., 1997b).

The printed and broadcast media have also been used as a platform for consolidating and strengthening the Welsh language. Indeed, Welsh-language broadcasting and publishing has grown steadily over the last thirty years. The national television station Sianel Pedwar Cymru (S4C) currently broadcasts an average of thirty-three hours of Welsh-language programming per week, with BBC Cymru Wales also providing a bilingual radio and television service. Welsh-language broadcasting constitutes a significant element of the output of independent radio in Wales, and a number of independent production companies produce TV programmes for S4C.

Information and communication technologies are seen by some Welsh-language advocates as a new space for Welsh as a 'living language' to thrive. As with the earlier arguments concerning the Internet as an ideal place to recreate a sense of Welsh community without constraints of distance and place, on-line fora are now being heralded as spaces where Welsh-speakers can freely communicate with each other without the constraints of proximity. The establishment of Welsh as one of the many languages of the Internet has taken place over the last ten years. This has taken the form of Welsh-language bulletin boards and user groups, the digital provision of Welsh-language texts and resources as well as the establishment of ICT-based Welsh-language learning courses (such as those forming an extended case study in a later part of this book). In this way, the Internet has been keenly appropriated as a place for the use of the Welsh language and for the learning of Welsh to develop and flourish.

Yet, whereas some see technologies such as the Internet as allowing a 'beneficial' space for the Welsh language to flourish (e.g. Lloyd, 1996), concerns over the increasing marginalization of the Welsh language on the Internet have led others to reiterate concern over 'how the old practices of linguistic and cultural imperialism [are] very much alive, kicking and colonising areas of new technology' (Atkinson and Powell, 1996: 81). Indeed, information and communication technologies have long been argued to be culturally restrictive, being ostensibly white, Western, male artefacts. The Internet, for example, overtly embodies American qualities, in terms of its language, technical development and users' values (Selwyn, 1999a). English is, and will remain for the foreseeable future, the lingua franca of the worldwide web, just as it is for the computer industry more generally.

Some commentators see this as inevitable, and are reasonably happy that it is so, reasoning that cultural homogenization is one of the 'entailments of a shrinking earth' (McKie, 1996), leading to greater understanding and less conflict. Others are less comfortable, and ICT is therefore being approached by some Welsh-language supporters with understandable caution. A justification for such concerns over the potential linguistic homogenization of the information age is the lack of support for Welsh on much computer software – a long-standing area of contention for a vociferous minority. Although the Internet may well be proving a fertile site for Welsh-language material, the dominant Microsoft packages such as the Office suite of programs have only included Welsh spellcheckers, for example, from their 2001 versions onwards. Although the inclusion of Welsh into such computer software may or may not turn out to 'profoundly influence Welsh over the following centuries' (Clark, 2000) it should certainly act as a check against the Anglicizing of computer-generated text. Nevertheless, as Clark (2000) concedes, the integration of Welsh into more influential software such as computer operating systems (e.g. Windows) and the fast-rising voice recognition software is more problematic, if not impossible in practice.

ISSUES OF ECONOMY

A final, and perhaps most prominent, issue for Wales in an information age is that of adapting the Welsh economy to the challenges of ICT, and building the so-called 'knowledge economy'. Traditionally, economic activity in Wales has mirrored the demographic divisions outlined earlier – with the bulk of economic activity concentrated in the area known as industrial

Table 2.2 Employee jobs in Wales, by industry

| | 1988 | | 1998 | |
	Wales	GB	Wales	GB
Agriculture, forestry, fishing	2	2	2	1
Mining, quarrying, electricity, gas, water	3	2	1	1
Manufacturing	23	22	22	17
Construction	5	5	4	5
Distribution, hotels, catering, repairs	19	21	22	23
Transport, storage, communications	5	6	4	6
Financial and business services	10	15	11	19
Public administration and defence	7	6	7	6
Education, social work, health services	20	18	22	18
Other services	5	4	5	5
Total	100	100	100	100

Source: Welsh Office/Office for National Statistics, 1999.

south Wales along with the environs of Wrexham in the north. These areas were dominated by the coal and steel industries – although since the 1980s they have benefited from the significant restructuring of the Welsh economy and the rising importance of the electrical and electronic engineering industries and the automotive components industry. Indeed, as table 2.2 shows, although the service industry has expanded in Wales as in the UK as a whole, Wales remains distinct from the rest of the UK. Only in Wales has the proportion of employee jobs in manufacturing remained constant over the last two decades – benefiting from considerable inward investment from overseas manufacturers. However, beyond the high-profile activities of multinational companies such as LG and Sony the bulk of the Welsh economy consists of small to medium rather than large businesses. For example, although there are over 158,000 businesses in Wales the vast majority are either sole traders (70 per cent) or small enterprises with fewer than ten employees (20 per cent). Less than 1 per cent of Welsh businesses had fifty or more employees. Outside the industrial heartland the rest of rural Wales remains predominantly reliant on small businesses in agriculture (especially livestock farming) and tourism.

Wales is by no means an economically prosperous country. At £9,400 per head, the Gross Domestic Product (GDP) of Wales is the lowest among all twelve economic regions of the UK apart from Northern Ireland. The west Wales and Valleys areas have a GDP per head of less than 75 per cent of the European average and therefore qualify for European Commission Structural Funding (Objective One) which provides up to three-quarters of the cost of economic development initiatives. Much of Wales is also eligible for additional European Commission Structural Funding, with industrial south Wales and rural Wales receiving £414 million of funding between 1994 and 1999.

The Welsh economy can be seen as fragile; remaining largely dependent on manufacturing – be it in the form of small indigenous enterprises or via inward investment from global corporations which have little loyalty to local communities – and with clear differences between subregions. For Welsh politicians such as Alan Pugh (2000: 22), therefore, the scenario is a simple one with a simple solution: 'Wales faces a twin challenge: moving manufacturing up the value chain while at the same time developing a service sector. This is a very tall order indeed. Using ICT effectively is part of the solution to these challenges.' Information and communications technology are therefore now seen by a majority of politicians and business-men as the answer to many of Wales's economic problems. This is the case both in terms of consolidating and revitalizing the traditional manufacturing and service sectors as well as offering the chance to forge ahead in the new Internet-based 'dot.com' sector and knowledge economy as a whole.

Yet, beyond enthusiastic headlines in Welsh newspapers such as 'Welsh New Media Sector Expanding at a Rapid Rate' (Mason, 2000: 2) the economic reality of Wales in the information age is less straightforward. The most noticeable counter-trend is the slow take-up of information

Table 2.3. ICT connectivity indicator

UK region	Penetration of ICT use by small businesses,* 1999	Penetration of ICT use by small businesses,* 2000
London	74	88
South East	62	84
West Midlands	65	83
Eastern	58	78
Yorks and Humberside	54	76
East Midlands	54	76
Scotland	54	76
North West	59	75
Northern Ireland	43	75
South West	52	74
North East	51	74
Wales	48	69

Source: DTI, 2000a.
*The ICT connectivity indicator is an index based on three components: (i) small companies' web-sites, (ii) frequent use of external Email and (iii) frequent use of electronic data interchange.

technology and a lack of e-commerce in Wales. For example, the Department of Trade and Industry's 'connectivity indicator' designed to measure ICT use amongst small businesses, placed Wales as the poorest-performing region in a comparison of e-commerce activity throughout the UK regions (see table 2.3). Similarly, with regard to the recent explosion of dot.com Internet-based businesses Wales is seen to have been increasingly marginalized. The vast majority of dot.com companies are located within a 'web-wedge' extending out from London to Nottingham and Bristol – leading to headlines warning that 'Wales Needs to Get Surfing' (*South Wales Echo*, 25 November 2000). Thus, from this perspective ICT (or the lack of it) is conversely being presented as an economic threat to Wales, rather than the agent of its salvation: 'By being the poorest online trading region in the UK, Wales runs the real risk of becoming effectively excluded from a high growth business area' (Pugh, 2000: 22).

CONCLUSIONS

A common theme emerges from these discussions: that of information and communications technology being seen as both a potential *saviour* and a potential *threat* to Wales in the twenty-first century. Of course, opposing perspectives are all part and parcel of any reasoned discussion. Yet such is the allure of ICT and such is the strength of conviction amongst its supporters and detractors alike that the real issues and impact of ICT on a country such as Wales may be overshadowed by the prevailing polarized hype. On the one hand, ICT continues to be painted in terms of revitalizing the Welsh language, community and culture, kick-starting the Welsh economy and reawakening the Wales of a bygone era into an empowered 'Cyber-Cymru' to be proud of for the twenty-first century. On the other hand, ICT is bemoaned as eroding the very heart of Wales and what it is to be Welsh – fragmenting communities, homogenizing national language and culture into a bland, corporatized, mid-Atlantic sludge, decentralizing economic control away from individual nations and towards the vagaries of global flows of capital and, at best, resulting in a diluted and disenfranchised Wales.

In trying to make sense of this *mélange* of rhetoric and counter-rhetoric we need to recall the points made in chapter 1 – in particular the folly of adopting an overriding technologically determinist view of technology and society. Indeed, throughout many of the debates reviewed in this chapter, it is still technology that is seen as the driving force of countries such as Wales in an information age; as technology changes, so Wales as a country and the Welsh people follow, for better or worse. Technology is seen as guiding and shaping Welsh society with its own logic, but otherwise autonomous from social influence. Thus, much of the current debate over the technological future of Wales has been presented in terms of what effect ICT will have on Wales, its language, its culture, its economy, its businesses, its people. Yet, as we discussed in chapter 1, such a viewpoint is overly narrow, obscuring many of the key questions that we should be asking. The next chapter explores the role of individual nations in dealing with the information age, in particular the policy frameworks being put in place to address some of the issues highlighted so far.

3

The Policies and Politics of an Information Age

Wales's contrasting rural heartland and urban fringes, its relatively small population compared with England, a history of reliance on manufacturing and primary industry, as well as its position on the periphery of the world and European stages, are all factors in trying to understand the practical possibilities for Wales in an information age. Having reviewed the possible effects of the technological on the social in chapter 2, we now draw attention to the possible effects of the political on the technological. In other words, to what extent can Wales make its own luck in the information age?

For some commentators, the rise of ICT and global economics leave little leeway for national agency, with nation-states increasingly seen to be curtailed by the rise of transnational corporations, supranational trading blocs and the rising prominence of telecommunications networks. This viewpoint is shared by those keen to predict the 'death' of the individual country in the borderless information age, looking instead at the power of the multinational corporations as the key actors in shaping the twenty-first century. Yet, as we have seen, many prominent politicians, business people and other Welsh 'leading lights' remain confident of Wales's ability to fight its corner and exercise a degree of self-influence in the information age. Moreover, as we have already begun to explore, there are some local reasons why this might be the case. But what can countries like Wales actually be expected to do in shaping their experiences?

THE INFORMATION AGE AS GLOBAL COMPETITION

If we accept that the information age is an international concern then we cannot begin to consider the fortunes of Wales in an information age without also considering the actions of other nations – both large and small, developed and developing – in responding to the economic, political and social changes outlined in chapter 1. For the most part, despite the harmonious imagery of 'global villages' and 'single marketplaces', the information age is certainly not being seen by individual countries as a time of general benevolence and coming together. Indeed, for some governments around the world the information age is seen as little more than a high-stakes race, with the potentially huge rewards on offer attainable only by getting a 'head start' on the competition. As the highly influential Bangemann Report (1994) to the European Union reasoned, countries must therefore 'progress or perish' in this new world order:

> The first countries to enter the information society will reap the greatest rewards. They will set the agenda for all who must follow. By contrast, countries which temporise, or favour half-hearted solutions could, in less than a decade, face disastrous declines in investment and a squeeze on jobs. (European Union/Bangemann, 1994)

For many countries the opportunities of the information age are there to be seized by the scruff of the neck – a chance to rewrite (or reaffirm) digitally the world order established by the onset of the Industrial Revolution. In other words, the information age is seen as a chance for some countries to 'win' at the expense of others. As the US Information Infrastructure Task Force aggressively asserted early in the 1990s:

> The benefits of the NII [National Information Infrastructure] for the nation are immense. An advanced information infrastructure will enable US firms to compete and *win in the global economy*, generating good jobs for the American people and economic growth for the nation. (IITF, 1993; emphasis added)

So before we go on to explore what Wales can realistically do for itself in this global struggle we would first do well to reflect on how some other countries are attempting to position themselves in the information age 'race'. By identifying themes and contradictions in the policy responses of major industrial powers such as the USA and UK as well as the emerging 'tiger economies' of East Asia, we can sketch out the global political context within which Wales finds itself in the information age.

NATIONAL RESPONSES TO THE INFORMATION AGE: THE RISE OF THE 'NATIONAL INFORMATION INFRASTRUCTURE' IN EUROPE, NORTH AMERICA AND EAST ASIA

For the last twenty years the identity and sovereignty of the nation-state have been challenged by the apparent globalization of national economies. Individual countries have been struggling to maintain their traditional decision-making power and authority against the mobilization of global financial markets and the increasing reach of the multinational corporations (Schiller, 1986). As we hinted in chapter 1, the collapse of national barriers to trade, production and service delivery has been significantly advanced by the development of information technologies which have contributed to an exponential increase in global information flows. Against this background, governments around the world have therefore been developing policy initiatives aimed at improving the quality of their human resources in an attempt to gain an advantage in the new global competition. In this way, a working familiarity with information technologies has become a key feature of both individual 'employability' and international competitiveness; thus prompting nation-states to invest in information technologies as a way of delivering and extending education and training, whilst also building and developing nationwide 'information infrastructures'.

The development of advanced information networks is now taking place in most industrialized countries, usually with the objective of creating 'national information infrastructures' (NII). In an organizational sense, such policy-making encompasses all computerized networks, applications and services that citizens can use to access, create, disseminate and utilize digital information (Martinez, 1997). In practice, therefore, NII policy programmes have tended to encompass the diffusion of technologies as diverse as POTS (plain old telephone service), digital broadcasting, the Internet and other multimedia, in both the private and public sectors.

A prime example of NII policy-making can be seen in the sustained efforts of the Clinton/Gore administration throughout the 1990s to position the United States of America as a front runner in the global information race. Indeed, the announcement in September 1993 of the 'US National Information Infrastructure' initiative by the Clinton/Gore administration (IITF, 1993) was widely acknowledged as precipitating the subsequent rush of NII policies throughout the rest of the world (e.g. Tan, 1995; Langdale, 1997). The broad aim of the US initiative was to create an information and communications network connecting homes, businesses and public institutions to the 'Information Superhighway'. Although the Clinton/Gore administration expressed concern that every American citizen should have equality of access to a fast and flexible network, the development and implementation of the NII has largely been left to the private sector. The US federal government presented its role firmly as one of promoting the NII and creating the market conditions for the private providers to flourish.

In the United Kingdom the vision of a national information infrastructure has been less pronounced than in the USA. The British government has traditionally been keen to adopt a 'hands-off' approach to the construction of telecommunications and information networks. Throughout the 1980s successive Conservative governments strove to develop a telecommunications infrastructure by being a 'referee in the market-place' (Garfield and Watson, 1998), primarily overseeing the deregulation of many sectors. Nevertheless, with the election in 1997 of the New Labour administration, a more cogent sense of an NII strategy in all but name began to emerge. As well as encouraging cable and digital broadcasting provision, the Labour government was quick to announce the development of (primarily Internet-based) ISDN networks within local and central government, post offices, the National Health Service and the establishment of a 'People's Network' of connected museums and libraries. An 'e-envoy' group has been established within the Cabinet Office and substantial work has been carried out to stimulate ICT use in business as well as establishing a system of Internet-based 'e-government' services. Education has formed a central plank of this ongoing strategy, with extensive billion-pound initiatives to integrate ICT into the school system (the National Grid for Learning) and adult education (the 'University for Industry').

Significantly, in East Asia many countries have pursued explicit NII policy agendas with even more vigour. For example, originating from an initial 1987 National Information Technology plan, Singapore has been following the extensive centralized 'IT2000 Vision' designed to establish an 'intelligent island'. This has been based around the integration of IT into eleven major sectors, namely: government; health care; education; leisure and tourism; construction and real estate; financial services; manufacturing; the IT industry; publishing and media; retail; and transportation. To some extent Singapore faces analogous problems to Wales – keen to use ICT to foster national advantage while fearing the impact of exposure to worldwide culture on a small and somewhat censorious island. The differences, however, outweigh the similarities – most notably the higher population density, superior transport facilities, and huge economic power of Singapore.

Malaysia's NII policy has been formed under the aegis of 'Vision 2020', a twenty-five-year plan for a 'technologically driven nation'. An integral part of Vision 2020 is the 'Multimedia Super Corridor' (MSC). Malaysia's Multimedia Super Corridor is a 15 by 50 km zone extending south from Kuala Lumpur, thus 'creating the perfect environment for companies wanting to create, distribute and employ multimedia products and services' (Ministry of Education, 1998: 1). The MSC consists of a physical infrastructure (highway, airport, garden cities), new 'cyberlaws' to encourage electronic commerce coupled with a high-capacity national telecommunications infrastructure. With this in mind, seven 'rapid development areas' have been identified: electronic government; tele-medicine; a multipurpose card; research and development clusters; world-wide marketing webs; borderless marketing centres; and smart schools.

As a final example, keen to reaffirm its technological reputation and position in the world, Japan is also striving to establish a 'Japanese Information Infrastructure' (JII). As Latzer (1995) details, the technical construction of the infrastructure alone is expected to cost up to 100 trillion yen, with educational and health institutions connected to the Internet by 2000 and all homes by 2010. Although most of the network is to be financed by the private sector, the health and education elements of network services are government-led. Indeed, the original intention to have all primary schools connected to the Internet by 2003 was accelerated by a combination of extra government funding and private-sector commitments to offer discount rates to schools.

THE NATURE OF COUNTRIES' NII POLICY-MAKING: CONVERGENCE OR DIVERGENCE?

These multibillion dollar examples are just the tip of an iceberg, with every developed country from Finland to Korea, Hungary to Chile, beginning to pursue similar policy agendas and fashioning national responses to the information age. Despite such a diversity of nations and political persuasions, what is immediately striking from this international perspect-ive is that there is a fair amount of congruence in the stated aims of all these countries in NII policy-making (Selwyn and Brown, 2000). Across all nations, for example, the national information infrastructure is, perhaps unsurprisingly, seen primarily as a vital source of economic competitive-ness as information processing, e-commerce, and virtual networking of individuals and companies are seen to be remoulding the nature of business. Yet, countries are also attempting to develop NII policies for a range of societal aims, expressed in terms of citizenship, life skills, and individual access to information and public services. Interestingly, a broad theme running throughout NII policy-making in all these countries is that of educational change. Indeed, the educational discourse of establishing information networks across countries and their educational systems has tended to be expressed in three different ways. These are: using ICT to improve educational opportunities; using ICT to improve educational standards; and, in a more radical form, using ICT to remould or transform systems of education.

Yet, beyond this similarity in emphasizing economy/society/education, who is responsible for initiating such changes and how this is to be achieved is less homogeneous. Indeed, our earlier examples of the UK, USA, Japan, Singapore and Malaysia are interesting in the varying roles that the public and private sectors are expected to play in shaping individual countries' fortunes in the information age. What is immediately striking about these national examples is the difference between the Western economies and their East Asian competitors. Countries such as Singapore, Malaysia and Japan have been quick to establish broad but coherent NII initiatives across public and private sectors. Countries such as the United Kingdom and the United States have relied more on 'stand-alone' programmes in areas such as education which are driven by market forces under the 'remote control' of the state. This difference can be explained from two different perspectives. From one standpoint it can be argued that the societal rather than piecemeal approach to the development of an NII in the Asian tiger countries is an attempt to 'catch up' with the mature economies found in Europe and North America. However, this loses much of its plausibility in the case of Japan, which has been a major international economic force for over thirty years. Alternatively, an explanation based on technological determinism can be used to make the converse argument that countries such as the United Kingdom are rooted in the smokestack era of industrial capitalism and have still to catch up with the 'high-tech' vision of countries found in East Asia. The latter take for granted the full force of the 'information revolution' in attempts to achieve national development.

It is also interesting to note how these examples mirror the well-established distinction between neo-liberal and developmental approaches to ICT policy-making (Ashton and Green, 1996; Castells, 1996). Neo-liberalism views most forms of state intervention as an impediment to the operation of a market which is seen as being the most cost-effective means of economic organization. Here the private interests of individuals and companies are allowed to define the demand for goods and services, given that the state can never achieve a monopoly of the information seen to be necessary for effective state planning. In this way, Moore (1998) suggests that in the neo-liberal model of policy implementation the state acts merely as a facilitator to ensure that IT markets flourish, whilst the private sector determines the scope of the NII policies. Examining the policy statements across the various countries, this approach is strongly reflected in both the US and UK models of implementation:

> The Federal government funded and developed early versions of the Internet for national security and research purposes. It will continue to provide funding for research and development on future Internet and high-performance computing technologies. However, most of the capital to build the computing

and telecommunications infrastructure is being provided by the private sector. (US Secretariat on Electronic Commerce, 1998: 50)

The [UK] government will not attempt to replace the private sector – competitive markets will bring the greatest benefits to the economy and consumers alike. (Central Office of Information, 1998: 5)

This reliance on market forces means that the connection of homes and businesses to information and communications networks has been left firmly in the hands of the private telecommunications sector, with as yet limited success. Although the UK government is attempting to set up public-sector IT as a 'quasi-marketplace' (Le Grand and Bartlett, 1993), it is the USA which provides the closest example of an ideal-typical model of neo-liberalism in respect to the development of national information infrastructures. A centralized approach to policy-making has been generally considered to 'run against the very grain of American culture' (Sawhney, 1993). Nevertheless, even here public services such as education have assumed a heightened importance, with the federal government paying particular attention to the connection of US schools and colleges to the Internet. Indeed, the boast of an Internet connection in every classroom was seen as embodying the public perception of the Clinton administration's drive throughout the 1990s towards an NII. Of course, perceived government involvement and concern over the educational element of NII policy has obvious political advantages. For many Western governments, pledging to 'wire up' schools appears to carry far more electoral significance than promising to ensure the connection of the commercial sector to the Internet. Hence the high-profile media images of Al Gore and Bill Clinton donning hard-hats and being seen to carry rolls of ISDN cabling into American schools. In this way education is a highly visible and laudable arena for Western governments to be seen to launch the idea of a national information infrastructure.

If the above provides an example of the state being treated as an impediment to the operation of market efficiency, in the case of developing states it can be seen as the supreme catalyst, with NII policy implementation firmly 'driven by the state acting in accordance with a predetermined set of objectives' (Moore, 1998: 154). This model typifies the approach taken by most East Asian governments, which have leant towards highly centralized 'visions' with strong state leadership and direction. Castells (1996) argues that a state is developmental when its main source of legitimacy is its ability to deliver consistently high rates of economic growth and modernization of the economy both domestically and in relation to the international economy. This presupposes a societal approach which 'in East Asia took the form of the affirmation of national identity, and national culture, building or rebuilding the nation as a force in the world, in this case by means of economic competitiveness and socio-economic improvement' (Castells, 1996: 182).

Thus, developmental governments can be seen as taking 'a proactive central role' rather than leaving 'their national information infrastructure to the hands of the private sector' (Teo and Lim, 1998: 122). For example, although differing somewhat in the degree of private involvement that has been encouraged, the Japanese strategy implies a strong belief in the 'hands-on' approach to building information communities: 'the political/ administrative system, with strong central power in the hands of the ministry at the local and national level, and an unusually close relationship between the civil service and industry support this approach' (Latzer, 1995: 527). Given this societal approach to NII development, the education system is treated as one element of a state-co-ordinated strategy. But as for all ideal-typical models, the broad view runs the risk of obscuring important differences in empirical realities, such as in the educational and economic policies pursued by the Asian tiger economies. Moreover, some countries such as Germany cannot be said to have adopted either an avowedly neo-liberal or developmental model, given the importance attached to the politics of co-determination (Streeck, 1992). Indeed, had we extended our focus beyond the examples discussed here the number of ideal-typical models would undoubtedly increase.

WALES AS A CELTIC TIGER IN THE INFORMATION AGE? THE IRISH PERSPECTIVE

Although we can learn much about the mechanisms for initiating change from these international examples there are obvious practical reasons why comparing Wales's position with that of the USA is of only limited benefit. Much of the excitement over the impact of ICT in Wales has been in terms of transforming the Welsh economy and, in this, the lead being set by economically powerful countries such as the USA and Singapore is less applicable to the economy of Wales (in addition to the political difference that the former are all fully independent nations). From this perspective, in looking for indications of where Wales could be heading in the information age, a great deal of attention has also been given to the Republic of Ireland's apparent transformation into a 'Celtic tiger' throughout the 1990s. Such an aspiration is an ambitious one as there can be no denying the transformation of Ireland's economic fortunes during this time. In ten years, the per capita GDP of Ireland rose from 63 per cent of the overall average for the European Union to 97 per cent – a figure now outstripping that of the United Kingdom. Therefore, there can be little surprise that the Irish comparison has been picked up by those seeking to establish Wales as a burgeoning twenty-first-century nation. As Rhodri Morgan recently argued:

> We need to do roughly over the next ten years what Ireland did over the past ten years. They've transformed themselves from a basketcase to a boom case in Europe. They've gone from the bottom of the league to the top of the league. If they can do that I reckon we can do half to two thirds what they've done. And if we could do that then I would be a very happy person. (Morgan, cited in Sweeting and Rawstron, 2001: 20)

Throughout the last decade the Irish economic resurgence was viewed with some envy around Europe, as the once economically peripheral nation experienced continuous high growth rates, a steady rise in living standards and an improvement (both in terms of quantity and quality) of inward investment into the country – particularly by a number of high-tech transnational corporations. It has been Ireland's apparent talent for profiting from the information age that has attracted most attention. For example, by 1998 Ireland's software industry was annually exporting over US$6 billion of products and was seen to be leading the way even for traditionally high-tech Asian tiger countries such as Singapore (Coe, 1999).

Ireland's apparent success has been attributed to a combination of factors. First, there is a ready supply of skilled workers to attract export-orientated direct foreign investment – due to both demographic change and increased levels of state investment in education (Breathnach, 1998). Ireland is seen to have benefited tremendously by taking full advantage of European Union funding although the relative contribution of EU funding to the Irish economy has actually been declining since 1991. Ireland has also been very successful in reinventing itself as a tourist destination. Finally, Ireland is argued to be favourably located in the midst of the highly lucrative transatlantic marketplace. As Coe (1999: 36) argues, 'Ireland has benefited from its position on the periphery of Western Europe, one of the largest markets in the world, to emerge as a key production location for US transnational corporations.'

So, to what extent can Wales be expected to replicate the apparent success of Eire? As Taylor (2000: 26) continues, '[Ireland] because of its agrarian history, huge out-migration rates and close linkages with a cash friendly USA, is not necessarily the correct analogue for Wales.' Indeed, although Wales and Ireland are separated by less than sixty miles of water the two countries are hardly comparable. In terms of political infrastructure, cultural identity and international presence, the Celtic connection between Wales and Ireland is at best tenuous.

This growth in Ireland has anyway been achieved at a price; there has been an increasing social and spatial polarization in Ireland towards those in skilled employment and towards the main cities (Breathnach, 1998). Moreover, there is very real concern about the long-term sustainability of Ireland's transition to a high-growth information age economy. Although the short-term benefits of inward investment by foreign multinationals is readily apparent, long-term success is based much more on the development of local economic and social networks (Dicken et al., 1994). Such has been Ireland's reliance on North American firms that Murphy (1997) argues that it is more accurately seen as the 'US High-Tech Tiger with the Celtic Face' – highlighting what Breathnach (1998: 315) terms 'the inherent instability of the economic base upon which the Celtic Tiger economy has been constructed'.

WHAT CAN BE LEARNT FROM THESE INTERNATIONAL EXAMPLES?

That said, there is much to be learnt from all of these international examples. First and foremost, is the importance of the development of some sort of national vision or framework of countries' progression with regard to the use of ICT across a range of areas. Whether in terms of developing the physical infrastructure of telecommunications networks or the organizational infrastructure with which it will be utilized, the role of the state in either passively facilitating or actively directing a national agenda is a recurring theme. The balance between the roles of the public and private sectors in implementing these national plans is a crucial area of development – but one which is also rooted in traditional national cultures and previous histories of policy-making. Finally, the comparison of the Irish example with the USA and East Asia serves as a reminder of the importance of non-economic factors involved in nation (re)building in the information age. The challenges to Wales in an information age are all too often seen in a narrow economic light but, as we have seen, formulating a national information strategy revolves around a host of economic and social issues – epitomized for example in the high profile of education and training strategies in all of the countries we have highlighted (see also chapters 5 and 6).

Although these comparisons have value it would be naïve to argue the case for Wales's ability to 'do a Singapore' or 'do an Ireland'. Although the notion of the information age can be seen as a new era in the economic, political and social fortunes of nations, it is also obviously rooted in their 'pre-informational' positions. Expecting Wales to mirror countries such as the USA, or even the Asian tigers of Singapore and Malaysia, in the direction of information age policy-making and action is to ignore the very different nature of such countries. For example, Singapore's relatively small land mass coupled with relatively high density of population means that the technical challenges of 'wiring up' the nation pale into insignificance in relation to the more expansive and sparsely populated Wales. Similarly, the centralist political administration in Malaysia makes the implementation of a nationwide networking initiative such as the Malaysian Multimedia Super Corridor a far more straightforward process than it would be in the multi-party, partially devolved Wales. For the reasons given above, even Ireland's apparent resurgence may not be the best example for Wales to be following in terms of developing an information-orientated economy which is also stable and long-term.

So, where can Wales be said to fit into this global background? Certainly Wales is a very different entity from those countries highlighted in this chapter – economically, politically, culturally, geographically and linguistically. Thus in viewing Wales in an information age it is perhaps best to take heed of the global context – be it Ireland, Singapore or Malaysia – but now look to Wales itself for some answers. Politically, economically, socially and culturally, Wales's position is unique and will continue to be so. How, then, is Wales positioning itself for the information age?

KEY ACTORS IN SHAPING THE WELSH ICT AGENDA

In answering this question we first need to be sure what we mean by 'Wales' and even whom we mean by 'actors'. Behind the construction of the National Information Infrastructure policies in other countries lie a host of public and private organizations and interests at national and local levels, all of which are instrumental in achieving the wider aims. So who in Wales is responsible for pursuing an information age agenda?

We have deliberately waited until now to address the question of Welsh politics, but it is clear that examining Wales in an information age must involve an element of examining Welsh politics in an information age. Politically, Wales has changed substantially since the mid-1990s. On the face of it, the creation of the National Assembly for Wales in 1999 marked a new political era in Wales – transforming the responsibilities of the Welsh Office into a directly elected legislature free from the constraints of Westminster party politics and cabinet collective responsibility. The National Assembly is now charged with overseeing much of what goes on in Wales, commanding a budget of around £8 billion and legislating on many domestic policy issues such as education, health, social services and housing, as well as making major decisions concerning economic development and agriculture.

Many people are therefore looking to the National Assembly for a proactive stance in leading Wales's affairs – especially in light of the perceived impotence of the old Welsh Office. As Griffiths (1999: 793) argues, until the establishment of the National Assembly of Wales, '. . . claims of exceptionalism (certainly in terms of policies) have been much exaggerated and . . . the "centre", Westminster and Whitehall, was able to impose its preferred policies in Wales, whatever appearances to the contrary'.

Yet, the nascent National Assembly has yet really to impose itself on Wales and in its first years has not enjoyed the most stable and effective of starts (Morgan and Mungham, 2000). In particular, the National Assembly remains totally financially dependent on London, and its legislative role is confined within narrow limits – making only secondary legislation. Thus, for Laffin et al. (2000: 224–5) the pressure is on the National Assembly to demonstrate at least some degree of power in influencing Welsh policy within this constrictive framework:

> The Assembly is under considerable pressure to demonstrate to the Welsh electorate that it is 'adding value' which would not be there without the democratisation of the Welsh Office . . . They must begin to develop some distinctively Welsh policies that can be sold to a sceptical electorate and score some noticeable successes.

Perhaps it is not surprising that the National Assembly has firmly indicated information age-related areas in which to demonstrate its lead. Indeed, the National Assembly appears confident of its ability to shape Wales's fortunes in the information age, arguing that it is nothing less than 'the job' of the Assembly to do so:

> Wales is in a period of exceptional change and unprecedented, but exciting, challenge. Global competition and ever-faster technological changes are reshaping our economy, altering the nature of work and having a powerful effect on our lives. Use of the Internet is growing at 90 percent a year . . . The job of the Assembly and its partners is to embrace change and tackle these issues head-on for the benefit of everyone in Wales. Wales has the commitment, drive and talent to rise to the challenge and the ideas. The new political environment created by the Assembly . . . provides us with a unique opportunity to make a real difference to people's lives. (National Assembly for Wales, 2000: 7)

Aside from the Welsh Assembly many of the key public actors in shaping Wales with regard to ICT emanate from the pre-Assembly Welsh

Table 3.1 Distribution of the UK software industry

UK region	Companies	Employees
South East	9785	72700
London	6580	48500
North West	2605	17400
South West	2570	15300
West Midlands	2061	16100
East Midlands	1599	10800
Yorks and Humberside	1432	9500
Scotland	1217	7800
East Anglia	1080	7200
Northern	607	4100
Wales	602	3100

Source: Foreign and Commonwealth Office, 1998.

political framework, which was dominated by quasi-autonomous non-government organizations (or quangos) and other non-departmental government bodies. The most prominent of these bodies has been the Welsh Development Agency (WDA), which has proved a vocal champion of information age issues in Wales over the last two decades. The WDA is a public body established in 1976 with the three-way brief to

> (i) further the economic development of Wales or any part of Wales and in that connection to provide, maintain or safeguard employment; (ii) promote industrial efficiency and international competitiveness in Wales; and (iii) further the improvement of the environment in Wales. (WDA, 1996: 1)

With this in mind the WDA has worked to attract inward investment by promoting Wales as 'the Winning Location for Information Technology' (WDA, 1995) via its 'IT Wales' initiative and, more recently, has been responsible for co-ordinating the European-funded 'Wales Information Society' project as well as a host of other IT-related initiatives.

A further group of key actors in shaping the information age agenda of countries comes from the private sector – and here Wales is lacking the physical presence of many of the large multinational IT corporations which have been actively involved in shaping government technology policy elsewhere. Indeed, as table 3.1 shows, Wales has proved a comparatively poor location for IT firms to operate from and, therefore, have a sustained influence on policy. Despite the establishment of inward investment from firms such as Sony and local success stories such as Newbridge Networks,

Wales lacks the presence of 'heavyweight' IT firms such as Microsoft, Dell, Apple, IBM, Compaq and others who are actively involved in influencing IT policy at an English and UK-wide level (see Selwyn and Fitz, 2001). Nevertheless, as we shall see, the activities of private-sector actors have still gone some way towards shaping IT use and infrastructure in Wales, if not directly shaping actual policy.

Having identified some of the key shaping concerns of Wales in an information age, we can now conclude this chapter by outlining their frameworks of action.

(i) The National Assembly – Cymru Ar-lein – Online for a Better Wales

Although the National Assembly is justifiably proud of its own ICT-based information and voting system for its members in the assembly chamber in Cardiff Bay (Pugh, 2000), its progress regarding the digitization of the rest of Wales has been less impressive. Like the similar session in the Westminster Parliament in 1997, one of the Assembly's first sessions in 1999 was a debate on the information age where the Assembly members overwhelmingly voted to

> recognise the importance of the coming information age to the economic and social development of Wales, and endorse the Assembly's role in enthusiastically promoting and supporting . . . the awareness, development and extensive utilisation of advanced information technologies in all sectors in Wales. (National Assembly for Wales, 1999)

Nevertheless, the Assembly's first strategic plan, belying the connotations of its *www.betterwales.com* title and on-line publication and consultation process, was surprisingly brief when it came to the subject of ICT, promising only the development of a 'widely-owned Information Age strategy for ensuring that Wales takes full advantage of the ICT revolution' by October 2000 (National Assembly for Wales, 2000: 2). Subsequently the Labour minister for Assembly business, Andrew Davies AM, was appointed as the National Assembly's first 'e-minister' and an ICT Strategy unit and then an Information Age Advisory Group were established soon after. Then, in January 2001, the consultation version of the Assembly's ICT strategy was launched as 'Cymru Arlein – Online for a Better Wales'. This document outlined the Assembly's vision of a Wales that:

- Is widely recognised in its application of ICT in the way we deliver education and training through our modern, effective, efficient and accessible public services and through the way our businesses use ICT to lever genuine market growth;

- Builds on its unique and diverse identity to match economic growth rates elsewhere in the UK and Europe;
- Has a prosperous, well-educated, well-trained, highly skilled and healthy workforce fit for the knowledge economy.
(National Assembly for Wales, 2001a)

Indeed the *Cymru Arlein* consultation document and the final strategy document published at the end of 2001 were clear in spelling out the role that the National Assembly sees itself playing; mirroring the role of the Westminster government in avoiding the extremes of *dirigiste* state control and *laissez-faire* free-marketism and, instead, acting as a facilitator and 'steward' in stimulating the use of ICT in Wales. Thus, whilst the *Cymru Arlein* document was careful to stress the need for the Assembly 'not to hinder or get in the way', it did outline a role for the Assembly in creating and influencing demand and take-up of ICT facilities as well as providing more detailed ICT policy direction in public sectors such as education and health. Tellingly, in terms of Assembly-led action, the consultation document spoke of the need for the Assembly to 'focus on doing a few big things really well, rather than creating many new projects and initiatives' (National Assembly for Wales, 2001a). As e-minister Andrew Davies outlined in his introduction to the consultation to *Cymru Arlein*, 'I think the time is right for some substantial interventions that will make a big difference for the whole of Wales.'

Despite a somewhat slow start, the National Assembly is now actively promoting ICT as one of its priority areas. As Andrew Davies has asserted, despite its limitations in other legislative areas, the Assembly is considered to be in an ideal position to shape and influence the use of ICT in Wales, given its unbounded implications:

> I would like to see Wales as an e-nation, with people having the means to access the latest technology and also having the skills to take advantage of it and to maximise the opportunities available to them. I think we're ideally placed to do that. This is an area where the Assembly can really make a difference because it cuts across economic development, education and training and health. It affects all walks of life. (Davies, cited in Hornung, 2000: 25)

(ii) The WDA and the Wales Information Society initiative

Prior to the National Assembly's renewed interest in ICT perhaps the most sustained lead in shaping Wales in an information age had not come from Cathays Park or Crickhowell House, but from the Welsh Development Agency in the form of their long-running 'Wales Information Society' (WIS) initiative. Originally established in 1997 as one of twenty-two European Union 'Regional Information Society Initiative' pilot projects, the initiative's principal initial aim was to develop a series of strategic business plans for Wales as well as acting as an 'awareness-raising' and 'consensus-building' exercise to 'accelerate the introduction of an Information Society in Wales' (WIS, 1998a: 15). In this way, the guiding desire of the WIS was to ensure that

> all of the key actors and interests within Wales should be involved in building consensus, in order … to generate the momentum to enable Wales to obtain the most economic and social benefit from the transition to the Global Information Society. (WIS, 1998a: 16)

The resulting strategy and action plan, as well as highlighting the need for widespread, easy access to ICT and strong leadership from a 'Wales Information Age Champion', identified four main areas for action: businesses, education and training, public services and, perhaps most ambitiously, 'transforming Wales into a world leader in the Information Age' (WIS, 1998b). The resulting WIS2000+ programme, running from 2000 to 2003, has therefore been based around stimulating activities in all of these areas as well as attempting to develop the Welsh ICT industry and access to ICT throughout the country. In particular the Wales Information Society WIS2000+ programme has converted the original action plan into four areas of activity: Transforming the Effectiveness of Public Services; Transforming the Skills of the People of Wales; Transforming the Quality of Life in Wales; and Transforming the Competitiveness of Welsh Businesses. Whilst these are remarkably similar to many of the National Information Infrastructure agendas that we reviewed at the beginning of this chapter, and certainly act as a useful framework for reviewing current ICT activity in Wales, in terms of the actual scope of the initiative itself the WIS is modest: the first phase of the initiative, for example, was costed at little over £700,000.

Nevertheless, the WIS initiative has produced a range of projects in all four of these areas and has supported several more. Subsequently there are a number of larger WDA- and European Union-funded initiatives which aim to fulfil the Wales Information Society brief. These range from the £5 million 'Wales smE-Business' initiative, which aims to provide one-to-one ICT consultation and support for 1,500 small and medium-sized enterprises across Wales, to the 'Computers for Young Enterprise' scheme which offers each secondary school in Wales a free multimedia PC in order to develop entrepreneurial skills amongst pupils. Another significant project is the £10.3 million Rural Wales Information Society which aims to establish up to 140 access points to ICT in public locations throughout rural Wales.

(iii) Other major ICT projects in Wales

The *Cymru Arlein* and WIS programmes sit alongside a variety of already existing programmes and initiatives in Wales, funded by a variety of European Union, Welsh Office and WDA grants as well as private finance. Indeed, in 1998 the WIS programme estimated that over 200 such ICT programmes were being pursued in Wales. Much of the current activity in the ICT arena has therefore not resulted directly from National Assembly or Welsh Office legislation but from community-level collaboration between public-sector and private-sector organizations pursuing a range of projects – some substantial and others more modest. For example, the ongoing Llwybr/Pathway project is a £6 million telecommunications investment programme aiming to introduce advanced telecommunications access to ten rural towns in Wales as well as upgrading forty-two smaller rural telephone exchanges. Similarly, a consortium of higher education institutions under the guise of Welsh Networking are in the process of establishing 'metropolitan area networks' for post-compulsory educational institutions in both south Wales and north Wales. A multitude of other, more locally based projects are also being undertaken; such as the Swansea Information Society Initiative and the Gwynedd Multimedia Development Programme supported by a range of local authorities, universities and other bodies.

CONCLUSIONS

At the time of writing this book, the reality of Wales in an information age is an amalgam of emerging nationwide strategies and frameworks for action, alongside a multiplicity of more localized activity. The degree to which these two elements converge will obviously be of fundamental long-term importance. However, in the short to medium term other pressing areas for discussion are raised by the issues discussed in this chapter. The first is the ability of Welsh institutions – the National Assembly, WDA and others – to make any real impact in the face of the global information context. Behind the promises of the Assembly's proposed five-year plans and associated ICT strategy units, the emerging information age agenda for Wales could be seen as paling into insignificance in comparison to the national information infrastructure policy agendas of the countries that Wales is supposedly looking to emulate.

Following on from this point is the issue of Wales's relative subservience to, or independence from, the wider UK policy agenda. As we highlighted in our national examples, the United Kingdom can now be represented as one of the leading nations in formulating a nationwide ICT strategy with the New Labour government in Westminster beginning to pursue aggressively a widespread ICT agenda in areas as diverse as e-commerce, education and training, health, e-government and social security. Whilst the National Assembly often has a degree of freedom as to how such Westminster initiatives are implemented, many are nevertheless implemented in Wales as they are in England. With this in mind, to what extent are the key actors in Wales able to construct and implement a distinctive and effective set of policies for Wales above and beyond what is already being implemented from London? Of course, many in Wales see the opportunities of the information age as a chance to rewrite Wales's role with relation to its partners in the United Kingdom. As Finch (1998) argues, ICT is potentially an area where Wales could 'break free' from the confines of English oppression: 'Things are dramatically changing. Wales needs to get in now before big brother next door does it to us again' (Finch, 1998: 14).

However, there is a danger that ICT becomes another case of 'For Wales, See England'; with Welsh policies merely replicating their English counterparts, or, even worse, becoming less effective, watered-down and often delayed versions of policies being implemented in England. Moreover, even if a distinctive Welsh agenda is pursued there is the alternative possibility that clashes will occur between policies drawn up in Cardiff and London.

On the one hand, examining Wales in an information age is to ask such 'big' questions regarding the role of nation-states in the twenty-first century, the ever-changing relationship between Wales and the rest of the UK, Europe and beyond, as well as what it takes for individual countries to prosper in the global information economy. On the other hand, equally important questions to ask about Wales in an information age centre on the reality of all these interventions and initiatives, policies and programmes in practice. What impact can localized ICT-based initiatives and programmes really be expected to make? How are the issues outlined in chapter 2 being resolved? For example, is the Welsh language being revitalized by on-line language courses? Are people in isolated rural areas enjoying access to services and resources hitherto denied to them by issues of distance? How is ICT impacting on the experiences of Welsh people? All of these questions are addressed, at least in part, by our primary research evidence presented in the second part of this book.

Looking back to chapter 1, we must be aware of the information age as 'problematic'. Thus, we should be *critically* thinking about Wales in an information age from wider perspectives than perhaps we are used to (or indeed told to). As Golding (2000) observes, it is often very tempting to slip into a futuristic analysis of a near future where ICT has led to an erosion of time and space, the loosening of the familiar ties of social and economic formation, and freedom from the mundane barriers of power, privilege and place. Yet, instead of being distracted by the sublime (yet never quite attainable) near future of the information age as constructed by politicians, technologists and other enthusiasts we should be concerned with the present (and often mundane) implications of new technologies such as the Internet which, more prosaically, allow existing social action and process to occur more speedily, more efficiently or more conveniently. Thus, in considering the implications of ICT in Wales we are not talking about a radically new Wales – geography and distance will obviously still be an issue in ten years' time just as they have been for the past 10,000 years; inequalities of opportunity and outcome will still exist. Yet ICTs *will* be associated with change – some beneficial, some less beneficial.

This will form the basis of the remainder of our consideration of Wales in an information age. The information age encompasses far more than just the knowledge economy and e-commerce; the information age encompasses issues that defined Wales in the pre-informational age, such as people, land and culture. Above all the information age is not a homogeneous Nirvana just waiting for the correct technological infrastructure and universal access to ICT. Similarly, Wales is not a homogeneous nation. Indeed, Wales is often seen as a country of two halves – be it rural Wales and urban Wales, English-speaking Wales and Welsh-speaking Wales, or 'rich' Wales and 'poor' Wales. Either way, as Morgan and Mungham (2000) argue, we must not be tempted into a popularly painted picture of resurgent Wales which is in fact often merely a Cardiff-orientated picture of south-east Wales – one often not reflected in 'the other Wales' with some of the most deprived regions in western Europe. In the next chapter we now wish to sharpen our focus on the social aspects of Wales in an information age, and examine in more detail how one aspect of information age policy-making – combating social exclusion – is being put into practice at both UK- and Wales-wide levels. This sets the scene for our empirical examination in later chapters.

4

Social Aspects of an Information Age

The very technology that has the power to empower us all also has the potential to increase the problems of social exclusion unless we act to bridge the digital divide . . . The Government is determined to help bring us all into the information age. (Michael Wills MP in DfEE, 2000a)

INTRODUCTION

As we have seen in the first three chapters of this book, the use of information and communications technology (ICT) is seen by some to be a primary factor influencing the continued social cohesion of nation-states throughout the early twenty-first century. Recently, the often evangelical zeal of futurologists and technologists has been taken up with equal determination by governments around the world. Spurred on by the apparent inevitability of an information society, governments in industrialized countries are beginning to initiate ICT-based programmes ostensibly aiming to ensure that their citizens do not get 'left behind'. The ability to use ICT is now seen by politicians as part of 'the indispensable grammar of modern life' and a fundamental aspect of citizenship in the ensuing information society (Wills, 1999: 10).

Over the last ten years, countries such as the UK, USA and France have also seen a more subtle shift towards a centre-left, 'socially inclusive' general policy agenda. Indeed, the issue of combating 'social exclusion' and establishing an 'inclusive society' now forms an integral part of academic and political debate in the UK; officially embodied in the Labour Party's establishment of the interdepartmental Social Exclusion Unit during their first year in office (Levitas, 1998). An intriguing aspect of recent social policy formation has been the attempted convergence of these 'information society' and 'inclusive society' discourses into an ongoing debate over the potential of ICTs either to exacerbate or to alleviate social exclusion. As Phipps (2000: 41) contends:

A risk is acknowledged that ICT developments may reinforce polarisation and create additional division through people and communities who are 'information rich' or 'information poor', whereby the failure to get plugged-in leads to a downwards spiral of economic activity with associated social fall-outs. ICTs can be seen as neutral in themselves, as an enabler. Positive and beneficial applications, enhancing democracy and accountability, are an active choice and responsibility for our society.

Indeed, in the UK as a whole this perspective has been quickly translated into an extensive policy agenda aimed at using ICT for social inclusive purposes. This chapter therefore explores both the Westminster and the Cardiff governments' ICT-based social policy drives through policy statements, official documentation and political discourse – examining the 'problems' that they set out to address, the substance of the policies, and the perceived rationales and benefits for doing so.

CONCEPTUALIZING THE PROBLEM: FROM 'SOCIAL EXCLUSION' TO THE 'DIGITAL DIVIDE'

Although much used by both policy-makers and academics, the concept of 'social exclusion' remains contested. Originating in France in the 1970s and 1980s, concern with social exclusion has become increasingly important to the policy agendas of Western nations; largely displacing the specific issues of poverty, deprivation and injustice in many countries' policy-making (Lenoir, 1974; Martin, 1996). For most, the concept of 'social exclusion' is distinct in being seen as a dynamic process rather than a static outcome. As Giddens (1998: 104) reasons, 'exclusion is not about graduations of inequality, but about the mechanisms that act to detach groups of people from the social mainstream.' In this sense, social exclusion is seen as being a far 'wider concept' than poverty (Parkinson 1998) and, it follows, more difficult to define adequately. Burchardt et al. (1999: 230) offer the following tentative definition: 'An individual is socially excluded if (a) he or she is geographically resident in a society and (b) he or she does not participate in the normal activities of citizens in that society.'

In defining 'normal' activities, these authors broadly concur with others in identifying five dimensions of participation in society that can be seen as constituting 'inclusion' (e.g. Berghman, 1995; C. Oppenheim, 1998; Walker, 1997). These are grouped as: *consumption activity* (being able to consume at least a minimum level of the goods and services which are considered normal for the society); *savings activity* (accumulating savings, pensions entitlements or owning property); *production activity* (engaging in an economically or socially valued activity, such as paid work, education/ training, retirement and looking after a family); *political activity* (engaging in some collective effort to improve or protect the social and physical environment); and *social activity* (engaging in significant social interaction with family or friends and identifying with a cultural group or community).

This multidimensional approach to defining 'social exclusion' has obvious conceptual advantages but also has equally obvious practical disadvantages. Addressing the 'problem' of social exclusion has proved to be a complex undertaking – reflected in the Social Exclusion Unit's initial eighteen areas of concern, ranging from housing to employment, political participation to use of ICT. The UK government, therefore, has taken a deliberately broad approach to conceptualizing social exclusion:

> Social exclusion is a shorthand term for what can happen when people or areas suffer from a combination of linked problems such as unemployment, poor skills, low incomes, poor housing, high crime environments, bad health and family breakdown. In the past, governments have had policies that tried to deal with each of these problems individually, but there has been little success at tackling the complicated links between them, or preventing them from arising in the first place. (Social Exclusion Unit, 2000)

In recent years, this concern over social exclusion has been augmented in the political arena by the looming impact of ICT on society, with the broad notion of social exclusion also exemplified in terms of 'digital exclusion'. Concern over 'digital exclusion' first emerged with regard to inequalities in access to technology between countries, and in particular to the technological disparity between developed and developing nations (Holderness, 1993, 1998; Rai and Lal, 2000). As table 4.1 shows, the disparities between countries' levels of access to ICT continues to be marked, leading some commentators to point to the emergence of the 'fourth world' in the information age, of people so marginalized that they are not even worth exploiting (Castells, 1996). The 1990s therefore saw the initiation of mainstream political discussion of 'information haves' and 'information have-nots' (Wresch, 1996), 'information and communication poverty' (Balnaves et al., 1991) and 'the digital divide' (Jurich, 2000; Parker, 2000; BECTA, 2001).

Yet, within European advanced capitalist societies, the supranational focus of these debates has gravitated towards the issue of technological inequalities within individual countries. In so doing, the prevailing view has broadly settled on combating a perceived dichotomous divide between those citizens who are 'connected' and those citizens who remain 'disconnected'. Crucially, digital exclusion is seen as a dual threat, with access to ICT and the ability to use it potentially creating a new form of exclusion as well as reinforcing existing patterns of exclusion from society.

Table 4.1 Levels of access to information technologies by country

Country	Per 1000 people					
	Personal computers	Mobile telephones	Telephone lines	Television sets	Radios	Daily newspapers
United States	406.7	206	644	847	2115	212
Singapore	399.5	273	543	354	739	324
Switzerland	394.9	147	661	536	969	330
Australia	362.2	264	505	638	1385	297
Norway	360.8	381	621	579	920	593
Denmark	360.2	273	633	568	1146	311
Sweden	350.3	358	679	531	907	446
Finland	310.7	417	556	534	1385	455
Netherlands	280.3	110	564	541	963	305
Canada	270.6	139	609	708	1078	159
New Zealand	263.9	149	486	501	1027	223
Germany	255.5	99	550	570	946	311
United Kingdom	242.4	151	540	641	1445	332
Ireland	241.3	146	411	455	703	153
Belgium	235.3	95	468	510	792	160
India	2.1	1	19	69	105	–
Syria	1.7	0	88	68	274	20
Ghana	1.6	1	6	109	238	14
Mozambique	1.6	0	4	4	39	3
Tanzania	1.6	1	3	21	278	4
Cameroon	1.5	0	5	81	162	7
Uganda	1.4	0	2	26	123	2
Yemen	1.2	1	13	273	64	15
Laos	1.1	1	5	4	139	4
Benin	0.9	1	6	91	108	2
Cambodia	0.9	3	2	124	127	–
Angola	0.7	1	5	91	54	12
Mali	0.6	0	2	10	49	1
Guinea	0.3	0	3	41	47	–
Niger	0.2	0	2	26	69	0

Source: World Bank Institute, 2000.

As these quotations from the prime minister and his then minister for learning and technology highlight:

> My point is this: this technology is revolutionising the way we work, the way we do business, the way we live our lives. Our job is to make sure it is not the preserve of an elite – but an Internet for the people. (Blair, 2000)

If the digital divide is not tackled, it will entrench existing exclusion for generations. Familiarity with ICT is the indispensable grammar of modern life. Those not empowered by it are disenfranchised. (Wills, 1999: 10)

The UK government's stance, as such, is constructed around broad notions of social justice for the information age and striving, as far as possible, to ensure a 'fair' information society:

In the Information Age the many must benefit, not just the few . . . A society of 'information have-nots' would not just be unfair – it would be inefficient. (COoI, 1998)

The left has always been dedicated to a fairer society where everyone is able to make the most of themselves. The challenge now is to equip the people of Britain with the tools they need to succeed in whatever they want to do. Deploying these new technologies should be as easy and natural to everyone as riding a bike. They are the bridge to the future and we cannot afford to leave anyone stranded behind as we cross over. (Wills, 1999: 11)

EMPIRICAL EVIDENCE FOR THE 'DIGITAL DIVIDE'

While dramatic, these concerns are reinforced by an emerging picture of inequalities in access to ICT. In the UK, a range of recent research suggests that access to ICT is patterned along the lines of socio-economic status, income, gender, level of education, age, geography and ethnicity (e.g. BRMB, 1999; National Statistics, 2000, 2001; MORI, 1999; DTI, 2000b). Although these figures vary, the emerging trend is that even within the UK's relatively high levels of ICT use, specific social groups are significantly less likely to have ready access to ICT. For example, in terms of socio-economic status, such inequalities of opportunity appear marked and enduring (see figures 4.1, 4.2 and tables 4.2, 4.3).

As well as differences in terms of socio-economic status and income, such access to home computers, the Internet and digital television also appears to be patterned in terms of gender (with higher proportions of males than females reporting access to ICTs), age (with access to all three technologies inversely correlated to age) and composition of household (with two-adult and one/two-child households most likely to have access).

Significantly, access to ICT also appears to vary greatly between different parts of the UK. For example, in terms of Internet access, Wales lags behind all regions of England apart from the North East (see figure 4.3, table 4.3). Yet, in terms of access to digital television Wales actually heads levels of take-up by region (see figure 4.4).

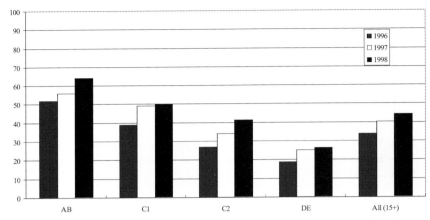

Source: BMRB International, 1999.

Figure 4.1
UK access to a home PC by socio-economic group
Percentage of each socio-economic group reporting access to a home PC in 1996,
1997 and 1998

**Table 4.2 Adults who have used the Internet at some time by social class. Data
are percentage of households**

Per cent	July 2000	January 2001
Professional	66	78
Intermediate	58	65
Skilled non-manual	46	52
Skilled manual	31	37
Partly skilled	26	33
Unskilled	20	27
All Adults	**45**	**51**

Source: National Statistics, 2001.

These figures should also be seen in an international context, with the
United Kingdom apparently heading a 'second division' of Internet users,
following 'leading' countries such as the United States, Sweden and
Finland (Booz, Allen and Hamilton, 2000). Of more urgency is the fact that
within this position Wales lags behind all but one English region in Internet
access, albeit being marginally ahead of levels of connectivity in Scotland
and Northern Ireland.

Table 4.3 Households with home access to the Internet, UK by gross income decile group: 1998–1999 and 1999–2000. Data are percentage of households

Per cent	1998–9	1999–2000
Lowest 10 per cent	3	6
Second decile group	1	3
Third	2	4
Fourth	3	6
Fifth	4	15
Sixth	7	15
Seventh	10	22
Eighth	16	28
Ninth	19	38
Highest 10 per cent	32	48
All households	**10**	**19**

Source: National Statistics, 2000.

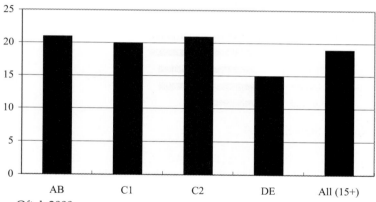

Source: Oftel, 2000.

Figure 4.2
UK access to digital television by socio-economic group. Data are percentage of each socio-economic group reporting access to digital television in May 2000

Of course, all of these figures should be read with a health warning. As Arthur (1995) reflected, attempting to quantify the number of people using the Internet is the modern equivalent to the religious academic exercise of trying to quantify the number of angels that could dance on the head of a pin. What each survey actually means by 'access' often varies, and such is the fast-changing nature of ICT use that such figures can only ever provide

Table 4.4 Households with home access to the Internet by country: 1998–1999 and 1999–2000. Data are percentage of households

Per cent	1998–9	1999–2000
England	11	20
Wales	7	15
Scotland	8	14
Northern Ireland	5	11
United Kingdom	**10**	**19**

Source: National Statistics, 2000.

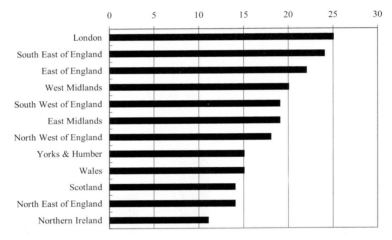

Source: National Statistics, 2000.

Figure 4.3
Households with home access to the Internet by government office region and country 1999–2000. Data are percentage of households

a 'snapshot' which is outdated as soon as it is published. Indeed, such is the fast-changing nature of these figures that attempting to extrapolate trends and forecast future growth patterns is fraught with difficulty. For example, only a few years ago, forecasters were happy to predict that by 2000 everyone on the planet would have their own web-page and be connected to the Internet (Arthur, 1995).

Nevertheless, such figures can give us an indication of the patterns of ICT access in the UK and, to a lesser extent, in Wales. It would seem the case that disparities do exist between different social groups in terms of access to ICT. Moreover, although technologists are keen to talk of such

Source: Oftel, 2000.

Figure 4.4
Households with home access to digital television by government office region and country. Data are percentage of households

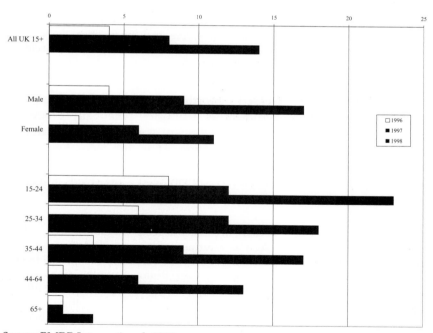

Source: BMRB International, 1999.

Figure 4.5
Use of home PC for the Internet by age and gender. Data are percentage of individuals reporting home PC use

patterns as merely reflecting 'early adopters' of technology whose levels of technology use are eventually matched by the majority of the population, there is strong evidence that such inequalities are actually being strengthened over time rather than alleviated (e.g. see figure 4.5). So what, if anything, can governments do to combat the digital divide?

COMBATING THE DIGITAL DIVIDE

Those groups most likely to be 'digitally excluded' in terms of access to ICT are remarkably similar to those who can already be characterized as being socially excluded more generally – especially in terms of low income and socio-economic status (Burchardt et al., 1999). For both the Westminster and Cardiff governments, therefore, the potential exacerbation of existing exclusion coupled with the scale of such divisions is seen as a cause for some concern. Indeed, New Labour's own commissioned research recently identified an 'acute emerging digital divide' of over a third of the population:

> At this rate, [Internet] penetration in the UK should pass 60% 'naturally' by 2003. However, far from evening out the emerging inequalities, the wave of growth is likely to exacerbate them in relative terms, leaving an unconnected or excluded group of over 20 million citizens. (Booz, Allen and Hamilton, 2000: 13)

Providing access to ICT-based opportunities for these disadvantaged groups is seen by the government as a priority; potentially promoting social inclusion and preventing the 'nightmare' scenario of twenty million excluded citizens from coming to fruition. Thus, the focus for the UK government is clear – overcoming a 'digital divide' defined in terms of lower levels of ICT access within 'disadvantaged', 'deprived' and 'low-income' communities:

> The rapid spread of ICTs is changing many aspects of modern life . . . [The Information Revolution] is seen as a turning point, a major leap for society equivalent to the industrial revolution. Much of the UK is well placed to take advantage of it. At the same time, however, Britain faces the problem of a society divided socially and economically. The gap between the worst off and the rest of the country has increased over the last two decades. In some of the poorest neighbourhoods people face severe deprivation. Access to the benefits of the 'Information revolution' is often the most difficult because of a lack of awareness, skills or opportunities. People living in deprived neighbourhoods should have the same opportunity to benefit from the rapid spread of ICTs rather than being further excluded by them. (Policy Action Team 15, Social Exclusion Unit, 2000, para. 1.1)

Since the inception of the Social Exclusion Unit in 1997, these concerns have been crystallized into a concurrent series of initiatives and programmes. In examining this policy the constituent initiatives can be broadly divided into two distinct phases – (i) initiatives aimed at widening access to ICT; (ii) initiatives aimed at providing services through ICT.

(i) Widening access to ICT: getting 'UK Online'

The UK government is attempting to ensure that exclusion from the 'opportunities of the information age' does not take place. The opportunities of the information age – for education, for entertainment or employment – must be open to all. The government's role is to make sure that we do not create a society of information haves and have-nots (COoI, 1998: 13).The government's drive to widen access to ICT has been constructed around the pledge to achieve 'universal access' to the Internet by 2005. Underlying this ambiguous target is a commitment to work with telecommunications companies to reduce Internet access charges and an envisaged commitment to 'promote usage on a regular basis by at least 70 per cent of individuals by 2003' (Booz, Allen and Hamilton, 2000: 3). As Tony Blair has argued, this focus on universal (or at least 70 per cent) access is firmly based on both social and economic rationales:

> Universal Internet access is vital if we are not only to avoid social divisions over the new economy but to create a knowledge economy of the future which is for everyone. Because it's likely that the Internet will be as ubiquitous and as normal as electricity is today. We cannot accept a digital divide. For business. Or for individuals. (Blair, 2000)

In practice this stated commitment to 'universal access' involves a variety of initiatives originating from a number of government departments, latterly branded under the umbrella term of 'UK Online' (DTI, 2000b). In terms of widening access to ICT these initiatives have largely focused on establishing distributed sites of ICT access. For example, at the beginning of 2001, the government announced plans to establish a network of 6,000 'ICT Learning Centres'. This initiative is focused on 'disadvantaged communities' in rural and inner-city areas of England and they will provide flexible access to new technologies for those without ICT facilities at home or at work, and will be located in a variety of existing sites such as schools and community centres (DfEE, 2000b). Above all, the focus will be on overcoming barriers of geography by bringing ICT 'to people's doorsteps' (Wills in DfEE, 2000c) with an overriding emphasis on flexible community access to ICT:

ICT learning centres will provide a *local* place for *local* people to meet, learn and achieve. They could be in a community centre, church, or a mobile centre, for example for those in rural or dispersed communities – whatever best suits the needs of the people who will use it. (DfEE, 2000b; emphasis in original)

Alongside these DfEE (now DfES) initiatives, £200 million of New Opportunities Funding has also been committed to the Public Libraries IT Network, aiming to link every public library to the Internet by 2002. Moreover, community access to ICT was also included as an integral element of the then Department of the Environment, Transport and Regions' 'New Deal for Communities' funding. The focus of these initiatives on community-based technological accessibility has latterly been reinforced by a series of financial announcements concerned with extending levels of home access to ICT among the UK population. In 1999 the chancellor of the exchequer announced a £15 million scheme to make 100,000 refurbished computers available to low-income families for as little as £5 per month. Subsequently a £10 million 'Wired-up Communities' programme was launched in 2000 aiming to provide high-quality access to ICT hardware, on-line access and training to 14,000 households in seven 'highly socially deprived' communities in England.

(ii) Providing access to public services via ICT

Complementing these initiatives, the second thrust of the UK government's ICT drive is the electronic provision of public services. As the title of the recent 'e-citizen, e-business, e-government' strategic framework suggests, this focus is on both the technologizing of public-sector services and promoting ICT-mediated private business (e-commerce). Indeed, much of this effort has been directed towards stimulating private-sector use of ICT with the ambitious yet ambiguous aim of making Britain 'the best place for e-commerce by 2002' (Blair, 2000).

The government has also undertaken a programme of making public services accessible via ICT. The *Modernizing Government* White Paper first outlined a strategy of 'citizen-focused' electronic delivery of government services (Cabinet Office, 1999a), with a later revised target that by 2005 the public will be able to do all of its dealings with government electronically through their television, telephone or computer (Cabinet Office, 2000a). Essentially, this element of the government's ICT drive is seen as affording a 'democratization' of access to information for the socially excluded, leading to eventual 'empowerment':

Society is not homogeneous. Government exists to serve those who feel excluded from developments in information technology just as much as it serves those who embrace new technology. The information age should increase the choice of how citizens and businesses receive services, not restrict it . . . We will develop targeted strategies to ensure that all groups have proper access to information age government. (Cabinet Office, 1999a: para. 6)

Increasingly the information provided so quickly will be a gateway to opportunity in every aspect, from offering competitive prices for goods to offering access to better healthcare and leisure and cultural resources. It offers vital weapons for democratic empowerment and civic activism . . . Those who fall behind will be left behind. And all today's problems of social and economic exclusion will be multiplied. (Wills, 1999: 10)

In theory, then, the provision of social security, employment, health and housing services via ICT is seen as 'unlocking the door of government' for the socially excluded (Cabinet Office, 2000b). Despite the emerging 'roll-out' of schemes such as NHS Direct and the computerized benefit payments systems in post offices, the most advanced aspect of this drive to date has been in the area of education and training. Indeed, New Labour has committed over £1.6 billion to a series of initiatives since 1997 aiming to widen access to educational and training opportunities via ICT. The government is focusing particularly on education as a primary area of social exclusion, and on ICT as a method of overcoming this.

CONCLUSION

We have covered a lot of ground over the last four chapters. So far we have seen how the notion of the information age is intertwined with myriad economic, cultural, political and social issues – many of which can be seen to be decidedly non-information age in their origins and impact. Whereas we could now go on to speculate about the development of Wales as an 'e-nation' in the year 2020, our previous discussion has instead pointed towards the need to take a careful look at the realities of the information age for present-day Wales. As we argued at the beginning of the book, the tendency to look only forward to what *may* happen, as opposed to looking at what *is* actually happening, is an underlying weakness of many contemporary discussions of the information age. We now, therefore, will balance our discussion of the many issues that the information age throws up for Wales with consideration of how ICT is actually beginning to be implemented in Wales and its impact 'on the ground'. In particular, we now go on to focus on education and training as a particular area of public policy in the information age. We do so both because, as we have seen in chapters 3 and 4, ICT policy is more mature in this area (and we can therefore assess its actual impact), and also because in discussing education we need to discuss many other areas of related policy, including the economy and social inclusion.

Much of the remainder of this book, therefore, focuses on these issues of education and training (under the aegis of 'lifelong learning'), social inclusion and economic development, utilizing primary data from a large-scale study of lifelong learning and the role of ICT in Wales. In this way we use a central policy to examine in considerably greater detail the points made so far, and return to the more general theme of the information age in the concluding chapters. The next two chapters set the scene for this examination: chapter 5 outlines the context for this extended case study by discussing the key issues for lifelong learning in Wales, and chapter 6 examines in more detail recent ICT-based initiatives for both school and post-compulsory phases. In particular, chapter 6 explains how the 'virtual education movement' is intended to improve participation in lifelong learning, benefiting Wales economically and, it is hoped, combating social exclusion.

5

Lifelong Learning in Wales

Education in Wales represents something of a paradox: a history and reputation of respect for learning combined with relatively poor measures of educational attainment in the present day in almost every assessment. If we are to consider education in an information age then we need to identify and understand the problems that are seen as outstanding. This chapter therefore presents a brief overview of pertinent issues at both compulsory and post-compulsory levels of education within a contemporary view of the 'learning society'.

A CRISIS IN WELSH EDUCATION?

In the UK, and in England and Wales particularly, education has been the subject of some considerable criticism, leading in turn to numerous initiatives delivered with the promise of 'salvation'. It is important in evaluating the impact of any current initiatives, such as those based on ICT (see chapter 7 and those following), to understand the nature of the problems they set out to solve. In particular they must be seen within the long-standing 'crisis' account of British education based on failing schools, falling standards, increasing inequity and so on (Boyson, 1975; Husen and Postlethwaite, 1985).

The basis of this now-established crisis account is expressed in many different ways, most commonly in comparison with education in other countries. For example, the real level of government expenditure on education in the UK went from 5.2 per cent of GDP in 1970–1, to reach a peak of 6.6 per cent in 1975–6, but subsequently declined to 4.8 per cent by 1990–1 (Hartley, 1994). In 1994, Britain spent 32 ECU per person on education, and 27 per cent of school-leavers achieved a GCSE, grade C or above, in English, a science, and mathematics. Both France and Germany spent 66 ECU per head, and 66 per cent of school-leavers achieved equivalent passes in the national language, science and mathematics (Hugill and Narayan, 1995). Pupils in upper secondary schooling in Britain learn the fewest foreign languages of all the EU states, fewer than half as many languages as the European average (Eurostat, 1995). Around 20 per cent of sixteen-year-olds do not achieve even a GCSE grade G in English or mathematics, and are thus not at the level of proficiency of the average twelve-year-old (Pyke, 1996). The proportion of the population in the age range twenty-five to fifty-nine who are only educated to lower secondary level is around 50 per cent, compared with a figure of less than 20 per cent for Germany, for example. This figure, which is even higher for females, is reducing more slowly than many other member states, and given the fact that the greatest decrease has been in the proportion of females with no post-compulsory education, the relative figures for males may actually be getting worse (Eurostat, 1995). Among school-leavers 'the UK . . . lags behind many of its European and international competitors' (ETAG, 1998: 11). In the population as a whole, only 45 per cent of those in the UK have attained the equivalent of National Vocational Qualification (NVQ) Level 2, whereas in France the figure is 65 per cent and in Germany 70 per cent (ETAG, 1998).

This crisis account generally derives from politicians, media commentators, and some academics and practitioners who push a version of the crisis for their own ends. There is little validity in any of it (see Gorard, 2000a), and indeed all countries could find *some* negative evidence in comparison with their neighbours. Viewed long-term and in proportion to other relevant changes, standards of British education are certainly being maintained, while indicators of inequality and injustice have been decreasing (although recent policy changes in England may have produced a more socially stratified school system than in the 1990s). A two-track system of education, leading to 'winners' and 'losers', certainly remains today but is less damaging than during the period of near-universal selection (Gorard et al., 1999a).

The problem for Wales is that whatever criticisms have been made about standards in England and the other home countries seem to apply more strongly here. There has been a tendency in the past to refer to Wales as being a nation of education-lovers, whose respect for education is almost 'primordial' (Roberts, 1983). It has been stated, for example, that the 'Welsh' value education, and have a deep-rooted desire for learning, although by the end of the 1960s some observers were suggesting that these attitudes to learning were changing (Lowe, 1970). Nowadays, however, it is more commonly suggested that secondary schooling is almost a complete irrelevance to 'ordinary', that is the majority of working-class, youngsters in Wales today (cf. Brown, 1987). There are thus two distinct histories of the development of education in Wales, and two versions of the current standard of education in the region. On the one hand, the people of

Wales are seen as having a unique respect for learning leading to early innovation in the delivery of quality education to a relatively large proportion of the population, and on the other, education today can be seen as élitist, constraining and of little relevance to most people. The British two-track distribution of educational experience is therefore seen to be at its most exaggerated in Wales.

ISSUES FOR COMPULSORY EDUCATION IN WALES

Perhaps the most obvious and most prominent contemporary issue in Welsh education is that of language, with a succession of educational legislation ensuring that Welsh is now taught in all schools as either a secondary or primary language and over 500 *Ysgolion Cymraeg* offering Welsh-medium education. These changes may have caused some problems, including staffing shortages in technical subjects, some parental disquiet, and relative weakness in modern foreign languages (Gorard, 1997a). They have also led to a divisive and erroneous discourse based on the purported superiority of Welsh-medium schooling (e.g. G. Jones, 1996; but see Gorard, 1998a, 2000b). Similarly Wales is seen to suffer from various other school-level disadvantages in relation to England (such as gender inequalities at senior levels, classroom expenditure, small size of schools and recruitment problems – see Reynolds, 1990). However, aside from these issues, the overriding problem that is seen to blight Welsh education is that of attainment

Given the problems of remoteness, relative economic poverty and the implementation of a bilingual educational programme across the whole of a predominantly monolingual region (see chapter 2), it is perhaps not surprising that many observers have been less than impressed by the levels of attainment in schools in Wales. The grammar school tradition, after 1944, polarized high attainment and high failure rates, wasting talent and encouraging social division (Istance and Rees, 1995). Until the advent of comprehensivization in the 1970s, schools in Wales had produced a high proportion of relatively well-qualified school-leavers as well as a high proportion that were completely unqualified. As early as 1974 some reports suggested that schools, or pupils, in Wales were under-performing to some extent. A national survey of non-attendance at school found the situation in Wales much worse than in England, even in areas with similar socio-economic disadvantages (Reynolds, 1995) but particularly in urban areas like Merthyr Tydfil and Cardiff in the 1980s (Reynolds, 1990). The 1981 Loosemore report found that Welsh schools seemed overly concerned with the most able pupils, and that consequently too many of the others were leaving school with no qualifications at all. In 1978, 28 per cent of pupils left school in Wales without any qualification (G. Jones, 1990). Even by 1989, when only 9.5 per cent of pupils in England left school with no qualifications and this figure was decreasing every year, the figure for Wales was 17 per cent, nearly twice the size (Reynolds, 1995). Progress towards any of the school-level targets has been slower in Wales than in England, the neighbouring country with an almost identical school system (see table 5.1). Therefore, 'in Wales overall . . . much under-achievement remains' (OHMCI, 1993: 2), leading Reynolds (1990) to describe Welsh youngsters as being, in some respects, 'schooled for failure'.

Table 5.1 Relative progress towards Foundation Target 1

% 5+ GCSEs A*–C	Spring 1991	Autumn 1995
England	53.5%	67.4%
Wales	51.2%	62.2%

In summary, there can be little doubt that despite shifts and changes from year to year, almost any educational indicator shows schools in Wales with a weaker position than those in England. School attendance figures, assessments from Key Stage 1 to A level and GNVQ, progress towards Lifetime Targets, and rates of participation in post-compulsory education and training all tend to show Welsh schooling in a worse light. For example, more students from Wales are leaving school with no qualifications than in the rest of the UK. As far as it is possible to estimate, other countries in the EU have qualification levels way in excess of current targets (G. Jones, 1996). Educational participation of 16–18-year-olds in Wales was 65 per cent of the age group in 1993, on a par with only Greece and Portugal in the EU. In fact, it is suggested that 'as a society, we lack a learning ethos' (Varanaya, 1995).

So clear are these differences that all political parties for the past twenty years have adopted policies based on the premise that Wales faces a problem of 'underachievement', in just the same way that they have read international comparisons to show that British education leads to chronic underachievement (see Gorard, 2001a). Underachievement in Wales continues to be the basis for educational policy for the National Assembly (e.g. ETAG, 1998; National Assembly for Wales, 2001b), backed up by findings such as 'Wales lags behind the rest of the UK in terms of the level of qualifications in the workforce' (ETAG, 1998: 11).

However, such political concerns are misplaced in reality. Where schools and students in Wales are compared with their equivalents in England, judged in terms of socio-economic background, there is no difference between the scores of the two countries. These findings, revealing a powerful link between the characteristics of students in each local education authority (LEA) and their results in public examinations, have been replicated in many studies and at many different levels of aggregation (from classroom to international). Clearly these findings do not imply that children from families in poverty are unable to obtain good examination results, especially since the analysis is not conducted at the level of the individual student. They *do* reveal how little of the variation in school outcomes can be attributed to school systems and processes themselves. It is patently unfair to compare the school scores of children living in Mayfair with those in Ebbw Vale (for example). In the context of the comparison between England and Wales, this means that there is no realistic evidence for the 'schooled for failure' thesis. Schools and students in Wales are attaining pretty much the level of results that would be expected from their socio-economic make-up, and there is no reason at present to suggest that schools in England and Wales are differentially effective with equivalent students (Gorard, 1998b). Coupled with other related findings about patterns of differential attainment and access to schools in Wales, the results suggest that if there are key problems facing Wales in an information age, then the standard of initial education is not one of them (Gorard, 2000a).

Indeed, the evidence suggests that the actual impact of schools on their examination outcomes is far less than in popular imagination. The key predictors of examination success instead appear to derive from the background characteristics of the student, and this is true *regardless* of the type of school attended. To put it another, perhaps more helpful, way, the inequalities in society far outweigh any differences between schools. Perhaps one conclusion from this is therefore that policy-makers should not accept the serious inequality in society as a given phenomenon and then try to engineer a solution on solely school-based initiatives (ICT-based or not), but that they should also tackle the inequality throughout society. With this in mind, in locating the true source of any 'crisis' in Welsh education we would perhaps be better looking at education as a whole rather than specifically school-level provision. We can now, therefore, turn our attention to the issue of 'lifelong learning'.

ISSUES FOR POST-COMPULSORY EDUCATION IN WALES

Today, the nature of lifelong learning in Wales is different, without being clearly better, from the traditional notion of Wales's religious and working-class industrial roots leading to an almost innate respect for continuous

Table 5.2 LEA-based adult education in Wales

	1991/92	1993/94
LEA centres	341	197
Male students	19,672	13,227
Female students	50,035	37,698

Source: Welsh Office, 1995a.

Table 5.3 Percentage of working-age population in job-related training, 1992

South East England	10.8
North England	9.9
Scotland	9.3
Wales	8.6

Source: Istance and Rees, 1994.

learning, resulting in a nation where 'public participation in various forms of education [was] very much greater and the habit of community co-operation [was] very much stronger than in England' (Lowe, 1970: 315). As we saw in chapter 2, the industry infrastructure of Wales has changed considerably over the last fifty years, and the training provision with it. The last Workers Institute in Wales was built in 1961, and all of them have gradually switched to being primarily places of entertainment rather than learning. All adult education in Wales has declined since the early 1980s, and that provided by LEAs has shown a significant drop since 1991 (Gorard et al., 1997b), so that more recent generations may not have the opportunities that their fathers, in particular, did (Rees and Rees, 1980). It is unlikely that this drop is simply due to lack of demand. It is also a result of the lack of some types of provision. Reducing the number of centres may make sense financially, but it increases the average travel time for students in an area of limited public transport. The massive impact, particularly on female students, can be seen in table 5.2. Of course, LEAs are not the only providers of adult education and training. The WEA and YMCA also provide classes for adults, but the numbers of these are still diminishing, with the only growth area being in university-department extra-mural classes. Crucially, throughout the 1990s, the number of people in training through work showed little change in Wales. Of 940,000 employees, only 14,000 had any training in the four weeks prior to one survey, of which 8,000 had training off-the-job, 4,000 on-the-job and 2,000 had both (Welsh Office, 1995a). These proportions had been constant for the last four years. Around 25 per cent of companies have a written training plan, which is a rise from 16 per cent in 1991, and the figures for companies with an agreed annual training budget are broadly similar (Welsh Office, 1996). However, plans and budgets are easy to increase. They are window-dressing, indicative of, but not the same as, training.

Vocational training in Wales, as in the rest of Britain, is largely deregulated and left to employers who tend to focus on a relatively low skills equilibrium, compared with Germany for instance. Qualifications such as National Vocational Qualifications (NVQs) are generally used to certify training that employers were already giving anyway. Very few small/ medium sized companies in Wales offer conscious multiskilling since they are dominated by the fear of poaching (Cockrill et al., 1996). Istance and Rees (1994) reported that the percentage of the working-age population who received job-related training in 1992 was lower in Wales than any other region in Britain (table 5.3). Wales consistently has the lowest proportion of 19–21-year-olds qualified at NVQ level 2, and in terms of the national targets for education and training, Wales had the lowest attainment of the Foundation Target 1 among the home countries by 1993, partly because of the relatively poor performance of males (Istance and Rees, 1995). A similar picture applies to Foundation Target 3, except that in this case, women are also performing poorly in Wales. The figures are improving (G. Jones, 1996), but not as fast as in England (DfEE, 1996a) and not as fast as needed to meet the targets, and this is despite primary evidence from this study that some employers are 'sharp-pencilling' NVQ certificates in order to meet their own targets. Much of the apparent improvement comes from natural inflation of qualifications as older people retire, rather than being due to an increase in investment in training for all ages (Gorard et al., 2000a).

Wales also has a low proportion of trainees gaining a qualification after Youth Training (39 per cent compared with 47 per cent nationally, DfEE 1996a). Of those of working age in Wales, 27 per cent had no qualification at all, 19 per cent have a GCSE, 24 per cent have an A level, 9 per cent have a higher qualification below degree, and a further 9 per cent have a degree or equivalent (Welsh Office, 1996). The number of people with no qualifications is higher in the older age groups, 43 per cent of 60–64-year-olds, 26 per cent of 35–49 and 14 per cent of 20–44 for example (Welsh Office, 1995b).

Despite recent increases in participation in HE and FE in Wales, there is still therefore a very real danger of Wales becoming a relatively low-pay, low-skill economy. In the first place there are insufficient opportunities locally for the number of graduates produced locally, so the exodus or waste of the highly educated continues (Delamont and Rees, 1996). Many students from Wales, around 8,000, attend universities outside Wales, and a

fair proportion of these may never return. In addition, the majority of
students at the University of Wales, 17,000 in all, are from outside Wales,
although this situation is changing with a shift towards study nearer home,
the expansion of FE in Wales, and the shift towards older less 'traditional'
students via Access courses and less traditional HE institutions, such as the
Open University (Istance and Rees, 1995).

RECREATING WALES AS A LIFELONG LEARNING SOCIETY

From this background Welsh education was in a relatively weak position
during the mid-1990s – with an indifferent compulsory education system
and a stagnant adult education sector. The dual problems of a low-
performing school sector and low levels of both work-based and outside
work-based adult training belied the older popular notion of Wales as a
'learning nation' (Gorard and Rees, 2002). However, over the last half of the
1990s there has been an apparent 'reawakening' and reassessment of
education and training by educators and politicians alike – as evidenced in
Tony Blair's now infamous pledge to concentrate on 'education, education,
education'. It is this renewed emphasis on education and its roots in the
economic and social aspects of the information age to which we shall now
turn.

Perhaps it would be misleading to argue that education suffered from a
lack of governmental concern over the past couple of decades in Britain, as
through much of the 1980s it was schools and schooling which provided
the focal point of policy-makers' attention. However, more latterly, this
focus has widened to encompass a broader conceptualization of 'lifelong
learning', which certainly continues to embrace the compulsory phases of
education, but also includes activities in further and higher education, as
well as continuing education and training throughout adult life (Coffield,
1997a). This is not to suggest, of course, that this shift in policy emphasis
has produced a coherent strategy with respect to education and training
through the life-course. Nevertheless, the change is unmistakable. For
example, the creation of a minister for lifelong learning within the Department for Education and Skills (DfES), along with equivalent positions in
the devolved Scottish and Welsh administrations, signals a formal acknowledgement of its significance. Similarly, a plethora of official reports and
other policy statements on lifelong learning have flowed from government
departments in recent years. Especially since the election of the New
Labour administration in 1997, official pronouncements about lifelong
learning have proliferated spectacularly. There have been three substantial
reports (Kennedy, 1997; Fryer, 1997; and Dearing, 1997), a major Green

Paper (DfEE, 1998), and most recently a White Paper on the reorganization of post-sixteen education and training. Certainly, lifelong learning has come to occupy a position which – symbolically at least – is at the centre of government strategy in both Westminster and Cardiff.

What is involved here is more than a narrowly technical adjustment to the organization of educational provision. It is instructive, for example, that the key Green Paper was given the portentous title, *The Learning Age: A Renaissance for a New Britain* (DfEE, 1998; our emphasis). What is suggested, then, is a transformation in learning opportunities, which is crucial to effecting a profound restructuring of wider social and economic relations. The intellectual basis for this is provided, in turn, by what has become a widespread consensus about the emergent requirements of the economy. Simply put, it is now widely argued that the production and distribution of knowledge are increasingly significant processes in the determination of economic competitiveness and development, which are reflected, in turn, in economic growth, employment change and levels of welfare. The capacity of both organizations and individuals to engage successfully in learning processes of a variety of kinds has come to be regarded as a crucial determinant of economic performance (for example, Lundvall and Johnson, 1994). For some commentators, this implies nothing less than a fundamental transition from an industrial to a knowledge-based or *learning society* (OECD, 1996; Leadbetter, 1999). Clearly, alternative accounts of the nature of the learning society are possible and many have been propounded at length in the literature (Gorard et al., 1997c). However, the ideological impact of this particular version derives precisely from the fact that it is rooted in a coherent – albeit contested – analysis of contemporary patterns of economic and social change.

The proponents of this sort of analysis recognize, of course, that the development of the learning society (even defined in these terms) involves a complexity of economic and social processes. On the one hand, it holds the promise of increased productivity and an improved standard of living. On the other, it simultaneously implies that individuals and organizations face major challenges in adjusting to new circumstances. The emergent forms of economic activity affect the characteristic nature of work and the types and levels of skills required in the economy. As a result, the security and general quality of jobs are being radically altered, with profound implications for the welfare of individuals. Accordingly, it is recognized that the nature of access to learning opportunities has implications not only for general economic competitiveness, but also for the employability of individuals and the consequent impact on their standards of living. In this way, then, this dominant view takes the effective organization of learning opportunities to be crucial to both economic growth and social cohesion (Brown and Lauder, 1996).

The policy implications of this analytical approach are, of course, profound. If an economy like Britain's – where factor costs are fairly high – is to be competitive, employers need to pursue innovative and technologically intensive strategies for the production of goods and services that have high value-added. Employees require not only good levels of general education, but also the capacity to adapt flexibly to changing skills requirements throughout their careers. Moreover, educational institutions should be organized in ways which ensure that these standards of general education are attained and also that the renewal of skills through continuing education and training is facilitated (for example, Ashton and Green, 1996). As Coffield (1997b, 1999) has argued, however, one of the striking features of UK policies is that they have concentrated very much on the implications of this analysis for educational institutions and for individuals. For example, the long-term preoccupation with raising 'standards' in schools and colleges is a clear reflection of the former.

As we have argued at greater length elsewhere, this emphasis on individuals reflects a model of participation in lifelong learning which is based upon a highly simplistic version of human-capital theory (Rees et al., 1997; Fevre et al., 1999). Hence, according to this model, individuals participate in lifelong learning according to their calculation of the net economic benefits to be derived from education and training (cf. Becker, 1975). Given the dominant consensus about the general direction of economic change towards more knowledge-based forms of production, it follows that a worker will seek to participate in lifelong learning in order to capitalize upon the benefits which will flow from skills renewal and development. In this account, the principal issue which government policy needs to address is to ensure the removal of the 'barriers' which prevent people from participating in education and training. These include 'situational' factors, such as finance and lack of time because of other commitments, as well as the features of educational institutions which make them unresponsive to potential learners (McGivney, 1990). Achieving a learning society often, thus, comes to be defined in these rather simple terms.

BARRIERS TO CREATING A LEARNING SOCIETY

So what, then, are these barriers preventing full participation in lifelong learning and seen to be hampering the establishment of a learning society in Wales? Research has suggested several barriers that potential learners face; and to widen, as well as merely increase, access to post-compulsory education and training, these barriers need to be recognized and faced. To a large extent they are presaged by the determinants of adult learning. Harrison (1993) categorizes the barriers neatly into situational (to do with the lifestyle of the prospective learner), institutional (to do with the structure of opportunities) and dispositional (relating to the learner's own attitudes).

Perhaps the most obvious obstacle that most people face when envisaging episodes of learning is the cost (McGivney, 1993; Maguire et al., 1993). This cost could be of the direct kind, such as fees, or more commonly indirect, such as the costs of transport, child-care, forgone income, time and even the emotional cost for those with families (Hand et al., 1994). These costs are clearly more restrictive for the poor (NIACE, 1994), and to some extent for women, who are still faced with the greater burden of child-care, for which support is generally poor (FEU, 1993), and with other domestic responsibilities (Park, 1994). There are anomalies in the benefits and grants systems (FEU, 1993) which confuse the financial issue. In addition to the problem of finding fees in one lump sum in some cases, since payment of fees by instalments is not generally allowable, learners are often surprised by the level of other expenses such as examination fees and stationery costs. The welfare system and the availability of cheap loans play a role here (Maguire et al., 1993). Benefit entitlement is incompatible with a grant from a local authority, and even when all of the costs of training are met by the individual, state benefits are often withdrawn. Unemployed people on training courses are therefore penalized by a system which says, in relation to going on a training or education course or programme, 'one of the conditions. . . to be entitled to unemployment benefit is that you must be . . . able and willing to take up any job which you are offered immediately. You might not satisfy this rule while you are on a training or education course or programme. . .' (The Employment Service, amended 1991). Currently sixteen hours per week (twenty-one before October 1996) are the maximum that one can study without losing benefit. In 1995, 20,000 people quit their courses because of uneven interpretation of these rules by benefits offices (Nash, 1996; Keep, 1997). General knowledge of the incentives available to train is sketchy (Taylor and Spencer, 1994). The much-lauded increase in students continuing to higher education (HE) has been accompanied by an increase in the number in debt, and the situation is worse for the mature students (Gorard and Taylor, 2001). In 1995, of those over twenty-six in HE many were already over £7,000 in debt (Garner and Imeson, 1996) and the situation will get worse with the ending of the older students' allowance. In general, adult education is the easiest sector in which central government/local government can economize when faced with financial stress (Kelly, 1992).

The loss of time, particularly for a social life, is another cost of learning in some cases (McGivney, 1993; FEU, 1993), especially in a country with a tradition of the longest average working week in Europe, for males in the manufacturing sector at least (CERI, 1975). For everyone, television has emerged as a powerful educational force, at least potentially, and a stimulant to new interests, but it can also be seen as disruptive. Adult education is now suffering not so much from lack of leisure time but from the multiplicity of opportunities available for that time (Kelly, 1992). Taking a course often involves an adjustment in lifestyle which may be possible for an individual, but is more of a problem for those with dependants or in long-term relationships. Relationships can be strained, particularly for women taking courses to progress beyond the educational level of a male partner – the 'Educating Rita' syndrome (FEU, 1993). Women, who are more likely to be employed part-time, less likely to be aware of opportunities stemming from the workplace and more likely to have domestic and child-care responsibilities, and generally poorer transport facilities, therefore face many threats to participation (Maguire et al., 1993). The most vulnerable women from the most disadvantaged backgrounds face the most barriers (Burstall, 1996).

The institutional barriers to training often come from the procedures of the providing organizations, in terms of advertisement, entry procedures, timing and scale of provision, and general lack of flexibility. Colleges of Further Education (FE), for example, still assume a seveteen-year-old norm which is fast changing, and they need to adapt to flexible opportunities for learning (FEU, 1993). Older learners differ from younger learners in many ways, but adapting to having them in a class could benefit the youngsters, since the adults can have a wealth of relevant experience. People want to fit learning around other tasks of equal importance in their lives, since they cannot always get time off (Park, 1994). They have interrupted patterns of participation and diverse progression routes (Istance and Rees, 1995). Non-completion of courses is now so high that it must be partly seen as an indictment of the quality of provision at all levels: schools, FE, HE (higher education) and YT (youth training). Drop-out is commonly caused by people discovering that they are on the wrong course (Pyke, 1996), with nearly half of students in one survey feeling they had made a mistake (FEU, 1993), and part of the blame for this must lie with the institutions in not giving appropriate initial guidance. Many learners are disappointed by the lack of help available in choosing a course and in staying on it. There is in general a low level of awareness of sources of information and financial incentives for training, such as the Training to Work scheme.

Part of the cause of lack of training must be the lack of appropriate provision (Banks et al., 1992). Even those studying may not have found what they actually wanted (Park, 1994). This is particularly true of non-work-related training and learning for leisure (NIACE, 1994), and is reinforced by the current emphasis on certified courses, heavily backed up by the incentives in the funding arrangements to provide accreditation of all adult education. Not only does this deny some people the opportunity to learn new interests and make new friends, it denies returners an easy entry route back into education (Maguire et al., 1993), especially for women who may be more intimidated by examination demands, according to one study (Burstall, 1996). It is often very simple provision, perhaps involvement in reading schemes for children, that can eventually lead to accredited continuing learning (Hunter-Carsch, 1996). Even where provision is available, knowledge of opportunities may be patchy for some parts of the population (Taylor and Spencer, 1994), giving many a feeling that 'you are on your own'. In addition, an estimated six million adults in Britain may have difficulty with writing or numeracy (Nash, 1996b), and perhaps one-sixth of adults have problems with basic literacy. These deficiencies appear to pass through generations of the same families (DfEE, 1996b), reinforcing their importance as a 'reproductive' determinant of adult non-learning.

Whatever barriers are faced, they are harder for the less motivated prospective student. The lack of provision of learning for leisure, and at home, with a focus only on the formal public arena, especially of work, means that learners may be seen as younger, better educated, and from higher income groups than they really are (Edwards et al., 1993). To some extent, this image becomes self-realizing. People with these characteristics tend to be selected for learning, and so social practice becomes reproductive, and education can thus be seen as middle-class and 'not for the likes of us'. It may be a poor experience of previous educational episodes that creates the obstacle for continuing education (Taylor and Spencer, 1994). If initial education has not led to the creation of basic studying skills such as numeracy, this provides a further barrier.

The influence of lack of motivation to learn may be underestimated by literature concentrating on the more easily visible barriers such as cost and entry qualifications (McGivney, 1992). Many people display an incorrigible reluctance to learn formally. In fact, perhaps 21 per cent of adults form a hard core of non-participants outside all attempts to reach them (Titmus, 1994). If all the barriers were removed for them, by the provision of free tuition and travel, they would still not want to learn. They have no desire, and given greater leisure time would want to 'just waste it'. Self-identity in Britain may be more strongly linked to a job than it is in other countries, where a greater emphasis is placed on learning (Bynner, 1989). Lack of drive thus becomes the most important barrier of all, since it is seen as too easy to get a job instead, and qualifications are seen as useless anyway (Taylor and Spencer, 1994). Some young people do not even bother to find out what their public examination results are (Banks et al., 1992), since they are only concerned with getting a job. Qualifications may even be seen as antagonistic to getting a job, and only concerned with entry to more education. Learning is something done early in life, as a preparation, but with no relevance to the world of adults (Harrison, 1993).

CONCLUSION: THE CHALLENGES FOR EDUCATION IN THE LEARNING/INFORMATION AGE

It is clear that education at the beginning of the twenty-first century is a key area of both social and economic concern, and that the goal of creating a learning society or learning age forms the focus for many Western governments keen to stimulate learning throughout the whole population. How this broad aim can be achieved therefore becomes the key issue for education in an information age. If nothing else, our brief account in this chapter indicates that achieving this goal will certainly not be easy.

At least three strands of a learning society arise in this brief discussion. These include a push for greater inclusiveness and the economic imperative, both currently in favour, and the older liberal view of a learning society as a cultured arena for civilized life. To a large extent these differing objectives require different approaches and benefit different sections of society. The economic argument tends to see people as human capital, only touching base with the inclusive argument when there is a shortage of appropriate labour, because of falling birth rates or a major war perhaps. The inclusive argument for recurrent education is based on movement towards greater equality rather than towards greater quality. It has become mixed up with the more liberal view of equal opportunity rather than equality *per se*, and what remains has a tendency towards rather condescending compensatory forms of adult education.

The concept of the learning society is therefore a difficult one to agree on, let alone legislate for in policy terms. Nevertheless, the aim of creating a learning society has been explicitly formulated by both the Westminster and Cardiff governments and, returning to our overarching theme, is one that is heavily based on ICT as an information age solution to long-standing problems. It is this that we now turn our attention to in chapter 6.

6

ICT as a Solution for Education

We described some of the problems facing education and training in chapter 5. In this chapter we now go on to consider how ICT is seen as offering a solution to many of these problems, and thereby outline the UK-wide policy agenda that has been developed as a result. As we shall see, the area of education and training has witnessed a raft of ICT-focused 'information age' policies over the last five years. Indeed, although education has traditionally been seen to lag behind other areas of society in terms of ICT use and application, in recent years educational ICT has been one of the noticeable growth areas of technological interest and activity amongst both politicians and the IT industry. In the schools sector, for example, ICT has been enthusiastically approached as a means of overcoming traditional problems of resourcing, crucially addressing perennial concerns over raising standards and attainment. In this way the promise of the 'virtual classroom' and 'smart school' has been seized upon by many politicians and educationalists as an attractive alternative to the present-day realities of the 'bricks and mortar' school system. Similarly, the allure of ICT as a ready means of creating the learning society/ies described in chapter 5 has also proved irresistible for many concerned with post-compulsory education. ICT, it seems, is the educational panacea of the moment.

UK ICT AND COMPULSORY EDUCATION POLICIES

From this background, it is also not surprising that during their first term in office, by far the most prominent ICT policy introduced by the New Labour government was the compulsory education-orientated National Grid for Learning initiative (NGfL); a co-ordinated, nationwide drive towards establishing widespread ICT use in UK schools. Until 1997 educational ICT was by no means a mainstream political priority; reflected in the *ad hoc* approach of the 1979-97 Thatcher and Major Conservative governments (Selwyn, 1999b). Similarly, the use of ICT in UK schools remained, at best, sporadic throughout the 1980s and first half of the 1990s. Then, prior to the

1997 general election the Labour Party announced its intention to connect every school to the Internet via a 'learning grid' (Labour Party, 1995) and subsequently commissioned the industrialist Dennis (now Lord) Stevenson to produce a report on the state of secondary school use of ICT. The eventual Stevenson report criticized schools' inconsistent approach to ICT and recommended that increased and more effective use of ICT in schools should become a national priority, setting up a framework which eventually became the basis of the NGfL. The Stevenson report reflected the received wisdom amongst politicians and educational technologists that teaching with ICT in schools is attractive for two reasons. Firstly, by using ICT in schools, children would become familiar with computers, and develop the skills needed in the future workplace. Secondly, it was argued that many schools found their pupils much more motivated and keen to learn when ICT was used in the classroom. This suggested that ICT could raise standards of pupils' achievement in non-technical subjects which, as we have seen, is of particular resonance to Welsh education. The Stevenson report went on to outline a role for government in 'construct[ing] an overall strategy', helping schools obtain up-to-date hardware and software, and training teachers to use the technology in the classroom (see Selwyn and Fitz, 2001 for a more detailed description).

After the 1997 general election this policy commitment was quickly (re)presented as the National Grid for Learning, heralded as an attempt to 'mov[e] the education service into the twenty-first century and creat[e] a "connected society" '(Blunkett, 1997) and was certainly seen at the time as an ambitious and much-needed impetus for a previously 'ICT-ambivalent' educational sector. The NGfL has subsequently evolved as a broad strategy aiming ultimately to promote lifelong learning and, in particular, to integrate the use of computers and digital technology in the learning process with an overall aim of achieving higher standards. The government intends the NGfL to have an impact in all levels of education, from basic skills and community-based adult learning to university-level teaching and learning. However, despite its lifelong learning allusions, in practice it is the school-based elements of the NGfL which form the most substantial element of the initiative.

In this respect the National Grid for Learning is best seen as an umbrella term for the government's various programmes concerned with integrating ICT into schools across England, Wales, Scotland and Northern Ireland (see Selwyn, 1998, 1999c, 2000). In spanning a diverse set of individual programmes, the NGfL encompasses the three broad areas of educational ICT use which were first identified by the Stevenson and McKinsey reports as underpinning the previous lack of effective ICT use in UK schools. This three-way focus of the NGfL can therefore be seen in terms of:

- *infrastructure* (i.e. hardware/connectivity to the Internet);
- *content* (i.e. educational software and on-line content);
- *practice* (i.e. teacher training and subsequent use of ICT by teachers and learners).

In terms of *infrastructure*, the initial implementation of the NGfL has concentrated on increasing the quantity and quality of computer hardware in schools as well as laying the foundations for a 'networked learning community' of schools, colleges, libraries and museums. Thus, much early effort has been directed towards ensuring that every school is connected to the Internet and, where possible, has a technological infrastructure to support networked on-line access within the school. This increased hardware capability is also seen as acting as a stimulus to UK software companies to produce quality education *content* as well as allowing schools to access educational resources from the Internet. Indeed, one of the first tangible outcomes of the National Grid for Learning initiative has been a range of 'approved' on-line educational content coming under the aegis of the NGfL web-site; including the 'Virtual Teacher Centre', 'Standards and Effectiveness' web-site and the digitization of library and museum resources. Moreover, with regard to the *practice* element of educational ICT, the government has also concentrated on teacher support and development, with a nationwide programme of initial and in-service teacher training set up alongside various financial incentives for teachers to purchase their own IT equipment for home use. This in turn is seen as stimulating innovative and effective use of ICT in the classroom.

Alongside these educational goals, the government have also designed the NGfL to help develop the UK educational software industry by creating a ready demand for digitally delivered educational content. Indeed, the involvement of the business sector is welcomed, as the title of the NGfL policy document, *Open for Learning, Open for Business*, suggests, and the government has made it clear throughout the initiative that various types of partnership working are the preferred way of meeting the aims of the NGfL. For example, the education sector is urged to 'consider the scope for working in partnership with other sectors and industry to develop content and make it available though the Grid', and the DfES frequently refers to the NGfL as a 'public–private partnership' (Selwyn and Fitz, 2002).

Thus, the *long-term* significance of the National Grid for Learning should be seen as extending far beyond issues of increased resourcing and staff training. Aside from broader concerns of providing Britain with a 'technologically literate' workforce and 'competitive global economy', the NGfL is ambitiously directed at fully integrating the use of ICT into *all* aspects of the school system with the explicit purpose of 'raising standards', both in terms of the use of ICT for teaching and learning and the use of ICT in the administration, management and organization of schools. Thus, the overtly 'top-down' nature of the present NGfL roll-out is seen as eventually resulting in schools themselves taking full responsibility for developing and extending their own use of ICT in full collaboration with the private sector. In other words, the NGfL's overall aim is to stimulate schools to become autonomous, empowered and confident consumers in an educational ICT marketplace. Significantly, substantial funds have been committed to achieving these aims – £1.8 billion committed to the NGfL from 1998 to 2002 – with most of this being spent on schools. The government promised £700 million to provide schools with money for ICT hardware, software and content. This was recently boosted by the promise of a further £1 billion between 2002 and 2004. The New Opportunities Fund (financed from the National Lottery) provided £230 million to train teachers to use ICT in the classroom.

ICT AND POST-COMPULSORY EDUCATION

The National Grid for Learning certainly represents an unprecedented government commitment to educational ICT and has set the ambitious target of technologically transforming the UK school system and directly addressing issues of raising standards of attainment and reducing inequalities between schools. Yet, as we saw in chapter 5, perhaps the most pressing problems faced by educationalists and politicians lie not in the reform of compulsory education but in addressing the less well-defined challenges of the 'learning society', that is, widening participation in education and training throughout the lifespan for both economic and social aims. From this perspective, we now go on to examine how ICT is being presented as a solution to these problems.

From a conceptual standpoint, the application of ICT as a ready solution to the educational and economic problems of low rates of participation in education and training is a logical progression. Indeed, the human-capital notion of a learning society outlined in chapter 5, servicing the needs of a globally competitive 'knowledge' economy, is clearly rooted in the notions of the information age as espoused by post-industrialists such as D. Bell, Touraine and Castells. For many commentators, the revitalization and transformation of education and training systems in a lifelong learning society is an essential prerequisite to (and vital sustaining factor in) the effective establishment of an information society. Moreover, given the determinist emphasis in the information age model on ICTs as a driving force it comes as little surprise that technology-based education is now forming a significant part of many countries' learning society strategies.

Given many of the barriers to establishing a learning society outlined in chapter 5 (i.e. barriers preventing people from participating in learning, such as time, distance, finance, institutional avoidance), ICT has been quickly seized upon by both educationalists and politicians alike as a ready means of overcoming them. The promise of 'anytime, anywhere' learning via ICT has long been highly attractive to those involved in lifelong learning, many of whom have proved keen to speculate on the effects that technology may have on learning (e.g. Tiffin and Rajasingham, 1995; Field, 1997; Wyn, 2001). Typical of such enthusiasm is Gell and Cochrane's vision of the imminent 'meltdown' of traditional education:

> ICTs remove the constraints of distance, time and location, which will undermine traditional educational monopolies and force a restructuring and revitalisation as a new 'training, learning and creativity' sector . . . Lifetime learning has become a necessity and will replace the old pattern in which education occurred in school and university before a person started a career. Meltdown in education is also likely to encompass all ages and bring remote capabilities into the home. (Gell and Cochrane, 1996: 252)

In a similar vein, influential commentators, such as Bentley (1998), have argued that ICT offers a 'new landscape of learning' unfettered by the enclosed spaces of traditional institutions. Educational technology is seen as leading to the 'delocalization of learning' with individuals free to learn whenever and wherever they choose. Thus, for some more radical commentators, there is little doubt how the learning of the near future will be conducted. As Naylor (1998) incredulously asked, why would any learner choose differently?

> If information is freely available, to anyone, anywhere, at any time, then why would anyone go to the trouble of travelling in order to access it? Why would they go to school, college or university at all, when simply by switching on their own computer near to them, the information and expertise once held at that school, college or university can come straight to them? (Naylor, 1998: xxiii)

Against this background the raft of present policies aiming to increase levels of learning via ICT arguably form the most coherent and advanced element of government information age policy-making in the UK and other 'developed' countries. The remainder of this chapter provides a brief overview of the role of ICT in lifelong learning policy-making in the UK now, outlining both the policies themselves and the rationales behind them, and thus setting the wider scene for our later empirical investigation.

THE RISE TO PROMINENCE OF 'VIRTUAL EDUCATION' IN POST-COMPULSORY EDUCATION

Much of the impetus for 'virtual' education is popularly seen as arising from a natural and inevitable convergence of telecommunications technology and the traditional distance education sector (e.g. Daniel, 1997). In practice much of the development of virtual education courses can, however, be traced back to the university sector and the so-called 'crisis in higher education'. Dumort (2000) provides the sobering thought that over five million new students are expected to enter the higher education sectors in Europe and North America throughout the first decade of the twenty-first century as the rhetoric of the learning society begins to be put into practice. However, such expansion of student numbers is set against a background of universities facing ever-constrained and restricted budgets and finite resources. From this perspective, the prospects of 'virtual campuses' and 'e-universities' are seen as convenient solutions for higher education administrators to a problem that would otherwise require the building and establishment of a 'conventional' university every day for the next ten years.

Traditional universities in the USA have offered on-line courses along-side their campus-based educational provision throughout the 1980s and 1990s. The University of Phoenix, for example, has been developing on-line courses for adults since 1978 and currently boasts nearly 10,000 on-line enrolled students within an overall student body of 70,000. A range of other traditional universities have since followed this example such as the University of Southern California, UCLA, the University of Washington and the University of Nebraska-Lincoln – with around half of US colleges and universities estimated to offer some on-line education facilities (Dumort, 2000). Alongside these traditional providers of higher education in the US there has also been an emergence of virtual organizations which act as on-line brokers of training services on behalf of universities and colleges, such as the National Technological University and California Virtual University. Although still not considered a 'mainstream' element of higher education provision, the virtual university is certainly an estab-lished feature of the US educational landscape.

In comparison, in the UK and Europe such activity has been less prominent amongst the largely publicly funded university sectors which have proved more wary of the virtual commodification of their public services. As Dumort (2000: 549) observes, 'until 1999 the development of the virtual university was ignored by most public authorities and universities of Europe'. Indeed, attempts by the UK Higher Education Funding Council to establish an 'e-university' continue to be frustrated by insufficient existing ICT-based learning activity in the sector (HEFCW,

2001). That said, the UK *is* widely seen as pioneering what have come to be known, rather clumsily, as 'mega universities' (Daniel, 1996), primarily through the development of the Open University. Since its initial establishment as the 'University of the Air' in 1969, the Open University (OU) has developed into a worldwide concern with a current student roll of 130,000, including over 10,000 postgraduates. The OU's success can be seen in those who have followed its lead. Indeed, in comparison with the fifty open universities created since the 1970s the OU's scope remains modest. Both the China TV University System and the Turkish Anadolu University, for example, boast student bodies of over 600,000 apiece. Similarly, the Indira Gandhi National Open University in India has over 350,000 students.

UK ICT AND POST-COMPULSORY EDUCATION POLICIES

As well as being highly successful role models for distance education, the success of the OU and the burgeoning virtual university movement is also now having a significant bearing on the current development of wider virtual education in the UK. Indeed, the initial development of a nationwide system of virtual adult learning initially conceived by the Labour Party during the 1990s drew heavily on the Open University 'mega university' model. In particular we are concerned here with the University for Industry (UfI), which has been introduced as the UK's key 'virtual' adult learning organization since the latter half of the 1990s. As Harris (2000: 581) describes:

> The UfI has been conceived and implemented as a genuinely 'virtual' form. It has no physical infrastructure or permanent faculty. The 'university' coinage is something of a misnomer, in that the UfI might be viewed more accurately as a learning utility, which uses information networks and 'networked' organisational forms to provide 'mass customised' access to vocational learning material and courses.

The original nucleus of the UfI concept came from the centre-left Institute of Public Policy Research. It was first outlined in a speech delivered by Gordon Brown (now chancellor of the exchequer) in 1994, suggesting 'a university which could do for vocational training what the Open University had done for higher education' (Wolf, 1998: 12). Since then the DfEE/DfES, the National Lottery, broadcasting companies, and private sponsors have provided initial funding for UfI pilots and associated projects. In doing so a major part of the case, at least rhetorically, for the provision of these funds has been based on notions of social justice, widening access to opportunities for lifelong learning and breaking down institutional, motivational and geographical barriers to educational participation. The University for Industry has therefore been quickly positioned in terms of widening participation in lifelong learning:

> the University for Industry will help deliver the widest available access to new forms of learning. The new opportunities of the new information age must be open to all – the many, not just the few. (Central Office of Information, 1998: 1)

In this way the government has reiterated the primary objective of increasing access to learning and thereby widening adult participation in lifelong learning. It is implied that information and communications technology will be the primary means by which programmes such as the UfI will overcome barriers to traditional lifelong learning. It is suggested that the UfI will help overcome the barriers which deter people and businesses – in particular smaller firms – from learning, by:

- harnessing technologies to make learning provision more flexible. The UfI will help people find the time to learn;
- stimulating new learning markets. The UfI will help bring costs down and make learning more accessible and affordable;
- offering reliable and accessible information and advice. The UfI will provide a clear route to learning opportunities;
- allowing people to learn at their own pace, in a familiar, convenient and supportive environment. The UfI will take the fear out of learning.
  (DfEE, 1998: 9)

In practice the UfI adopted the public brand name of 'learndirect' in 1999 under which services are delivered to learners and employers. Learndirect most prominently takes the form of a telephone-based helpline for directing individuals to approved and kite-marked learning opportunities. In addition, a series of franchised ICT-based learndirect centres are being established around the UK in venues as diverse as football grounds, pubs, shopping centres, funfairs and more 'conventional' sites such as colleges and community centres. This network also maps onto the wider government plans, discussed in chapter 4, to increase access to ICT under the aegis of 'UK Online'. For example, the government announced plans in the budget of 1999 to establish a £252 million network of 1,000 'ICT Learning Centres' focused on 'disadvantaged communities' in rural and inner-city areas of England. These Learning Centres have the overall aim of providing flexible access to learning technologies for those without ICT facilities at home or at work, and will be located in a variety of existing sites such as schools and community centres (DfEE, 2000b). Alongside these ICT Learning Centres is a parallel initiative to establish eighty-five City Learning Centres, based in inner-city schools, to provide technology-based learning and teaching opportunities for school-aged learners as well as the DTI's already established 'IT for All' centres in further education colleges and libraries.

The Library and Information Commission has produced concurrent plans for a New Library Network (or 'People's Network') connecting all libraries to a national digital network and, therefore, giving libraries 'a fundamentally new role as managers of electronic content and gateways to a vast wealth of on-line information' (LIC, 1997: 1). The People's Network aims to connect all 5,000 public libraries in the UK to the Internet and the National Grid for Learning at a cost of £100 million. In this way libraries are seen as being managers, organizers and creators of local and national information, with library access to ICT acting as an alternative outside-school means for learners to connect to the National Grid for Learning (LIC, 1997).

As we also saw in chapter 4, the focus of these initiatives on techno-logical accessibility has been latterly reinforced by a series of financial announcements concerned with extending levels of access to ICT among the UK population. In 1999 the chancellor of the exchequer announced a £15 million scheme to make 100,000 refurbished computers available to low-income families for as little as £5 per month. Moreover, at the beginning of 2000, Tony Blair stated New Labour's intention to achieve 'universal access' to the Internet by 2005 (Blair, 2000). Beneath this ambiguous, and some would argue contestable, target (Compaine and Weinraub, 1997) is a commitment to work with telecommunications companies to reduce Internet access charges and an envisaged commit-ment to 'promote usage on a regular basis by at least 70 percent of individuals by 2003' (Booz, Allen and Hamilton, 2000: 3).

EXAMINING THE UK GOVERNMENT'S LIFELONG EDUCATION POLICY DRIVE

In initiating such a policy agenda the UK government clearly see ICT as a primary means of overcoming traditional barriers to widening participa-tion to lifelong learning and, therefore, the creation of the learning society. Before we go on to consider how this information age policy-making can be tested empirically, it is worth examining further exactly what the effect(s) of these policies can be expected to be. In other words, how is the ICT-based learning society being presented by its supporters and how can we therefore judge its actual impact later on?

It could be argued that the ideological significance of these initiatives overshadows their actual impact on lifelong education in the UK. Although initiatives such as the UfI have been thrust upon the education sector in a blaze of publicity and hype, their 'physical' construction promises to be a slower process. In the first instance, therefore, a major step in the 'construction' of policies such as UfI, NGfL and the People's Network has been their formation within government and official discourse. Indeed, the importance of this has been readily recognized, with the UfI spending £10 million on marketing the learndirect initiative in its first year of operation (McGavin, 1999). This discursive construction is important inasmuch as it shapes expectations among both the education and business communities and consequently influences the future effectiveness of the initiatives. The final section of this chapter will, therefore, examine how ICT-based lifelong learning is being discursively constructed by government and official actors at a macro level through policy and advisory documents, official statements and other rhetoric. In particular, we explore the extent to which such policies are being shaped within a restrictive technocratic and determinist discourse of the 'technical fix', thus conforming to the traditional narratives of society, technology and the information age outlined in previous chapters.

THE ROLE OF LIFELONG LEARNING IN 'TRANSFORMING' THE UK FOR AN INFORMATION AGE

Much of the government's positioning of the technological 'reconstruction' of lifelong education has been firmly based around well-worn notions of the 'information age' and 'information society'. At a fundamental level, it is suggested that the wider societal momentum of the information age has prompted such changes in education:

> The Information Age will transform education, at all levels and for all ages. Education in turn will equip people with the necessary skills to profit from the Information Age. We want to open up these opportunities to everyone. (Central Office of Information, 1998: 7)

The government has been quick to point out that technological change is not being made merely on 'technophilic' grounds, but rather that the need to change has been forced upon the education system from outside. In this way, as the then secretary of state for culture, media and sport argued, the People's Network can be seen as a 'necessary' attempt to keep the UK library system relevant in light of technological changes in other sectors of society:

> Our proactive approach to introducing new technologies and the necessary new skills into the library service is not driven by some unthinking love affair

with new technology but by the knowledge that if we do not do it now, libraries will be left permanently behind the action, always striving to catch up with services available in schools and homes. (Smith, 1999: 13)

From this perspective the government is merely attempting to deal with the information age on behalf of the citizen. Therefore, the government's primary duty is presented as one of technological broker, 'harnessing' ever-changing technologies and providing individuals with opportunities to 'make full use' of this new age of information:

> The Government's priority is to provide people with the skills to play a full part in the Information Age, to take part in learning and so make the most of themselves . . . The goal is for people to learn how to use ICT to enrich their lives, improve their skills and make full use of the technologies in the Information Age. (DfEE, 2000b: 8)

> Learning is the key to our social and economic prosperity. We must ensure that people are able to realise their potential to learn and have the opportunity to return to learning throughout their lives. ICTs are expected, over time, to change the patterns of people's lives. We have the opportunity to harness these technologies to help people access a wealth of information and to benefit from new ways of learning. (NOFa, 2000: 3)

At this societal level, the inevitability and wholly 'natural' nature of technological 'progress' is stressed at every opportunity. At one extreme, as expressed here by the then minister for ICT in education, is the notion of technology-based learning as a fundamental and natural step towards a Fabian ideal of a 'fairer' society:

> The Left has always been dedicated to a fairer society where everyone is able to make the most of themselves. The challenge now is to equip all the people of Britain with the tools they need to succeed in whatever they want to do. Deploying these new technologies should be as easy and natural to everyone as riding a bike. They are the bridges to the future and we cannot afford to leave anyone stranded behind as we cross over. (Wills, 1999: 11)

At another extreme, although acknowledging more dystopian fears of technological change, is the underlying premise that the state (or in this case the British Broadcasting Corporation) knows best:

> The technological revolution may take five years or twenty five. It may be fast and frightening or slow and messy. But if I didn't believe it will ultimately be a good thing, I wouldn't have made on-line services and BBC Knowledge such priorities. The BBC believes in them. So should you. (Drabble, 1999: 19)

THE ECONOMIC ROLE OF TECHNOLOGY-BASED LIFELONG
EDUCATION

The economic necessity of technology-based lifelong education is perhaps the most prominent strand of the discourse surrounding initiatives such as the UfI, People's Network and NGfL. From President Clinton's early assertion that the 'information superhighway' was the means through which the USA could 'win the global economy', ICT-based policy-making around the world has been firmly located within economic rationales (Selwyn, 1999d). Thus, initiatives such as the UfI are being portrayed principally as an easy means of 'priming' Britain's workforce for the demands of the global economy:

> The vision of the UfI is a bright one, with the learndirect service bringing together social and economic agendas; raising skills levels and improving competitiveness . . . The flexibility of the new way of learning will put people in a better position to enhance their careers and get better jobs, while improving the competitiveness of their businesses and ultimately of the UK. (Wright, 1999: 17)

> The University for Industry has been founded to increase skill levels in Britain. (Sainsbury, 1999)

Lifelong learning is seen as a lifelong reskilling of the workforce:

> The UfI [will] encourage people to reskill throughout their working lives . . . within five years of launch, we expect 2.5 million people and businesses a year to be using the UfI's information services, with over 600,000 a year following UfI-brokered programmes of learning. The UfI will focus on making people ICT literate as one of its initial priorities. Within five years of its launch, we estimate that 200,000 people a year will be acquiring ICT skills through UfI. (Central Office of Information, 1998: 12)

On an individual basis, technology-based learning is seen as leading to improved employment prospects for workers: 'Access to ICT and confidence in its use in turn opens up access to learning, chances to acquire skills and a better chance of gaining and keeping a job' (DfEE, 2000a: 12).

On a collective basis (be it in terms of family, community or society) ICT-based education will lead to economic competitiveness:

> Lifelong learning can enable people to play a full part in developing their talent, the potential of their family and the capacity of the community in which they live and work. It can and must nurture a love for learning. This will ensure the means by which our economy can make a successful transition from the industries and services of the past to the knowledge and information economy

of the future. It is clear that we will not keep pace with the modern economies of our competitors if we are unable to match today's skills with the challenge of the developing information and communications age of tomorrow. (Blunkett, 1999: 41)

SOCIAL INCLUSION AND TECHNOLOGY-BASED LIFELONG LEARNING

Following on from a faith in individual empowerment, a third prominent strand to the official discursive construction of technology-based lifelong learning is the issue of social inclusion. Allied to the earlier assertions that the government's role is merely one of facilitator in the face of fundamental societal change, is the oft-voiced assertion that technology can be used to ensure that education is 'for all, not the few':

The University for Industry will help deliver the widest available access to new forms of learning. The new opportunities of the new information age must be open to all – the many, not just the few. (Central Office of Information, 1998: 1)

Thus, the government are claiming to be aware of the challenges faced in avoiding a 'digital divide' between 'connected' and 'non-connected' learners, a consequence again seen as stemming from the autonomous 'information revolution':

For the excluded and the ill-educated – and the two are increasingly synon-ymous – . . . there is now a real danger that the information revolution is putting up new walls further barring them from real progress. If the digital divide is not tackled, it will entrench existing exclusion for generations. Familiarity with ICT is the indispensable grammar of modern life. Those not empowered by it are disenfranchised: job prospects and security depend on it. Access to these technologies is a key tool for lifelong learning. Increasingly the information provided so quickly will be a gateway to opportunity in every aspect . . . offering vital weapons for democratic empowerment and civic activism. (Wills, 1999: 10)

Nevertheless, in general, such a bleak scenario is more often presented throughout official rhetoric in a more positive light, with the assumption that providing access to technology for previous non-participants in learn-ing will somehow automatically lead to increased learning and decreased social exclusion:

[ICT Learning] Centres will help bridge the digital divide by increasing access to ICT, helping people develop ICT skills and opening up opportunities for further learning and employment. This demonstrates our determination to ensure that all our people will be able to take advantage of the opportunities offered by the Information Age. (DfEE, 2000b: 5)

ICT has the potential to transform learning at all levels and for all ages. In particular, ICT can play a key role in breaking down the barriers to learning that people face, offering new opportunities to access learning for the most disadvantaged and those who have not traditionally taken up learning opportunities. ICT can bring learning resources to new locations which are accessible and acceptable to communities and offers new interactive learning methods. (NOF, 2000a: 5)

Easy access to a high-performance network will encourage adults to use libraries for self-directed and informal learning and for reskilling, and will encourage a rapid acceleration in the amount of instructional material made available online. (LIC, 1997: 2)

However, beyond notions of inclusion from 'taking advantage of the information age' and developing ICT skills, the underlying nature of this discourse is clearly connected with exclusion from the economy rather than any other issues of social welfare. Thus, at a basic level, this social agenda for technology-based lifelong learning has clear economic under-pinnings:

For individuals, the opportunities and benefits the new [knowledge] economy offers must not be the sole domain of elite knowledge workers. Learning is the key to individuals succeeding in the new economy. At school, in further education, throughout people's working lives. The key capability for people to survive and thrive in the new economy is their capacity to learn, and then to apply that learning. (Blair, 2000)

CONCLUSIONS

It is clear from even this brief policy analysis that the Westminster government is committed to establishing an ICT-based learning society via initiatives such as UfI. As such, then, if the political rhetoric outlined above is to be believed, the imminent 'transformation' of adult education and training may well be being put in place. Certainly, that is the favoured position of a substantial number of educators and politicians. Yet if we move beyond unquestioning faith in the information age a host of specific questions concerning this ICT-based establishment of the learning society in the UK begin to emerge, even more so from a specifically Welsh perspective.

In particular, these questions are encapsulated by the Open University's Diana Laurillard when asserting that 'Virtual [Education], if it does anything at all, ought to make real the rhetoric of lifelong learning' (Laurillard, 1995: 1). This, then, is the approach that we should be taking when considering the impact and implementation of these ICT-based learning policies. For example, to what extent are social exclusion and economic upskilling rationales compatible? To what extent are public and private interests compatible? What are the realities of learners' experiences behind the political hype? To answer these questions we need to examine both the present state of the 'learning society' in Wales and the potential of ICT to impact on this situation. How we can do this is discussed in the next chapter.

7

Researching the Information Age

So far, we have seen how information and communication technologies are being heralded by both politicians and educators as a ready and effective solution to a very real problem of the information age – that of widening participation in education and training. So far, so good – and many presentations of information age policy-making would be content to stop at this point. In *theory* ICT appears to be capable of achieving a range of educational, economic and social aims outlined in chapter 6. All that remains to be done is to wait for the policies, initiatives and programmes to take effect and then watch the ICT-based learning society materialize in front of our eyes. Indeed, the *potential* societal and economic benefits of technology have been used as the primary justification for the establishment of schemes such as the UfI and, in doing so, have perhaps overshadowed some other potential questions. As Robertson (1998: 6) asserts 'The futuristic associations of multimedia technology appear to have been a substantial attraction to politicians: affordable and accessible training could be offered in a Millennium wrapper, "on-demand" and "on-line".'

However, in considering learning and exclusion in an information age it seems appropriate that we should focus on the realities of ICT-based policy-making as well as the claims. Although in theory ICT appears to be capable of achieving the range of educational, economic and social aims, what is actually happening *in practice*? Moreover, what is happening in Wales? How are all of the information age issues for Wales that we have mapped out so far in this book working out? To date, very few authors have attempted to 'flesh out' their accounts of the information age with any sustained 'empirical' evidence, above and beyond statistics detailing economic and social trends at national and international levels. That said, the fact that we lack a solid empirical base of what is actually happening 'on the ground' is not surprising. Until recently many areas of ICT-based activity have been at the stage of small-scale development with little or no real progress being made. Perhaps this is beginning to change. It might, therefore, be possible to begin to point to the real effects of ICT policy-making in the UK as a whole, and in Wales in particular.

With this in mind, the remainder of this book is used to present an empirical study of how information age policy-making in Wales is coming to fruition – using case studies of ICT-based education and training. The choice of education and training for our investigation is quite deliberate. There are, as already described, ICT-based policies in a range of other areas such as business, health or social welfare. However, education and training policies such as the National Grid for Learning, University for Industry and learndirect have, to date, proved to be some of the most advanced aspects of the UK government's ICT policy agenda and, therefore, the most suitable in terms of providing solid indications of their early successes and failures. There is also, as we shall soon see, a considerable amount of activity by Welsh organizations to complement this UK-wide policy agenda. The ongoing attempts to provide ICT-based education and training programmes encapsulate, perhaps most explicitly, the range of economic, social and cultural objectives within the concept of the information age.

RESEARCHING ICT-BASED EDUCATION AND TRAINING: FORMULATING QUESTIONS FOR RESEARCH

Widening participation in learning – a primary objective of the virtual education initiatives outlined so far – *is* testable. Our research should therefore begin to consider how far that objective is being achieved, and if difficulties are encountered, to suggest remedies for them. As we show in chapter 8, we are quite clear about the general characteristics of those who currently participate and those who do not; and those who do not, make up nearly one-third of the adult population. These individuals can, therefore, provide a real benchmark for the success or failure of the current technological initiatives described in chapter 6. If the various projects (hereafter termed the 'virtual college movement') are successful they should widen access to learning by taking in a range of that third of current non-participants. These initiatives could, as their supporters would have us believe, at last lead to a substantial widening of adult participation in lifelong learning. Yet, within our guiding approach of treating the information age as problematic, there is clearly a need for closer scrutiny of the development of technologically-based learning provision. The key research questions for our empirical study are as follows:

- What strategies are the virtual education providers using to attract learners?
- What political, economic, cultural, social and technological factors are impacting on the implementation of virtual education programmes?
- How effective are these strategies in attracting potential users?

- What is the evidence that such opportunities have widened access to include those previously disenfranchised from lifetime learning?
- What are the reactions and experiences of users to the quality of the learning experience provided?

HOW TO ASK THESE QUESTIONS

Over the past three decades there have been many ground-breaking and exemplary pieces of research focusing on the role of technology in education and training. However, throughout the literature there are also a number of recurring limiting features. Some writers tend towards an optimism which, in its extreme form, has approached a utopian outlook on technology. Whilst an optimistic view of technology is not in itself a bad thing, a reluctance to consider negative or less successful aspects of educational ICT can be been seen as fundamentally restricting the field (Maddux, 1989; Kearsley, 1998). In many ways, this optimistic rationalism stems from a failure to take into account the 'wider picture' of education technology beyond the 'efficiency' of the technology in question. Moreover, there has been a tendency to mistrust, or even avoid, theoretical approaches when formulating the direction of research – despite many attempts to introduce theoretical perspectives to an education technology audience (e.g. Bryson and de Castell, 1998; Seels, 1997; Wilson, 1997; Carr et al., 1998). All of these characteristics have been translated into a body of research which, while substantial in size, remains somewhat narrowly focused and executed. Much research on the use of technology in education and training continues to take the form of small/medium-scale surveys and case studies, experimental descriptions and classroom-focused analysis. In short, as Kenway (1996: 217) has argued previously, much of educational technology research is 'too micro-focused and unwilling to engage with wider concerns'. How, then, can this situation be redressed and research begin to reflect the increasing importance of information and communications technology both in education and society at large?

Perhaps the most obvious area for change is the way that researchers go about asking questions. Here, the opportunities to improve our methods are twofold. Despite a predominance of small and medium-scale survey approaches to research in this field, there has, as yet, been a lack of large-scale analyses prevalent in some other areas of educational inquiry. It can be argued that education technology research is lacking the large-scale data-sets necessary to illustrate how ICT is 'working out' in practice – across local districts, regions and whole countries – and not just in smaller case studies of localized institutions which cannot necessarily be considered indicative of any wider context of technological implementation. By providing larger-scale pictures of educational ICT use it should be possible to highlight patterns and conditions of success and failure, good and bad practice and the strategies which lead to the effective implementation of technology.

Yet, there is also an equally pressing need for more in-depth approaches to be adopted when researching education technology. Unlike a majority of other areas of social science research, education technology has remained seemingly impervious to 'qualitative' methodology and analysis. The addition of such a dimension to education technology research allows a focus on what *does* happen (as opposed to what has apparently happened or what *could* happen) when ICT is used in educational settings. Indeed, in an example of research concerning students' attitudes towards ICT and subsequent achievement, Weinholtz et al. (1995: 388) were anxious to show: '. . . just how ambiguous and misleading results from quantitative studies can be if not supplemented by qualitative data . . . Use of supplemental qualitative methods by quantitative researchers can serve as a prudent hedge against obtaining inconsequential or erroneous results.'

In this way, qualitative findings can be used to 'illuminate' quantitative data (Parlett and Hamilton, 1972), reducing the need for speculation or subjective interpretations on the part of the researcher. Such use of 'triangulation', in terms of a combined methods approach in social science research, has been well established (Williamson et al., 1977; Denzin, 1978). As Connidis (1983: 334) points out, 'the usual assumption underlying this view is that any single method has its own inherent weaknesses; combining approaches helps fill the gaps left by each one.' However, perhaps founded in traditional misconceptions of such methods as lacking 'rigour', educational technology research has largely shied away from a qualitative approach to data gathering and analysis; aside from a few notable exceptions (e.g. Singh, 1993; Schofield, 1995).

Allied to this pressure to broaden methodological horizons is the fundamental need to start asking wider questions of educational technology and its relationship to society. If we are to attempt a more objective, detached analysis of ICT in education then it would seem appropriate to move beyond the linear 'cause and effect' model of technological and social determinism and explore alternative perspectives of society and technology. We must move beyond the limitations of some previous analyses if we are to gain a deeper understanding of the use of technology in education and training. Above all, researchers need to be aware of the social, cultural, political and economic aspects of educational computing, the 'soft' as well as the 'hard' concerns. By considering alternative theoretical perspectives we can begin to form a multidimensional view of what is a very complex area of educational provision. Given the increasing salience of ICT, research cannot afford to spare educational technology the analyses that technology has been subjected to in other areas of the social sciences. Thus education technology research needs to make a conscious effort to move away from positions of either technological or social determinism towards a perspective that avoids drawing a technology/society distinction, and focus on the social, cultural, political and economic contexts where technologies are developed, and the ones where they are used (Bromley, 1997).

THE EMPIRICAL BASIS OF OUR STUDY

From this background we were careful to construct a research design which combined various sources of data as well as asking questions both at the macro level of government, business and educational providers and at the micro level of individual learners. Our case studies therefore reveal many of the opportunities but also several potential pitfalls for Wales in an information age. In summary, we have enumerated individuals' patterns of lifelong participation in education and training, both formal and informal, over the past fifty years in Wales. From these, and the characteristics of those on different learning 'trajectories', we have identified a set of key socio-economic determinants of participation, and modified these in terms of the individual learner identities revealed from subsequent in-depth interviews. Our question, then, was: in what ways and to what extent can information technology obviate these determinants, overcome any relevant barriers to access, and so assist policies of social inclusion and economic regeneration in Wales today? To answer this question we draw upon, to a greater or lesser extent, eight main sources of information which are now briefly described (more extended descriptions and justifications for the main research methods can be found in the Appendix, and in the ensuing references to our previous studies).

(i) Secondary data

We used existing data from the census of 1991, via the National On-line Manpower Information System, to select the sites for a household survey, and the electoral register of 1996 to select households systematically from these sites (Gorard, 2001b). Three sites were selected to represent the coalfield valleys north of Cardiff which have faced economic decline over fifty years (Blaenau Gwent), a long-established manufacturing area with mixed fortunes (Neath Port Talbot), and a newer industrial centre forming part of the revival of fortunes in south Wales (Bridgend). The census figures were disaggregated by electoral division. Further details appear in Gorard (1997b). We used figures from the Labour Force Survey (1992–9), also via the National On-line Manpower Information System, to examine qualification trends in Wales over time.

(ii) Household surveys

As part of a much larger project forming part of the ESRC's Learning Society Programme from 1996 to 1999, we conducted face-to-face structured interviews with 1,104 householders in three sites in south Wales in 1997. The sample was selected systematically from the electoral register, and stratified proportionately by age (sixteen to sixty-five), gender and area of residence. The primary response rate was 74 per cent. Questions covered the respondent's background, family, a full work history, formal education, training, leisure learning and informal learning. We also gathered simplified histories of respondents' employment careers; and of the educational and training careers of respondents' family members, and in this way we gathered learning histories for 2,482 individuals.

Following extensive preliminary analysis, there were two major elements in analysing the data derived from the questionnaire survey. Firstly, the complexity of the individual education and training histories was reduced by converting each one into a sequence of episodes (an educational programme, new job, economic inactivity etc.) in which participation in education and training did or did not occur. These sequences, in turn, were classified into eleven 'lifetime learning trajectories', which describe almost all of the variations in individual histories. For most analyses, these can be further grouped into only five types. The patterns of participation of all individuals in the survey have been encapsulated in these five classes of learning trajectories. A learning 'trajectory' is an overall lifetime pattern of participation which is predictable to a large degree from the educational and socio-economic background of the respondent (Gorard et al., 1998a, 1998b). The structured interviews attempted to capture all and any episodes of formal learning including one-off health and safety training, leisure reading, and evening classes as well as the more usually reported induction training, and further and higher education. *Non-participants* reported no episodes at all despite, in many cases, numerous and varied vocational changes. *Immature* trajectories describe those still in continuous full-time education, and these individuals are not used in the analysis below. *Transitional* learners reported only full-time continuous education or immediate post-compulsory work-based training so far. *Delayed* learners have a learning gap after compulsory school until at least age twenty-one, but then reported at least one substantive episode of education or training. The *Lifetime* learners reported both transitional and later episodes.

Additionally, one of the authors is a member of the research advisory group of the National Institute for Adult and Continuing Education for Wales (NIACE Dysgu Cymru). We co-operated with them in the collection and analysis of two surveys of adult participation in learning (e.g. Tuckett and Sargant, 1999). One survey interviewed a sample of 483 respondents in Wales, and collected background information, employment and learning histories, and details of access to information and communications technology at work and home. This provides useful additional information to our main survey.

(iii) Household interviews

One hundred and ten of those householders already described (a 10 per cent sub-sample) were selected for an even more detailed follow-up interview. The selection was purposive, based on age, gender and area, but also seeking variation in terms of the trajectories discerned from the first interview data. These household interviews allow further investigation of why people did and did not participate, particularly via a consideration of the choices they faced and the opportunities that they saw as appropriate (their subjective opportunity structure). The interview narratives also allow a consideration of those whose trajectory determinants are *not* neatly explained by the earlier analysis of their life histories. The ensuing stories are used in chapter 8. We wanted to find out about their existing use of ICT but, above all, we wanted to find out about the experiences and motivations of informal learners and autodidacts – a clear target group for the virtual college movement, and one which is considered to be particularly prevalent in Wales.

(iv) Interviews with key informants

In order to understand the position of traditional trainers we conducted thirty interviews with training organizations and companies in Wales. Further details appear in Chambers et al. (1998). We then conducted a further eight interviews with people involved in setting up and running on-line training provision in Wales. These included executives from the University for Industry and the Wales Digital College (WDC), executives from S4C, heads of sector-wide organizations representing educational providers in the further, higher and adult education fields as well as Assembly Members (AM) from the National Assembly for Wales. These interviews are discussed in chapter 9.

(v) Participant observation

One of the authors was invited as a researcher to join the Access Group of the Wales Digital College. The purpose of this group was to advise the college on making on-line and digital television learning available and attractive to everyone in Wales. The author performed his duties as a member of the group, but also acted as a researcher recording the story of the creation and early development of the college (see chapter 9). The ensuing field notes and document and web-site contents also formed useful sources of insight at this stage of the project.

(vi) Analysis of on-line learning activity

In order to examine the nature and extent of learning taking place the study adopted both a user-based and content-based analysis of Wales Digital College learning web-site. This involved a content analysis of the on-line learning materials as well as a cumulative log file record for the WDC/Acen Welsh Language Learning web-site covering a thirteen-month period from 1 August 1999 to the 31 August 2000. Such logs, maintained by the web-site providers, cover who was visiting the site (via individual Internet addresses); when they visited (in terms of month/week/day/hour/minute/second level data); where they came from; what aspects of the site were being used and what software (and often hardware) they were using (see chapter 10).

(vii) Email survey of on-line learners

In order to find respondents for interview (see below) who were recent participants in on-line learning we designed a brief email-delivered questionnaire. We sent this to all of the registrants on what was then the only 'live' course run by the Wales Digital College. We felt that email delivery was appropriate because the nature of the course provision entailed access to an Internet-capable computer. It was completed inter-actively by the recipients. Our primary concern was with widening participation, and we needed to see whether the kind of people using web-based instruction were different in any significant way from those following more traditional courses at the same level (see chapter 10). In essence, has technology broken down the barriers faced by those previously excluded from learning in adult life? Or has it reinforced them? We already knew that patterns of participation in traditional adult learning varied by gender, age, location, employment, social class, and prior educational attainment. Therefore, this is what our questions asked about. The temptation to include questions about the nature of their learning experiences and other superficially interesting matters was very strong. We resisted it because we added one final question: 'Would you be willing to be interviewed as part of this project?' It was in the follow-up interviews with a sub-sample that we decided to approach questions about attitudes, learner identities, the nature of barriers, and possible tranformative experiences. Email questionnaires constructed by the researchers were sent via the Wales Digital College to fifty-nine registered learners. Responses from eighteen registered learners had been received a month after mailing – yielding an overall response rate of only 31 per cent. These responses were used to provide tentative indications of the characteristics of registered learners.

(viii) Interviews with participants in ICT-based education

Finally, because of the limited number of respondents in the original sample of 1,104 who reported learning involving the use of ICT we increased the size of that sample purposively. We therefore also conducted face-to-face or, in exceptional circumstances, telephone interviews with a further thirty-six people who had recently or currently participated in learning on-line or learning via ICT. These interviews were taped, transcribed and thematically coded in the usual way. They provided us with useful indications on at least two important issues: the nature of on-line learning and how it is experienced by the learner, and the background characteristics and previous lifelong learning trajectories of the participants (see chapter 11). In this way we can begin to answer questions about the quality of ICT-based provision, and its ability to break down the barriers to more traditional participation.

CONCLUSION

The methodological strategy of an in-depth analysis of a single economic region has been justified by the results obtained. It makes practicable the use of a variety of data sources, both contemporary and historical. Whilst there remain issues to be resolved in integrating the different kinds of data thus derived, the overall picture is greatly enriched by this diversity of information. Using Wales as a 'social laboratory' to chart trends over time, moreover, permits the uncovering of fundamental relationships and processes in the determination of participation in lifetime learning which provide the starting-point for our examination of ICT-based episodes of training. The following chapters describe some of the key results of these investigation as they relate to Wales in the information age.

8

Examining Welsh Patterns of Participation in Education and Training

With Gareth Rees

INTRODUCTION

The main purpose of the following chapter is to describe the results of our more general study of adult participation in learning in Wales, thus setting the scene for our subsequent investigation of ICT-based interventions. What are the realities of educational participation and, therefore, what is the present basis of Wales as a learning society? The study is focused on three sub-regions rather than on Wales as a whole to allow a detailed knowledge of the actual opportunities for participation, and of the economic history of the area, to underpin the analysis of choices. We also chose to focus specifically on *individuals'* learning histories to allow the detection of trends in patterns of participation over time. In this way we have mapped actual patterns of participation in lifelong learning, their changes over time, and their social and economic determinants. Thus, we know a great deal about how and why people in Wales do, or do not, participate in various types of education and training. Using this knowledge as a background will enable us later to judge more accurately the actual and likely future impact of ICT usage on these patterns. Since that is our major purpose here, there is insufficient space to describe all the findings of this particular part of our research in detail. Readers are referred to Rees et al. (1999, 2000) or Gorard and Rees (2002) for a summary.

In order to explore the nature of lifelong learning in an information age we need to ask what the patterns of participation through the life-course actually are and how best we can understand their determinants. This is important not only to strengthen the social science of this field, but also to provide a proper basis for the formulation of policy (Coffield, 1997a). The present study therefore explores empirical patterns of participation in lifetime learning through the concept of individuals' 'trajectories'. At one level, what is involved here is the attempt to describe characteristic sequences of learning episodes through the life-course by aggregating individual experiences into a set of typologies (cf. Banks et al., 1992). However, there is a clear analytical element too. Hence, the 'trajectory' which people join is largely determined by the resources which they derive from their social background. Moreover, an individual's capacity to take up whatever learning opportunities are available is constrained by their previous history in this respect. Yet, 'trajectories' do not simply reflect the constraining effects of structured access to learning opportunities. The individual educational experiences of which they are comprised are simultaneously the products of personal choices, which themselves reflect 'learner identities'. What is central to an adequate analysis, therefore, is to produce an account of the interaction of 'learner identities' and the individual choices to which they give rise, with wider structural parameters (Rees et al., 1997).

MAPPING THE LEVEL AND NATURE OF LEARNING IN WALES: THE 1999 NIACE SURVEY

Before trying to uncover the specific factors and influences underlying people's patterns of learning we first need to gain a general picture of the level and nature of learning currently taking place in Wales. For this we can turn to our analysis of the 1999 UK survey sponsored by NIACE, which included 483 responses in Wales, for the most recent overview. It is noteworthy that of the twelve UK regions used for the analysis Wales shows the largest percentage of 'current' learners (28 per cent compared with 22 per cent overall), and the largest percentage 'likely' to participate in the near future (46 per cent compared with 38 per cent overall) (Tuckett and Sargant, 1999). Of the four home countries Wales shows the largest percentage of respondents either currently learning, or having done so in the last three years (43 per cent). In this respect, the relative patterns of participation in Wales and elsewhere are similar again to those reported in the corresponding 1980 survey, where Wales had the highest level of participation (28 per cent). In the 1990 and 1996 surveys, the picture for Wales was markedly different, with relatively low levels of participation. This difference, in a sense, provides confirmation of the accuracy of the latest NIACE figures, since despite the overall growth in participation by 1999 Wales shows the lowest percentage of 'recent' learners, which is therefore consistent with the finding of few current learners from 1996.

There may be several specifically local factors that may help explain the recent change, at least in part. The increasing need for Welsh-language proficiency, perhaps especially in light of the enthusiasms created by the new National Assembly, may account for some of the picture. Such a demand for language skills does not appear to be mirrored in either Northern Ireland or Scotland despite their concurrent programmes of devolution. However, this can only be part of the picture since the percentage of learners reporting the Welsh language (or indeed any language) as their main subject of study remains very low. The main growth has been in 'computer studies'. A complementary explanation may be based on the rural nature of much of Wales, since it is also clear from the overall study that participation tends to be slightly higher in rural than in urban areas. The overall pattern of participation in Wales is therefore closest to that of East Anglia among the other regions. However, the difference between urban and rural areas is slight, and does not appear to generalize to Scotland or less developed areas of England like the South West.

Although over half of respondents in Wales have not reported any learning for at least three years (58 per cent), the figure for those who have not participated *at all* since leaving full-time continuous education (ftce) is 34 per cent, the lowest for all regions. This could be seen as evidence for the often reported tradition of respect for adult education and training in Wales (Burge et al., 1999), and it is interesting that current trends of participation when aggregated by home country are almost the inverse of patterns of attainment in initial education. Northern Ireland and Scotland have elevated levels of initial qualification in comparison with England, while Wales generally has the lowest scores on any indicator of educational attainment (Gorard, 1998b). In summary, the determinants of full-time compulsory education and later learning are different, and might be considered in the light of these recent survey findings to be almost antagonistic. Adult participation is highest in the region with the lowest levels of initial qualification, and lowest in the regions with the highest levels of qualification. Although logical, this result will be a surprise to those who see 'front-loaded' and later adult learning as being positively related (such as those who believe in the accumulation of prior learning hypothesis that encouraging the one leads to an increase in the other).

EXPLORING PATTERNS OF PARTICIPATION IN EDUCATION AND TRAINING: RESULTS FROM OUR SOUTH WALES STUDY

Despite this apparent improvement in terms of numerical participation in Wales since 1996, it still remains clear from the recent data that a third of the population (34 per cent) reported no episodes of learning since full-time continuous education. So how can we characterize patterns of learning and, crucially, what factors underlie people's propensity to engage or not in learning after leaving full-time compulsory education? Here, then, we turn to the results of our own south Wales study. The 1,104 adult education and training histories derived from the questionnaire survey (see chapter 7) can be aggregated into a typology of five 'lifetime learning trajectories' which encompasses almost all of the individual variations for those aged sixteen to sixty-five (table 8.1).

Table 8.1 Frequencies of the 'lifetime learning trajectories'

Trajectory	Frequency	Percentage
Non-participant	339	31
Transitional	222	20
Delayed	144	13
Lifelong	353	32
Immature	42	4

The 'immature trajectory' describes the small number of respondents who have yet to leave initial full-time education (and they are not used in the analyses described below). The 'non-participants' are those who reported no extension of their education immediately after ending compulsory schooling, no continuing education in adult life, no participation in government training schemes and no substantive work-based training. The 'transitional' learners reported only the continuation of full-time education or a period of initial work-based training immediately after completing compulsory schooling, and no subsequent education or training. Those on the 'delayed trajectory' have a gap in participation between reaching school-leaving age and at least twenty-one years of age, but followed by a minimum of one substantive episode of education or training. The 'lifelong learners' reported both transitional participation and later episodes of education and training as well.

Whilst the nature of these later episodes of lifetime learning varied widely, it is significant that this 'lifelong trajectory' accounts for almost a third of respondents, neatly balancing the 'non-participants'. For a substantial proportion of respondents, their experience of lifelong learning ended with initial schooling. Although this needs to be qualified in light of the evidence from the semi-structured interviews (see below), it nevertheless confirms previous accounts of the size of the task confronting policy-makers seeking to promote lifetime learning, whether through the use of ICT or more traditional forms.

To begin to explain this pattern of participation in lifetime learning, our statistical analysis can be used to identify those characteristics of respondents which enable good predictions of which 'trajectory' they follow. For example, a respondent who is a fifty-year-old woman, born and still living in Neath Port Talbot; whose father was unqualified and in an intermediate-class occupation and whose mother was unwaged; whose family religion was Anglican; who attended secondary modern school and left with no qualifications; who herself has an intermediate-class occupation; and who does not have a hobby requiring study or practice, has only a 16 per cent predicted probability of being a 'lifetime learner'. This is confirmed by her survey responses which report no education or training since leaving school, and this actual example from our data-set encapsulates the kind of socio-economic determinants that our model uncovers.

The general determinants of lifetime learning patterns (i.e. relevant to both components) include gender, family background, initial schooling, occupation and motivation. The full model includes over forty independent variables – from the much larger life, work, and learning histories of each individual. However, the most significant factors may be summarized as time and place (Gorard et al., 2001). Their significance lies as much in their interactions with the other variables as in themselves. Where and when an individual is determines their structure of opportunities such as access to courses, but it also determines the relevance of gender, family background, initial schooling, occupation and motivation in mediating those objective opportunities. For example, the apparent appropriateness of higher education for a women depends to a large extent on when and where she is.

TIME AS A DETERMINANT

The age of respondents today, and therefore the periods at which they left school or moved jobs, is a major determinant of participation. Generally, the frequency of participation in formal education or training has increased over the fifty-year period of the study. More respondents in each generation report staying on in school or college after school-leaving age (even though, or perhaps because, this age has also increased twice during the same period). Formal participation decreases with the age of the individual however (Greenhalgh and Stewart, 1987) but age is not a simple linearly changing determinant of participation in south Wales, which has witnessed a dramatic boom, bust and retrenchment in the past fifty years (Gorard, 1997b). For example, it may be that adverse economics have more impact on the employment prospects of younger cohorts at any period (Gershuny and Marsh, 1994). The training and socialization available in the three local nationalized industries (coal, steel and rail) have disappeared along with lifetime job opportunities for many. The effect of time is an important one for the dependent variable (in this case training, in their case unemployment) but the effect of time varies for each birth cohort. Even where the working lives of two individuals overlap, they may have an age-related differential proneness to participation in training.

There is considerable evidence that the pattern of typical 'trajectories' has changed very substantially over time. When respondents were born determines their relationship to changing opportunities for learning and social expectations. It is significant that respondents with similar social backgrounds from different birth cohorts exhibit different tendencies to participate in education and training. Time may be a composite proxy here for a variety of factors such as changes in local opportunities, economic development, the increasing formalization of training, the antagonism between learning and work (see below), and the changing social expectations of the role of women (see Gorard et al., 1998c). Older respondents often reported quite radical changes of job or responsibility with no training provided at all. Examples from our interviews included coalminer to catalogue shop manager, steelworker to electrician, librarian to upholsterer, and plasterer to market-gardener, and all with no training at all. Such people thought that learning was simply common sense. 'No, nobody worried about things like that then. It's quite a new thing isn't it?' To some extent these feelings are also common in the reactions to the apparently more formal systems of training today. One woman said of her government training scheme, 'It was a complete waste of time. They didn't teach you anything. You had to learn it for yourself . . . It was a case of here's the stuff, have a go . . . but all they were there for was drinking coffee and having a fag . . . my mates all thought the same.'

By dividing our respondents into two equal-sized age cohorts, it is possible to gain some indications of changes over time in the social determinants of participation. Table 8.2 shows that the major change in terms of patterns of participation over time has been a large increase in transitional participation (i.e. immediately after compulsory schooling). There has not been an equivalent change in later participation (whether the individual 'stayed on' after school or not). This lack of change is not simply due to right-censoring of the trajectories of the younger cohort (who have had less time to participate), and this can be demonstrated in two ways. The average age of all episodes of later participation is within the age range of the younger cohort as people tend to spend a lower proportion of their lives in education and training as they get older. The actual age of respondents within the age cohorts is not related to either transitional or later learning. It is also the case that episodes of later learning such as work-based training are decreasing in length, as well as frequency, over time.

Table 8.2 Changes in the frequency of participation (percentages)

Age	Transitional	Later
21–45	67	45
46–65	46	47

Table 8.3 Personal characteristics (and associated changes in odds)

Predictors	All cases immediate	All cases later	Younger immediate	Younger later	Older immediate	Older later
Age	0.96		0.93		0.96	0.96
Male	2.15	1.69		4.35	3.03	
English spoken		0.36				0.29
Born local		0.56	0.33		0.40	
Born local male				0.37		1.88
Other religion/ none	0.60	0.56			0.51	0.39
Anglican	0.68	0.77			0.63	0.72

In general the relevance of age to patterns of participation is uncomplicated. The continuous increase in immediate post-school education and training ('immediate') means that it is much more common for the younger respondents in both age cohorts. In fact, the probability of immediate post-school education and training decreases by a factor of 0.96 for every year in the age of the respondent (table 8.3). In general, age is much less relevant for predicting patterns of participation in later formal learning episodes ('later'), since these have not changed much over the fifty years of the study. While males are more likely to participate in formal learning at any age when the sample is analysed as a whole, this overall picture conceals an interesting change over time (for more detail on this regression-type analysis, see Gorard et al., 1999a). Whereas in the older age cohort gender was only relevant to the decision to participate in immediate episodes, with later lifelong learning being gender-neutral (in quantity if not in type), in the younger cohort immediate participation is now gender-balanced, and the difference lies only in later learning. It is almost as if the women who are now staying on in education and training longer and are the basis for the increase over time in immediate participation, are doing so in replacement for later participation. This could be part of the explanation why it has already been observed that the decrease in non-participant trajectories over time has not created a proportionate increase in lifelong learners. 'Peter' has been robbed to pay 'Paul'. The same finding also demonstrates that the link between immediate and later participation is not causal. Although it is true that those participating later in life have a higher level of general education, it is not true that simply extending initial schooling will necessarily affect later patterns of participation (as implied by Tuckett, 1997, for example).

PLACE AS A DETERMINANT

Where respondents are born and brought up shapes their access to specifically local opportunities to participate and their social expectations. Those who have lived in the most economically disadvantaged areas (such as Blaenau Gwent) are least likely to participate in lifetime learning. Again this may be partly to do with the relative social capital of those in differing areas, or the changes in actual local opportunities to learn. However, those who have moved between regions are even more likely to participate than those living in the more advantaged localities. It may not be an exaggeration to say that those who are geographically mobile tend to be participants in adult education or training, while those who remain in one area, sometimes over several generations, tend to be non-participants. Some people appear to be trapped in an area by the relative cost of living, and lack of transport. One man, like all of his friends, went into the coal-mines aged fifteen, 'but that was closed then in 1969. I had an accident just before it shut and it was while I was out that Llanhilleth shut.' He was clear that none of the local jobs now required any special skills or training, and that there was no point in learning except to get a job, and no point in looking for a job elsewhere. 'I'm not brainy enough I suppose. Well, I never looked, to be honest.'

The importance of place in understanding the determinants of adult participation has been argued elsewhere (Rees et al., 1997). Empirically, place has so far been found to play three roles in this study. Firstly, Wales is different in many ways from other regions of the UK – against the national trend it has a decreasing proportion of the workforce who are self-employed, and a lower proportion of job-related training than every region of England outside the east Midlands for example (DfEE, 1997a). Similarly, the chances of participating in government employment and training programmes, and hence the chances of taking NVQs, have regional variations (Shackleton and Walsh, 1997). This has to be taken into account when examining the frequency of training episodes. Secondly, in much the same way as Daines et al. (1982) found differences between their six research sites, there are clear differences between patterns of participation in the three Welsh research sites, with Neath Port Talbot coming closer to the ideal of a learning 'community' whose members have a more wide-spread participation in formal lifelong learning, and Blaenau Gwent offering fewer and fewer chances for job-related training. Thirdly, participation, especially later in life, is more common for individuals and their families who have moved into the research sites from elsewhere. There may be two processes at work here – trained and educated individuals are more likely to be part of a nationwide occupational labour market and have to move with their jobs, while those who are prepared to countenance moving to get a job are also more likely to enrol in courses.

Most respondents in this study are local, having been born and educated in south Wales, and they reveal the influence of geography in two main ways. Those who had been away were more likely to participate in later learning. Partly this is a function of occupational class and educational attainment for those in national labour markets, or who had been to university in England. However, since most respondents had not left south Wales, the biggest influence of place was a direct one based upon the availability of local opportunities for education and job-related training (mainly in steel and coal for men at the start of period under study). These opportunities have clearly changed over time. The restructuring of local employment opportunities – the trends towards services, assembly, female employment, and contingent working – is one clear example. In general, employees no longer have the training (or the danger) associated with the nationalized industries, and the places are more frequently temporary, or part-time and have in the main been taken up by women.

To some extent the local views of the value of training are clarified by a training for work manager in one of the research sites:

> People can't move out of the area, to Newport for example because of the house prices, and there is no public transport at night or early morning for shift workers, so unless they have a good car people can't commute . . . Bosch, Sony, and Panasonic are always advertising for jobs, as their workers leave through boredom with the conveyor belt production. But they go on to another similar job hoping it will be less boring, or to benefit, and not to training [except for the limited induction training accompanying the new job].

GENDER AS A DETERMINANT

Although the significance of gender changes over the period of this study, it remains one of the clearest determinants of participation throughout, affecting not merely the frequency and length of learning episodes but also their type and outcomes. In general, women were more likely to be non-participants from the 1940s to the 1970s, and have been more likely to be transitional learners since. Women have traditionally been under-represented at every level of learning above initial education (cf. Hopper and Osborn, 1975), and this is still the case today. In fact, the differential between the genders in terms of later participation is increasing (Gorard et al., 1999a).

Part of this difference is related to differences in the pattern of work and the training opportunities that ensue. Men are still twice as likely as women to work full-time (DfEE, 1997b), perhaps because of child-care. In general, women without children are more likely to have jobs, while for women with children their employment cycle is job, family, workforce re-entry (Gershuny and Marsh, 1994). Most training is full-time for those working full-time, and so is more common for men, and single women (Greenhalgh and Stewart, 1987), and episodes are also longer for the same groups. In fact married women who receive full-time training show a net movement out of the workforce, so that those without any training actually increased from 1965 to 1975. More women are now working (economic activity up from 57 per cent of those aged sixteen to fifty-nine in 1971 to 71 per cent in 1995), while fewer men are (a drop from 91 per cent to 85 per cent over the same period). However, the rise in employment has been chiefly in part-time posts (DfEE, 1996c), which are less likely to lead to training and qualification (Shackleton and Walsh, 1997). Some of the same factors determining employment prospects for women also apply to off-the-job learning. Women often face more of a barrier to participation than men due to having children and other relatives to care for (Frazer and Ward, 1988) and are, in consequence, unable to travel as far to institutions. On the other hand, women are more likely to gain an NVQ via government programmes, and a recent report suggests that, in fact, women and men train equally often, but that women's episodes are briefer (DfEE, 1997b).

Moreover, when these changes over time are analysed separately for men and women, distinctive patterns emerge. For men, the increase in post-school participation took place chiefly for those completing initial education during the 1950s and 1960s; whilst for women, it occurred a decade later, for those finishing school during the 1970s and 1980s. The increase in participation for men is attributable to the growth of 'lifetime learners', although only up until the 1980s. For women, in contrast, it is the result of more 'transitional learners'. Hence, gender remains a significant determinant of participation in lifetime learning, even where it has been eliminated as a determinant of extended initial education.

PRIOR EDUCATION AS A DETERMINANT

Experience of initial school is another important marker for further study. A sense of failure at school has been found to reduce the chance of further education (Gambetta, 1987), and in some cases gaining qualifications is an essential precursor to continuation. The probability of experiencing most kinds of training rises with school attainment (Tan and Peterson, 1992). However, the clearest simple indicator of success at school is family background (Gorard, 1997c), and a depressed social-class background not only reduces the chance of further education, it also interacts with failure at school, so that those from poorer families may be less likely to compete for educational resources throughout their lives if they face a problem. Some writers have suggested there may therefore be a cycle of disadvantage for an underclass excluded from formal settings as a result of their inadequate schooling, resulting from their background. A study of the first cohort to stay in initial schooling until age sixteen found that 50 per cent had later problems with arithmetic, while 20 per cent had problems with reading. It also suggests that few had taken any steps, even by the age of thirty-seven, to overcome these problems, and that the penalties for illiteracy were getting worse (Bynner and Parsons, 1997).

Experience of initial schooling is crucial in shaping long-term orientations towards learning; and in providing qualifications necessary to access many forms of further and higher education, as well as continuing education and training later in life (although see below). There are important 'age effects' here, however, relating especially to the reorganization of secondary schooling in the maintained sector. For the older cohorts, the eleven-plus was a clear watershed, even, perhaps especially, when they did not sit the examination, and the ways in which the story played out from then on are clear from the subsequent interviews.

For example, this man is now in his fifties, still living in the Valleys, never been away, and now unemployed:

When it came to my eleven-plus I was in a family that had nothing kind of thing, you know. I was in a very poor family. My father and mother was afraid in their hearts that I would pass for County school because it meant then that they would have to get me a uniform. Where I could go with the holes in the back of my trousers to an ordinary school. But then you had to have your books and your satchels and you know, so they kept me back from my eleven-plus. I didn't go to school that day.

The female teacher described above had a very different experience. Although her parents had no higher qualifications themselves, 'Well the thing is when I took this scholarship . . . my parents were very very supportive. Yes, they thought it was wonderful.' Another man explained that he had left school aged fifteen, and his father had left school at fouteen to be a coal-miner, as 'it's just the normal thing I think around here unless I went to a grammar school or whatever'. Even in the later comprehensive system, many stories described life chances that were apparently impossible once initial schooling ended. A man who is still illiterate said, 'Well, I didn't take no exams at all because I wasn't very good in school. When I left school then I did the job I wanted was to be a care assistant but I can't 'cause I didn't get the papers.' Such accounts are plentiful, and they illustrate only one of the many relationships between family, school, work and later learning. In several cases, where initial schooling was ended solely for economic and family reasons, the frustration became a platform for the motivation to return to study as an adult.

FAMILY AS A DETERMINANT

Parents' social class, educational experience and family religion are also important determinants of participation in lifetime learning. Family background is influential in a number of ways, most obviously in material terms, but also in terms of what are understood to be the 'natural' forms of participation (as is indicated by the importance of family religion). A woman aged forty-four had left school as soon as possible to get a job and so leave home. 'There were thirteen of us and we all left home at sixteen. Our dad was . . . we never got on with our father.' These findings of the importance of family relationships as determinants of participation are clarified by many such stories from interview (see below, and Gorard et al., 1999b).

Focusing on the data-sets relating to parents and children in the same family suggests that despite large changes in educational and training provision since 1945, individual participation trajectories remain very similar within families. The analysis here uses three indicators of participation in lifelong learning: the highest lifetime qualification so far, the age of leaving full-time continuous education, and the individual's learning trajectory. The first of these indicators is the highest qualification of origin (parent) and destination (child) as shown in table 8.4. 'A level' refers to A level-equivalent qualification or above, using the DfES standard classification for National Training Targets (Marshall et al., 1997). 'Elementary' refers to qualifications below A level, including employer-based certificates. The frequency of each level of qualification is higher among children than their parents, but despite this growth in qualifications more children have the same, or lower, level of qualification as their parents than do not (54 per cent). There is clearly some form of family relationship here. A similar, though somewhat weaker, pattern is observed when qualifications of the smaller number of grandparents and their grandchildren are considered (i.e. the parents and children of the respondents). Thus, whatever the mechanisms of this relationship are, they continue over at least three generations. All of these patterns are observable for both male and female respondents, and although men are generally more highly qualified in all three generations, the biggest change has been the increase in the qualifications of women over time. Also, the table of reproduction, like that for occupational class, is more similar between each generation when it contains only cases of one gender.

Table 8.4 Qualification of parent and child

Parent\child	None	Elementary	A level	Total
None	798 (44%)	538 (27%)	490 (28%)	1826
Elementary	52 (18%)	99 (32%)	103 (50%)	254
A level	72 (20%)	135 (31%)	195 (49%)	402
Total	922	772	788	2482

One would expect there to be more lifelong learners in the younger generation than the older one. There are, but it is noteworthy that half of the children who are lifelong learners have parents who are lifelong learners themselves (46 per cent). Similarly, more than half of the children who are non-participants have parents who are non-participants (61 per cent). It is clear that, for whatever reason, patterns of participation 'run in families' to a great extent.

THE ROLE OF OCCUPATIONAL CLASS

Finally, current occupation or social class does not appear as a general determinant of later learning. This may seem surprising since the correlation between occupation type and training is well established. The point made here is that when the independent variables are fed into the model in life-span order from birth to the current position, occupation is not a key predictor of any variance left unexplained by earlier events, such as qualification at age sixteen. Such a finding is in agreement with that of Greenhalgh and Stewart (1987) that those people already qualified are more likely to receive further training. For example, although professionals may be more likely than other workers to undertake voluntary adult education, the DfEE (1995) estimated that over 60 per cent of professionals have a degree-level qualification from their full-time continuous education, whereas over 70 per cent of plant and machine operatives have no qualification higher than a GCSE.

Of course, the social determinants of early educational trajectories and of transition to work mean that occupation has been found in other studies to be strongly related to later participation. In this study, occupation (net of background determinants) is really only a good indicator of on-the-job training, which is itself difficult to predict using other social factors. Those with higher occupational status (Greenhalgh and Stewart 1987), and those working in the public sector or in larger firms are more likely to receive job-related training. They still tend to be younger and already better qualified (DfEE, 1997b). Occupation also affects the type of training one receives, the choice of content where it is available (NIACE, 1994), and the type of qualifications available at the end (Felstead, 1996). Therefore changes in patterns of employment will affect patterns of participation as much as changes in education policy and provision do. Since 1979, for example, the number of skilled workers needed in traded goods have dropped sharply, and the introduction of technology such as computer-aided design and manufacture (CAD/CAM) has added to the loss of specific jobs (Greenhalgh and Mavrotas, 1994). Places for plant and machine operatives have declined most sharply. Newer jobs have appeared at senior or highly skilled levels, and in distribution and services. This may be partly why employers feel that the skills needed by the average employee are increasing (DfEE, 1997b), and why unemployment and inactivity has risen for men, while participation has risen for women.

THE IMPORTANCE OF INFORMAL LEARNING

In the further interviews with 10 per cent of the respondents from the first two waves of the study, interviewers were concerned to find out about learning episodes that had perhaps not been covered in the survey stage. There were many interviewees who reported no informal learning experiences, and no leisure interests involving study or practice. In most cases, where a reason was given, this was ascribed to lack of interest, by someone who had not attended school regularly and had left at the earliest opportunity for example, or to lack of time, by someone like a consultant surgeon who had spent most of his life in formal study. In very general terms, where an interviewee described any genuine interest at length, they also described others, whether of a formal or informal nature. In a sense, as suggested by the survey findings, there are people who seek out things to learn, and people who do not. Books and magazines were more frequently cited as sources of information than other people, or broadcasts, with information technology reported as the least useful. In specific examples, magazines were used to learn sports like golf, the use of software such as spreadsheets, and how to build a radio transmitter. The use of books included learning musical instruments like guitar, languages, calculus, and practical skills like building a garage or wiring a house. It is important to recall in reading the accounts below that many of these people contacted via the systematic sampling procedure have little or no formal education after compulsory schooling.

One man, for whom there was little separation between work and home, had taught himself pottery (with his wife), electrolysis for metallizing, simple electronics, wax casting, and furniture modelling. He has a perspex-cutting room in his house, a gold-plated frog in his living room, and he once made a scale model of the Challenger space shuttle which is now on the desk of a four-star general in NASA. In some cases he has been successfully employed on the basis of self-taught skills:

> So as I say . . . I haven't got a GCE or a B.Sc. or whatever they're called these days . . . but as I say you don't have to be academic to be able to do things . . . Because of the books I read and I like reading science books etcetera, and with the television my favourite channel is the Discovery channel.

This story of a genuinely multiskilled but mainly self-taught interviewee is very similar to that of another respondent. He was a self-taught plasterer and electrician, who loved opera, but worked as a steel foundryman, and explained how he had read about the care of the 7,000 bedding plants he had in his garden:

> Well, you see when I was doing those I used to send off for those books. Once a month you get books from them. They come in volumes. There are twelve volumes. So if ever I was stuck I look, I used to look through the books and say 'oh'. Read it up oh that's the way to do it. It's the same with the bricklaying. I ordered a bricklaying book and I read it up . . . with plastering now a friend of mine is in the library and she got me a book, so . . . if I got to do a job I'm not quite sure I get the book and read it up and say 'oh well' this is the way.

Although the differences can be overemphasized, there is a pattern in these stories in the types of skills and activities undertaken by men (as above) and by women (as below). To some extent the gendered differences in the distribution of learning trajectories (see Gorard et al., 1998c) may be replicated by gendered differences in informal learning outside work. There are clear differences in the fields in which their informal learning generally takes place, but more intriguingly women may be even more likely than men to describe informal learning episodes as simply 'activities' and so to downplay their reporting of what must have been transformative experiences in many ways.

A woman in her forties has taught herself to crochet and do quilting from books, building on skills in knitting and sewing she gained as a child. She organizes a local 'ladies' club' and a coffee club to raise funds for her children's school. Again there are similarities with her earlier work as a bookkeeper which she undertook with no reported training, and where she taught herself how national insurance worked from pamphlets, for example. But she speaks for several respondents when she points out the pressures on her time. 'Yes, I think when you've got a family you tend not to . . . Can't seem to get around to do all the things I would like to do.'

What is surely significant about all of these accounts is that none involve the use of ICT either in finding out about opportunities, or in delivery. Of course, many of these accounts relate to events some time ago, but even so the absence of any reported use of ICT by informal learners is interesting. For that reason, principally, we extended our sample purposely to talk to participants in existing ICT-based learning in Wales, and to compare their accounts with the more general picture presented here (see chapter 11).

CONCLUSION

It is important to note that all of these factors reflect characteristics of respondents which are determined relatively early during the life-course. Hence, those characteristics which are set very early in an individual's life, such as gender and family background, predict later 'lifetime learning trajectories' with 75 per cent accuracy. Adding the variables representing initial schooling increases the accuracy of prediction to 86 per cent. And this rises to 89 per cent and 90 per cent respectively, as the variables associated with adult life and with respondents' present circumstances are included.

The analytical implications of this are profound. It provides strong empirical support for the utility of the concept of 'trajectory' in analysing participation in lifetime learning. Not only is there a clear pattern of typical 'trajectories' which effectively encapsulates the complexity of individual education and training biographies, but also which 'trajectory' an individual takes can be accurately predicted on the basis of characteristics which are known by the time an individual reaches school-leaving age.

This does not imply, of course, that people do not have choices, or that life crises have little impact, but rather that, to a large extent, these choices and crises occur within a framework of opportunities, influences and social expectations that are determined independently. At this level of analysis, it is the latter which appear most influential.

Despite the improvement in terms of numerical participation in Wales since 1996, both the NIACE survey and our own suggest that almost a third of the population reported no episodes of learning since full-time continuous education. Of course, both studies may be overemphasizing the importance of formal participation and certified episodes as opposed to more personal experiences of substantive learning. As we saw at the end of the chapter, non-participants sometimes reported important periods of substantive but informal learning, which is nevertheless downplayed in official reports, and therefore the research based on it, since it does not contribute to the rhetorical impact of National Training Targets (Gorard et al., 1999c). Thus, informal learning should therefore be seen as constituting an important element of patterning levels of participation in formal education in Wales.

Having mapped out existing patterns of participation we can now move on to the main focus of our study, the introduction of technological initiatives and their capacity to have an ameliorative impact on these levels of learning and social inclusion, via the implementation of the emerging 'virtual college' solution in Wales.

9

The Rise of the Virtual Education Movement

As we have seen in chapter 6, the somewhat bleak scenario of substantial levels of non-participation in post-compulsory education and training, and the barriers faced by the 'learning society', *are* seen to be solvable. The widening of educational participation and the overcoming of entrenched non-engagement with learning are considered 'treatable' through technological solutions. Learning in the information age is seen to be very different from before. This is the thrust being taken by the New Labour government via initiatives such as the UfI and learndirect, as well as the many more localized and specialized ICT-based 'learning solutions' being implemented by other educational organizations. The information revolution is to be primarily a learning revolution.

Yet our recurring theme of treating the information age as 'problematic' reminds us to take a more cautious approach. How exactly is technology-based learning being implemented in Wales? Who is responsible for the shaping of the ICT-based learning? How is the local context of virtual education in Wales interacting with nationwide and global-wide contexts? In the first of our three chapters specifically setting out to 'map' empirically the realities of learning in Wales in an information age, here we examine the roll-out of ICT-based lifelong learning at macro and meso levels. We examine, in particular, the politicians and business people, education providers and other educators in Wales attempting to implement the initiatives and programmes already outlined. Drawing on our interviews with key actors from the National Assembly, UK-wide and Wales-wide ICT learning programmes, private companies, and broadcasters as well as leading educationalists and learning providers, this chapter offers a snapshot of the political, economic and cultural realities of the country in the information age.

The chapter addresses some key questions regarding the cohesion between UK-wide and Welsh political and educational agendas, the relative influences and motivations of key actors behind the promotion and implementation of ICT learning solutions as well as the practical problems faced when implementing the programmes. We examine the history of the rise of virtual education in Wales, the present situation 'on the ground' as well as the future views, concerns and expectations of those responsible for developing and implementing ICT-based lifelong learning in Wales.

FOR WALES, SEE ENGLAND?

We commence our analysis with the initial observation that at an all-Wales political level the rise of ICT-based learning discourse throughout the 1990s appeared to do little more than replicate policy commitment from Westminster. This was the case with the ICT elements of the Welsh Office's *Learning Is for Everyone* White Paper and the Education Training Action Group (ETAG) report. In these documents, following the lead set by the then Department for Education and Employment, the Welsh Office did little more than echo the sentiments of the UfI in establishing technology-based lifelong learning for socially inclusive reasons:

> Modern information and communications systems, including digital developments, present both opportunities and threats in adult education. ICT can minimise the constraints of time and space: people can learn or gain information about what is available, whenever and wherever they wish – providing they have access to modern technology and the confidence to use it Traditional and new systems of learning must be carefully combined if maximum advantage is to be gained for a wide variety of adult learners with different needs. (ETAG, 1998: 30)

The discursive construction of ICT-based lifelong learning over the last half of the 1990s could easily be seen to be another case of 'for Wales, see England' (or vice versa of course). Yet, this is not to say that no distinctive progress was being made in Wales. For example, and of particular interest to our study, there has been the emergence of the Wales Digital College (or *Coleg Digidol Cymru*) as a distinctly Welsh provider of ICT-based learning opportunities alongside the parallel implementation of the UK-wide University for Industry into Welsh education provision.

THE DEVELOPMENT OF A WELSH 'DIGITAL COLLEGE'

The origins of the concept of a Welsh 'Digital College' can be traced back to the mid-1990s when the Welsh-language television company S4C began to consider its response to the upcoming changes in broadcasting legislation regarding digital television. Although responsible for output on Wales's Channel Four, S4C only produces around forty hours of original programming per week. At one level, therefore, the concept of an ICT-based education initiative arose from a need for S4C to commit itself to providing twenty hours per day of programming on its proposed digital channel without entailing a huge financial commitment, whilst also addressing its public service brief. As the S4C chief executive explained:

> OK. I think the idea originally came about when we became aware of the essential potential of digital television to offer more broadcasting time to us, and this goes back to about 1995 when the first inclines of what became the 1996 Broadcasting Act was starting to be laid out. It became clear that we were going to argue for and we eventually won the right to have a full channel of our own, but we know that we weren't going to have any additional money to make it into a 24 hour entertainment channel [. . .] So we started thinking about what we might be able to do with that additional broadcasting time which would be a value to Wales but which wouldn't be costing us as a broadcaster the same sort of money as it costs to provide an entertainment service. And we started thinking in terms of education and there was a key idea with different people, a theme of education and what might it be. [Eventually] the core concept was that there might be certain lifelong learning type of skills which Wales could identify as being its needs, not necessarily those that are the same across the UK, that then led us to talk to a whole range of organisations and people and over the subsequent two or three years the thing has solidified into what is now its final form.

After an initial feasibility study the project was taken forward by the then recently retired BBC director of education who had just returned to Wales after working in London. This serendipitous appointment crucially allowed the forging of a partnership between S4C and BBC Wales to co-fund some development work with the intention of eventually acting as joint programming providers to a self-funding Digital College. As the project matured from an initial feasibility consultation to a more substantial commitment, the fledgeling WDC team then enlisted the help of Acen, the Welsh-language education organization, to assist firstly with a Welsh-language element to the WDC and then adapt into a general steering role:

> There was also the question of working with other broadcasters and the BBC being the obvious one. So we got into a situation of an agreement with the BBC that the BBC and S4C would co-fund this development work [but] as we got deeper into to it 'of course the requirements the administrative requirements, the work to be done grew and we needed help and we turned to Acen and Elen specifically because I think we had talked to them because of the Welsh-language expertise that they had and this was clearly a strand that you would want to have in the Digital College. So they had been drawn in on that front and I think clearly they were interested [in the wider] plan. (S4C chief executive)

The early enrolment of Acen into the development of the WDC is significant, adding a clear Welsh-language dimension to the project above and beyond S4C's commitment to bilingual broadcasting. Indeed, Acen (translated as 'Accent') began in 1989 as a scheme within S4C to teach Welsh to adults through the production of a series of television programmes. With a mission statement of *Yn gwasanaethu dysgwyr y Gymraeg*/ 'Serving Welsh learners', Acen had been a multimedia company in its own right and had developed a reputation for providing Welsh-language learning provision through residential and workplace-based courses, conventional reading materials, television subtitles and the provision of web services for Welsh-language learners. Moreover, Acen had already been considering the prospect of expanding their broadcasting material in line with the emergence of digital television when they were approached by S4C and therefore saw the prospect of the WDC as potentially offering a convergence of different bodies independently working towards a similar goal of a Welsh-orientated education provision via digital television and the Internet. Thus, alongside the prevailing political rhetoric of lifelong learning emanating from the Welsh Office at the time, the development of the WDC appeared to be 'of the time':

> Now this is going back really to, as an idea, to 1996, 1997 and really it was a case of 'look the technology is changing' and Acen knew that it had to adapt and look to what was happening. Now we started discussing the general idea with a lot of other bodies and saying 'look you know, we're really having to rethink here.' Now about the same time S4C *in particular* was also thinking about digital [television] and really it was a case of both of us coming together, really only on an ideas level at the time and saying 'well, if we are going to do it we might as well do it properly and it should be across a *multitude* of different disciplines and looking at the skills needs of Wales' and so on . . . So the aims and objectives were set fairly early as enabling learning in Wales in a *general* sense. [Also we thought that] we should be widening participation and that of course was very much in step with various Welsh Office documents at the time, the 'LIFE' paper and so on . . . and they were all kind of moving in the same direction. (WDC executive)

By 1997 these early consultations and burgeoning partnerships were consolidated with the formal announcement that a 'Digital College' would be established as a technologically based broker for adult learning in Wales, both directing potential learners to existing provision and extending learning opportunities through digital television broadcasts and the Internet (Wales Digital College, 1998). Reflecting its broadcasting origins and S4C's initial intentions, the eventual model had a distinct emphasis on the use of telecommunications technology in its delivery of learning materials. Although other media such as the telephone, fax and paper-based materials were intended as integral parts of the programme, the dual use of digital television (DTV) and the Internet were presented as fundamental to the successful implementation of the Wales Digital College in its official launch literature:

> Anyone interested in learning new skills – vocational or non-vocational – would be able to benefit and exciting and effective access procedures would be put in place to attract and support traditionally non-participating groups such as the young unemployed and adult returners. Television is a powerful medium and can prove an effective access point. It was foreseen that the service would be particularly useful for job-seekers, those seeking new directions and challenges early or late in life and those seeking open learning opportunities. (Wales Digital College, 1998: 15)

As this quotation from an early 'prospectus' for the WDC highlights, the creation of a 'digital college' in Wales was also overtly presented as a ready means of widening access to learning opportunities for those currently excluded from participation in lifelong education and training. While embracing the economic imperative for lifelong learning, the Wales Digital College therefore pinned its success or failure very early on in its development on the ability to overcome traditional barriers to accessing adult learning opportunities. As Professor Bob Fryer (later director of the UfI) exhorted at the business launch of the WDC, in attracting adult learners the initiative *could not* be seen to merely recruit the 'usual suspects . . . this would not only be a failure but deeply hypocritical' (Fryer, 1999).

Crucially, in attempting to widen educational participation the WDC was being firmly developed and presented as a *broker* to learning rather than a provider of learning. As the chief executive of the WDC explained:

> The idea is certainly not to put a degree course on screen. It's to *motivate* people and it is to *move* them on and give them the key information they need and then make sure they are in contact with the people, those providers who can help them move along their chosen paths.
>
> [Interviewer]: *Right, so they get a sort of taster and then there will be information about how to move on?*
>
> That's right, that's right. And that could be moving on to a multi-media course which *could* by the way be accessible through the Digital College as the technology develops as well, either through PC or through the television, but it could well be that the way forward for a lot of people will be saying to them 'Look do you know there is a literacy course in your area . . .' It's driving people onto whatever is the best provision for them and making sure that they have got quality information in their hands as well as a feeling of 'Yes! I want to do this'. (WDC executive)

Moreover, the WDC development plan was also based on a partnership approach, both with existing providers of adult education and private firms such as NTL who had won the franchise for the 'cabling up' of much of Wales. From an educational perspective, the WDC was designed to complement both educational and technological structures already in place in Wales:

> Where we do provide we are providing with our partners. For example we don't register students, the students are registered with the colleges or whoever the training organisations are. We see really the role of Digital College as one of a front door, it's getting people in and getting them through to the people who [can provide education], whether they be colleges or whatever. (WDC executive)

THE EMERGENCE OF THE UFI IN WALES

However, the launch of the WDC in 1998 was followed in a matter of months by the initial launch of New Labour's flagship lifelong learning policy – the University for Industry (UfI). Crucially, for S4C, Acen and the other bodies already committed to the WDC, on the face of it the UfI represented a far larger organization with very similar aims to the WDC. As we have suggested in chapter 6, the UfI was publicly developed throughout the latter half of the 1990s under a range of expectations – from being an 'Open University for Adult Education' through to being a 'virtual on-line university' awarding its own degrees. Nevertheless, by 1998, notwith-standing its ambiguous public image, the aim of the UfI was similar to that of the WDC – as a broker of adult learning working in partnership with local learning providers, businesses and other organizations. As the head of UfI Wales explained, in being similar to the WDC the scope of the UfI's task meant that partnership with local educational initiatives was essential:

> As far as support is concerned for learners UfI has to ensure that there are partnerships around there to provide that support. Because UfI as an organization is not able to provide the support for the learners on the ground solely, it has to work in partnership with learning providers, with FE, with HE, with businesses, employers, trade unions, in order to provide that on-the-ground support for the learners. To produce the materials we have to be working with the broadcasters and the publishers in order to get to the materials of quality.

Like the WDC, the UfI also had an explicit focus on increasing social inclusion within its more work-based approach to brokering learning opportunities. One manifest example of this continues to be UfI's emphasis on community-based ICT learning centres:

> That *is* our target group – those who have been turned off learning. [We have] ensured that learning is accessible by having learning centres in places where people go. So we put them in those community areas where the people are. So again that is part of the joined-up thinking, put learning centres in places where we know there is a need. For example, in north Wales, Caer Park and Plasmadog, those are places of social deprivation. You put the learning centres there and you put in the learning centres people who *live* in Plasmadog and Caer Park, people who are normal individuals. So the learning centres are in appropriate places and they should be staffed appropriately to the needs of that particular place again, so that the learners, the potential learners are not put off. I think there are lots of learners out there, potential learners out there, but they are often put off through not wanting to go through the door of a college, not wanting to go through the door of what looks like a threatening learning centre. (UfI executive)

The launch of the UfI certainly caused the WDC to rethink its position. In the early stages there had been a fair degree of confusion and misinformation concerning the respective roles of the two initiatives, with the WDC even promoting itself at one point as the 'Welsh Node of the UfI'. Yet, on a practical level the impact of the UK-wide University for Industry on the ongoing development of the Wales Digital College was primarily restrictive – both in terms of the WDC quickly having to relinquish its initial links with BBC Wales (as the BBC as a whole developed links with the UfI), and then in terms of slowing down political momentum in Wales for the WDC – especially within the 'UfI-friendly' Labour government in the National Assembly anxiously waiting to usher the initiative into Wales:

> [There's been] a few political problems. A *major* setback was actually caused by another body set up for the same purpose and that was the UfI. Now that was really, I mean it wasn't UfI's fault at all, it was because we were working very close with the BBC at the time. The BBC in *London* had got themselves into contractual arrangements with the UfI in Sheffield, therefore BBC Wales felt they couldn't move forward unless things were sorted in Sheffield, unless there was a formal agreement between ourselves and the UfI and they actually put the brakes on things for a period and we got held back for about a year. Now it wasn't *totally* held back because we were still developing content ideas and so on so it wasn't a major problem but it was a bit of a problem at the time. For instance, it affected certain decisions made in the Welsh Office and the National Assembly because there was all the politics involved, this was a New Labour idea coming through, UfI, there were political tensions within the National Assembly. For a while UfI really was centre stage and was controlling almost what was happening. Now I think it was about November 1999 when

we made the break and said 'look either we are doing this or we're not, we can't be held back'. So we moved UfI from centre stage at that point and just said 'that's it, let's get on with the job, get the commissioning done and go for it'. Now this meant that the BBC could no longer be the full partner perhaps that they had been before. (WDC executive)

The decision of the WDC to break away from the UfI was further expedited by the subsequent setting up of UfI Wales as one of the regional UfI teams. As the head of UfI Wales described, as such UfI Wales was overtly intended to add a Welsh perspective to the UK-wide implementation of UfI, leaving the WDC in a position only to act as a potential provider of Welsh-orientated learning materials to UfI:

We have *influence* to develop UfI in Wales to meet the needs of the people of Wales. Our remit to do that and in that sense our autonomy is to ensure that the materials that are produced meet the needs of Wales. And that is quite a broad thing really, we need to meet the needs of Northern Ireland, we need to meet the needs of all the home countries – not to *dilute* materials but ensure that they are appropriate. (UfI executive)

Thus, up until the end of the 1990s, the background of 'virtual' lifelong learning in Wales can be seen to have developed largely in a piecemeal fashion – akin to ICT developments in other areas such as health and business. Already we can see a range of information age 'issues' coming to the fore: for example, potential tensions between nationwide/UK policies and more local initiatives, the involvement of a variety of actors and interests (from S4C to FE colleges to commercial companies such as NTL) and a recognition of avowedly 'Welsh' demands when it comes to developing ICT-based learning provision – be it in terms of language or the existing context of further education. Yet, how the WDC and UfI were subsequently taken up in Wales provides us with a first practical indication of the complications of the realities of Wales in an information age beyond the rhetoric.

In particular, in attempting to map out the virtual learning landscape some significant practical issues quickly emerged when trying to implement these initiatives. The most prominent recurring theme emerging from our interviews with key players was the nature of the implementation of initiatives such as UfI and WDC against the pre-existing structure of learning provision in Wales. In all of our interviews, it was felt that the 'goodness-of-fit' between the old and the new varied from initiative to initiative. Here, then, we can begin to map out some of the practical and political tensions which characterize Wales in an information age.

'SURF AND TURF WARS': THE IMPORTANCE OF 'FITTING IN' WITH
WALES IN AN INFORMATION AGE

Although aware of disquiet 'on the ground' the UfI certainly saw
themselves as complementing the existing education sector, firmly asserting that they were bringing new learners into the existing marketplace:

> We are not entering into the same market as the FE Colleges or the HE
> Colleges. It is a different way of learning, it's an additional way of learning
> which will support their general activities but also bring on new learners who
> will then feed into the system [. . .] But, it is a very complex system. And I think
> that part of the difficulty with the UfI is that when we say we are providing
> materials for social inclusion, other people say 'well we do that already'. But I
> don't think that anyone does [what we are doing] and that's the difference. It's
> the *way* that this is going to be done which is different. The associated support
> structures for identifying job needs, providing support for learners on-line.
> There isn't an integrated package which does that and UfI will do that. (UfI
> Wales executive)

This view was certainly not shared by our interviewees from within the
Welsh education sector. For example, there was a strong concern from
those representing education and training organizations that the UfI
'supported and strengthened' the adult learning sector rather than simply
'cutting across it' (national training organization executive). In other
words, it was felt that there is a need for UfI to enlarge the adult-education
sector rather than competing for existing learners. A consistent fear was
therefore that the projection of the student numbers that the UfI intended
to enrol meant, in practice, that they would merely be taking learners away
from existing learning providers. As one representative from a higher
education institution argued, colleges therefore faced the scenario of
having revenue for educating students 'creamed off' by UfI – an obvious
source of concern:

> Provided UfI can reassure us that these students are brand-new, they wouldn't
> have come into educational training unless it had been for learndirect then
> they'll have everybody backing them. But if they're going to say this is a UfI
> student and in reality it's a student that would have come to Newport,
> Glamorgan, Swansea anyway then there's going to be serious big problems.
> We wouldn't mind that if there's additional funding, but if it's the existing
> funding then its eroding our resource base and, given that we tend to operate
> in the community at a loss anyway, that is bloody serious. Now at the moment
> we reckon that UfI is going to want 25 per cent, and if that's a 75 per cent
> funding base for us, well we're going to be in very serious trouble as regards
> our community operation. (HEI representative)

In contrast, concerns over the replication of existing provision, being seen as a 'threat' to colleges and adding little to Welsh education were certainly *not* seen to be issues in the case of the WDC, themselves keen to stress their care 'not to tread on anyone's toes – especially in terms of recruiting students'. Thus, amongst our interviewees representing the FE and HE sectors in Wales the WDC was seen to be far more of an 'honest broker' – as the same HEI representative also contrasted:

> Now, the Digital College will, in my opinion, increase student recruitment, I think they would for example take a module that could be produced by us and they would make sure that people can glimpse the module through the television or through the web-site and people would get curious and come to us or whatever. I think it's going to work. (HEI representative)

Yet, there was evidence of the disquiet surrounding the UfI and contrasting enthusiasm for the WDC being rooted in more than just financial concerns. Although many of these preceding concerns centre around issues of increasing and decreasing colleges' and universities' revenue and client-base there was also a strong sense of key players' reactions to on-line learning initiatives being guided by the extent to which the initiatives 'fitted in with Wales' – whether in terms of existing Welsh structures of education, particular Welsh needs or their overall compatibility with Wales and Welsh education. Thus, in its most extreme sense, there was the view that UfI was simply not a 'Welsh' initiative:

> The UfI is obviously a UK government-favoured and -led initiative and has not grown from a particular need in Wales and has not found its way into settling in Wales and getting colleges of further education to understand what it can help to deliver. I think there might be an element of competition there and certainly a lack of understanding as to what the role of the UfI is. (National Assembly Member)

In particular, this sentiment was reflected in an indignation that the implementation of the UfI did not appear to take Wales's existing education provision into account. It was argued, for example, that an initiative such as UfI added little to what was already going on in Wales in terms of community education provision and, if anything, posed a threat to the effectiveness and continued improvement of 'traditional' forms of community learning:

> The colleges are already in the communities, why on earth do we want a multi-million pound investment in something that talks about hubs and learning

centres? Swansea College have got over 180 centres, or 180 learning environments outside the main campus. So why do we need to be told by a government-financed agency that we should have learning in the communities? It's been going on for years, and it's already happening now. So there's a high degree of cynicism around UfI. There's a problem with the tail wagging the dog in terms of UfI dictating the criteria for the quality of learning materials. (FE sector representative body)

That said, on the other hand the WDC was praised by many of our respondents for appearing to be strongly Welsh, working 'from within' Wales and with a distinctive 'Welsh identity':

The Digital College has worked with various education providers in Wales and in certain areas in Wales in particular, and is *creating from within*. I think that is very important in terms of recognition and in getting the participants in the sector to actually be signed up to the work . . . I feel that the Digital College will have more credibility because its been designed by players in the sector in Wales who recognize what the sector is currently achieving and what it aspires to achieve. (National Assembly Member)

The UfI, on the other hand, was seen to be an imposition from outside Wales on Welsh education – despite the acknowledgement that it set out to address very real needs in Wales:

There's a recognition by everybody [in the Assembly] that Wales certainly needs that push in this direction because we are lagging behind on some of the application of IT and the infrastructure to support the various elements [. . .] But because the UfI is a UK initiative then we [the Assembly] have little influence on it although Assembly funds go towards UfI. The government here in Cardiff, because it's a Labour government as it is in Westminster, is sort of signed up to the principle of UfI. (National Assembly Member)

We can see from these brief accounts how the realities of Wales in an information age are just as much bound within the existing infrastructure and meso-politics of Wales as they are about creating new ICT-based infrastructures and frameworks. Both the UfI and WDC can be seen as innovative initiatives, boasting a good use of technology for social and economic ends and could be argued, in theory, to exemplify information age education. Yet, despite their apparently similar frameworks and objectives, as we have seen, both initiatives were quickly faced by very different responses from their prospective 'partners'. We make no judgement of the relative value of these viewpoints, since our main concern is to show that the implementation of an ICT strategy for Wales, however well-meaning, is beset by problems and rivalries of precisely the same kind that it is intended to solve. The emergence of such 'turf wars' and 'nimbyism' will, of course, come as no surprise to even a casual observer of Welsh affairs over the last twenty years. The stories of the development of the WDC and UfI serve as pertinent reminders of the cultural, social and political contexts which enable or constrain such developments (even where all of the actors are purportedly working towards the same end).

THE FUTURE OF ICT-BASED LIFELONG LEARNING IN WALES

The somewhat negative view that existed of the UfI amongst our inter-viewees is perhaps exemplified by this executive from a representative body of the FE sector in Wales who argued that, in the long term, the beneficial effect of UfI would only act in a constructive way as a 'kick up the pants' for the Welsh FE sector to reorganize and represent themselves in light of technological developments in the sector:

> When you look at the cost benefits in the long run you will find these millions [spent on UfI] to be prudent only in that they will have acted as a catalyst, and a kick up the pants for the 24 Colleges in Wales [. . .] Others might cynically call UfI a stalking horse and say 'well it's there to get the private sector off its backside'. But I don't really care which theory it is as long as it gets colleges and other institutions off their backsides to do something, of a collaborative nature as well as something with in-house, in terms of their own internal managed environments. (FE sector representative body)

Several of our interviewees expressed more specific views on both the UfI and WDC which we conclude this chapter by examining. On a more positive note, the hope was expressed that both the WDC and the UfI would support lots of things that they have previously found difficult, especially in the case of encouraging previously apathetic SMEs (small and medium-sized enterprises) in Wales to address seriously the question of education and training. However, the scope of the UfI in particular was seen to be a problem. As the manager of one UfI learning centre argued, in practice the ethos of trying to be 'all things to all people' was limiting the effectiveness of the centre's provision. As a learning centre it would be best if they cut down on what was offered (in terms of learndirect packages), offering more specialist provision rather than general taster courses and low-level IT skills. The scope of the UfI was seen by another interviewee to be nothing less than marketing lifelong learning, seen to be a 'huge task' (S4C chief executive).

Despite the overall negative reception for the UfI most, if not all, of our interviewees nevertheless remained enthusiastic about ICT-based learning. After all, this was the area in which they worked, and through which we contacted them. For many, such developments were inevitable and strongly directed by technological development. Thus, the perceived use of ICT in school was seen as producing upcoming generations of individually empowered learners – fundamentally changing the role of the FE and HE institutions to one of facilitators of learning – in keeping with the UfI and WDC brokerage model:

> I believe that the whole thing is going to be individually demand-led . . . I think a lot of kids are learning this for themselves now through access to IT in the schools, now if they can start to be switched onto experiential learning through the use of IT, which a lot of kids are, and they begin to gather this concept of learning how to learn, I believe that the Colleges of tomorrow will be facilitators of learning . . . they will become vehicles for, if you like, they'll almost be search engines for learning materials. (FE sector representative body)

An alternative perspective to this individual empowerment argument was the stated concern from another institutional representative that ICT-based initiatives ran the risk that 'people may start to think that they can teach themselves' (UfI learning centre manager), thus undermining existing structures of provision. Moreover, despite a general enthusiasm, reservations remained over the day-to-day practicalities of delivering learning to those individuals who may not be highly literate or skilled in the use of ICT:

> You look at something like UfI and learndirect, it's all based around ICT, but it's making enormous assumptions on even the most basic of skills like hand–eye co-ordination and use of a mouse, how to turn a computer on [. . .] What about reading? Are people going to be able to learn in this respect? So I just have a worry that if people who are used to learning have difficulty trying to understand the costs and the access and different types of technology and the pace at which it's all changing, what hope has somebody got who comes from an under-privileged background, has not got access, perhaps doesn't see the benefits to learning? I don't see how its going to solve it. (FE sector representative body)

It was also felt that a wholly ICT approach would miss out on the vital 'social' and 'face-to-face' elements of adult education which were seen as integral to the sector:

> You must identify the difference between the technology hype and what actually works. Nothing will beat the face-to-face contact in the community

centres, it's as simple as that and as soon as people realise that and look into their own experiences of learning then there's no threat with all this technology. It will facilitate and it will help people get to that centre, but the first thing you think about when you're running an adult education course in a community centre is where's the coffee-making equipment? It's all to do with the social aspect of learning, as well as the intellectual aspect. (HEI representative)

From the providers' point of view, another perceived drawback to both the UfI and WDC was one of technological problems – with the need for ever more powerful Internet connections, a changing landscape of digital broadcasting and the self-confessed 'ropey' nature of some of the on-line learning material (WDC executive) seen as only temporary and fast-changing. Interestingly, the issue of access to ICT which we raised in every interview was consistently and confidently not seen as a problem. From the UfI's perspective the Westminster government's promise of universal access to ICT was seen as alleviating the problem of unequal access to ICT across the potential client groups:

[The digital divide] is an enormous task, but we're not dealing with them individually – these are issues for government, and these are issues for those who have the vision, to make sure that we have these things put in place. I can't speak on behalf of government but I know that there have been promises made that people will have access, and if the promises have been made then presumably they have got budgets put aside for this to happen. (UfI Wales executive)

Similarly, from the WDC's perspective, the rapid convergence of the Internet and digital television and their eventual emphasis on digital broadcasting was seen as overcoming barriers of class and socio-economic status, as the following quotations from the chief executive of S4C and an Assembly Member demonstrate:

I think that the key differentiating factor is the involvement of television. I think it is very clear now that digital television will take over from analogue television in the same way as colour television took over from black and white. It will take time and there is an investment in the domestic sets which you cannot ignore, but we are in the process of setting this up so that when that full-scale transfer to digital happens then this is one of the key things which will be available in Wales. (S4C chief executive)

Most houses have television. The only houses that don't have televisions are those that do not want a television, sort of high-middle class more than anyone else. It's going to be a very competitive field I'm sure and the prices of transferring digital technology will continually decrease so it becomes something which is hopefully affordable. (National Assembly Member)

Indeed, aside from basic issues of access, with regard to educational provision then having to compete with entertainment provision on the Internet and digital television, most of our respondents were confident that many, if not all individuals would place sufficient value on education to utilize the opportunities, thus overcoming barriers of motivation and disposition:

[with television] people value entertainment, entertainment has an important part in everyone's lives, but equally most people feel that there is a value to them from education. Now what this will enable to happen is that formal education which has been a barrier to many will decrease as a barrier as education becomes more accessible and is seen as part of something which happens in your living room. [So] it's not a matter of competition with entertainment, it's just a matter of having it as accessible as possible and there will be times when people want entertainment and time when they want education and you know that it will vary considerably amongst individuals as to how much education they want and when they want it and whether they want it. But having that access to it is a key development. (National Assembly Member)

Similarly, both the WDC and UfI were confident, but unsure of how to measure their success beyond viewing figures and the retention of clients. Interestingly, the collection of specific data on the social background of learners was not considered important:

[Interviewer]: *How are you going to be measuring the success of the Digital College?*
   What we are doing is obviously we'll be looking at the simple measurables, viewing figures, as far as S4C is concerned that's got to be an important one, obviously.
   [Interviewer]: *Because you are not actually keeping registration data?*
   No, because we are not registering them . . . But what the colleges have agreed to ask them [is] 'where did you find out?.' Where it's Digital College they will flag it up and let us know. So we *will* get this through, although it's not been formalised yet. (WDC executive)

[Interviewer]: *How would you measure in however many years' time that you've achieved the things you set out to do?*
   I think the success of UfI in the long run will be seen in, well how would you segregate it really? Things like companies staying on board with it, that would be a success measure. Large companies, smaller companies coming on board

and staying on board with us. Success measure is demand, organizations wanting to have more learning centres, pushing to have more learning centres, I think that's a success measure. (UfI Wales executive)

It is certainly not the case that either UfI or WDC appear particularly concerned, at least at this stage, about the type, learning history or background of their users. They therefore have no way of knowing whether they are simply recruiting the 'usual suspects' for the mixture as before:

[Interviewer]: *Where do you see the widening-access goal fitting in the Digital College? Is it right at the top, or is it a bit further down?*
I would say that it's a bit further down the way it's panned; it's because they have dedicated projects they presumably have to sort out technology, they've had to sort out who leads the projects and I think we kind of sit below that just in terms of this material looks good, this material doesn't, this issue is important, or it isn't. (HEI representative and chair of WDC Access Group)

Our experience of the Access Group for the WDC confirms this rather pessimistic interpretation. Its members were generally unaware of the scale of the problem facing them, both in terms of the numbers of people not involved in learning in Wales, and the barriers and determinants that led them to be like that (see chapter 8). A discussion intended to lead to choice of a photograph for the front of the first advertising material was very revealing. The one favoured by the group, and eventually used, was taken in the photographer's own home. It showed a white family of four in a large living room with a pine fireplace, minimalist décor, widescreen television, computer, and around £2,000-worth of stacking stereo units. Added to the fact that none of the 'actors' were actually looking at the screen, we felt that this scene was inappropriate. No one else could see why. A later discussion centred around telephone access, and one group member was heard to claim that everyone in Wales has a telephone, and that as second lines are almost free (they had had one installed recently) the necessity for a dedicated line for some on-line activities should not be a problem. This ignorance of the actual living conditions of the poorest in Wales, those least likely to be learning and in whose name these initiatives were set up, is endemic in a particular set of the Welsh 'intelligentsia'.

The UfI, on the other hand, have realized that access at home could be a problem. Their solution is distributed learning centres (we examine the effectiveness of these in chapter 11). But to imagine that two or three such centres in Wales, in towns and cities already provided with traditional colleges, is sufficient is to underestimate the scale of their need:

We will then have some flagship learning centres which will be developed from scratch and these will be from scratch, well some may already be in existence but we are looking at sort of Rugby Clubs, some Football Clubs, to develop the flagship ones which will be, um, a place where people will say well yes, that's a learndirect centre, fully branded it's a high quality thing, it's something which is new, different, public face really, of the learning centre.

[Interviewer]: *And what will make them flagships then? The size, the scale?*

The size, the scale, the location, the umm . . . the fact that they will probably be in large towns, lots of things will go into making the flagship learning centre. If you can imagine something like the Millennium Stadium, that could be a flagship learning centre, it's that sort of thing which will catch the eye really, more than anything else.

[Interviewer]: *Roughly what number are we talking about for the flagships?*

Off-hand I couldn't say, in fact this question came up yesterday in a meeting with um, and off the top of my head I thought we would have, probably, in Wales, two or three. (UfI Wales executive)

The setting up of these virtual platforms for learning is very slow. During the two-year period of our research in the WDC the starting-date for going live was put off three times, for over a year in total. Even this pace has led to problems, however:

Now at that stage you have to recognize the problems the Digital College has got in that they went ahead and did things, but perhaps the rest of the sectors, the statutory sectors anyway, started to get left behind, because they are probably working at a slower pace and have a lot of other things to contend with. But the Digital College as soon as they heard about UfI were in there, and as soon as they heard about the possibility of conventional televisions being converted for digital signals, they were in there and negotiating. So in some ways the Digital College moved too quickly and higher education, further education sectors were wondering what's happening? (HEI representative)

The potential problems are great, the teething troubles are significant, and none of those involved has a clear plan to measure their success in meeting their prime objective. Nevertheless several respondents made it clear that they cannot be seen to fail:

The cynical view is that it's Old Labour, Open University, New Labour, UfI. Digital bandwagon. I mean if you see a bandwagon in my view it's too late, yes, that seems to me, but . . . so that's the cynical view; Gordon Brown's baby is going to work, he's pumped money into it . . . Of course UfI will be a huge success, so they'll sell it as a success of going concern just as the Dome was a huge success. (FE sector representative body)

We have a UK government which likes initiatives and we've had a tendency for all UK governments to be driven by short-term initiatives because it meets the short-term political agenda. I think that what is possibly behind the UfI was a general perception that there was a need that needed to be addressed in terms of lifelong learning and it was led by the need for an initiative in this sector. (National Assembly Member)

In making these points we, and our respondents in this chapter and the next, are providing local illustrations of what is clearly a widespread malaise throughout the UK. The pilot study for the UfI in England also revealed problems in almost all areas except publicity (TES, 1999), and even then very few small firms had heard of the UfI. There were inaccuracies in the database of registrants, and inability to distinguish between willingness to receive promotional material by post and a desire on the part of the registrants to follow through to actual courses (Morrison et al., 1998). Some registrants on the learner database were unaware that they had been registered and for what. One is reminded here of the confusion, corruption and 'sharp-pencilling' that surrounded the introduction of NVQs and the Investors in People Award (Chambers et al., 1998). In needing to prove themselves successful there was some apparent collusion between employers and the providers of newly created qualifications.

In the first, trial, year of learndirect only 46 per cent of callers got through first time, and 35 per cent did not get the information they wanted even when connected (Johnston, 1999; Bysshe and Parsons, 1999). Other teething problems include regularly crashed web-sites, untrained tutors and advisers, misinformation sent to students and colleges (Johnston 2000a), and reports that the learndirect web-site ran so slowly that students were unable to use it in practice (Johnston, 2000b). Delays in setting-up, finance and organization were ignored as the UfI was under intense political pressure to deliver in an unrealistic time scale (Johnston, 2000c). By June 2000 there were fifty-six UfI hubs operating 251 development centres, testing 200 courses (Tester, 2000). The UfI was under pressure to accept all applicants to boost numbers, but these may be leading to very low completion figures. In addition to technical shortcomings, learndirect has also been accused of being 'too focused on FE colleges, threatening the original vision of enticing new learners rather than recycling traditional ones'. We shall have more to say on this in chapter 11.

CONCLUSIONS

This overview of the emergence and implementation of ICT-based learning initiatives in Wales is useful in contextualizing our results 'on the ground'. Certainly, all of our interviewees remained largely positive over the potential of ICT to overcome barriers to learning and widening participation. This was due, in no small part, to a strong faith among many of our respondents in the power of technologies such as digital television and the Internet to attract and retain the interest of a broad spectrum of learners. Indeed, the perceived need to utilize technology can be seen to be the fundamental driving force behind the WDC, with its overt publicly and privately orientated emphasis on digital television and the Internet as the means through which Wales can be most effectively enrolled into becoming a learning society.

Yet within this technology-fuelled confidence, significant and not wholly surprising tensions remain. The culture and context of Wales as a pre-information age nation appear paramount in the effective implementation of initiatives such as the University for Industry – at least at this macro level. These are all themes which we shall revisit over the remaining chapters. Yet some overriding questions remain of Wales in an information age. Most critically, and a question often overlooked, is what the realities of initiatives such as the WDC are 'on the ground', at the level of the learner. Even taking an apparent 'success' story, such as the made-in-Wales WDC, are our key actors correct in their assumption that the key aims of the learning society can be met in this way? The next two chapters address this very question.

10

ICT Solutions to Non-participation: Early Indications

INTRODUCTION

Despite the obvious tensions, mediating factors and political, technical and economic barriers to successfully establishing ICT-based learning in Wales, the overriding story from chapter 9 is still one of a learning revolution 'waiting to happen'. Even if the politics were not seen to be as conducive as they could have been, all of our key actor interviewees, without exception, remained optimistic about the potential of virtual education. In particular, the broad issue of widening participation in education remained almost unchallenged by those involved in the setting up of ICT-based learning programmes – once various technical, political and institutional problems could be solved then attracting new and diverse sets of learners to varied and meaningful learning episodes was assured.

Whilst gathering these data at the macro level of government and educational institutions has proved invaluable in illuminating the complicated realities of implementing ICT-based education and training programmes in Wales, further analysis needs to take place at the level of the individual learner. In many ways, viewing the realities of ICT-based learning programmes such as UfI and WDC through the eyes of learners is the most important part of examining lifelong learning in the information age. For beyond talk of multibillion pound government initiatives and private-sector investment it is the individual learner who is the ultimate 'end user' of ICT-based education programmes. Who these learners are and what they gain from their experiences form the basis of the overall effectiveness of the ICT-based learning agenda. With this in mind, the next two chapters concentrate on the ICT 'learning revolution' in Wales from the point of view of the learners themselves.

As already outlined, there are two main models of educational participation via ICT. First, there is the distributed learning centre model where learners will access learning via ICT located in various learning centres in community and educational settings. Second, there is the remote model where learners will access learning opportunities via technology in the home (or perhaps at work) – be it the Internet via a personal computer or digital television broadcasts. Both models form part of the UfI and WDC provision and both seek to widen participation in different ways. We go on to cover the experiences of learners using ICT in distributed learning centres in chapter 11. In this chapter we concentrate on learners accessing learning opportunities via technology in the home. In particular we examine the role of the Internet in providing effective access procedures to adult learning and, moreover, gain a sense of *whom* such methods are attracting and *what* learners are beginning to use the Internet for.

As a case study, we chose to concentrate on the Wales Digital College's on-line learning course for learners of the Welsh language. This case study was selected for a variety of practical reasons but primarily because, at the time of writing, it was one of the only tangible manifestations of the WDC or UfI in existence in Wales. This was chiefly due to the delays and technical problems discussed in the last chapter. The digital television broadcasts promised by the WDC for November 2000 had yet to commence, and the Internet-based Welsh-language provision, dually presented with Acen, represented the major element of learning. The fact that the provision of the virtual college movement at the time of writing largely consisted of an on-line course for learners wishing to learn the Welsh language is itself a significant finding – especially when seen in relation to the information age rhetoric presented in chapter 9. Nevertheless, although this on-line programme of learning was still being developed as we studied it, it was at least up and running. The 'Online Welsh' web-site, therefore, allowed us to begin to examine the role of the Internet in providing effective access procedures to adult learning. Our study asked the following questions:

- **How** is the 'On-line for Welsh Learners' course being presented on the Internet? What features of the Internet are being used to attract adult learners and what content is currently being made available?
- **When** and **what** are learners using the 'On-line for Welsh Learners' web-site for? How do patterns of usage correspond with existing patterns of Internet usage and reaching 'non-traditional' adult learners?
- **Who** is accessing Welsh-language learning via the Internet and how does usage of the web-site reflect the Wales Digital College's overall goals of extending participation beyond those social groups already engaged in learning?

THE CONTENT OF THE 'ON-LINE FOR WELSH LEARNERS' WEB-SITE

Just as any analysis of Internet *usage* is by its very nature transitory, so too is the analysis of the *content* of specific web-sites. It is important to note that this section presents a content analysis of the 'On-line for Welsh Learners' web-site carried out by the researchers at the time of writing. This point is of particular significance in view of the fact that the 'On-line for Welsh Learners' web-site was subject to ongoing development. Nevertheless, the web-pages were presented as a service that has been 'especially established for adult Welsh learners who wish to actually study the modern Welsh language *on-line through multi-media experiences*' (Acen, 2000; emphasis added). This section therefore focuses upon the extent to which the web-site delivered its promise of providing learning opportunities through 'multimedia experiences', and how it differed from more traditional texts aimed at teaching Welsh.

(i) First steps: registering with the on-line Welsh course

In order to use the 'On-line for Welsh Learners' web-site, the individual learner first had to register. Although during the first eight months of the initiative learners could register free of charge, all new users were now required to supply either their credit card details or their company details if their employer is paying for their participation on the course. Those on low incomes could apply for an Acen trust grant upon presentation of written evidence of their low-income status. From April 2000 a registration fee of £9.95 was implemented, and users were thereon also charged a membership fee of £14.95 per month. When the user completed the course or chose to terminate membership, a further £9.95 was charged by way of a termination fee. Registrants must also agree to Acen's conditions, mainly concerned with the protection of on-line material and secrecy of passwords. The registration was dealt with in a series of pages in which the registration details are explained and an on-line proforma is completed by the applicant giving personal and financial details. All of these pages were sparsely presented with standard Windows text-boxes and minimum embellishment. Once registered, similar pages can then be accessed detailing the learners' account. When users terminate their account with Acen they are required to fill in another on-line proforma giving details such as their main reason for un-subscribing and suggestions for improving the service.

(ii) Units of learning

Once registered as a learner the main body of the on-line Welsh course was structured into conversational topic areas or 'units'. At the time of data collection (September 2000), although six units were listed, only four were fully operational. The four working units covered the areas of 'greeting and introducing yourself'; 'discussing work and the workplace'; 'discussing where you live'; and 'discussing going places'. Each unit of learning was subdivided into ten separate sections:

- Vocabulary   (Geirfa)
- Patterns   (Patrymau)
- Tasks and activities   (Tasgau a gweithgareddau)
- Assignment   (Aseiniad)
- Visual memory aids   (Ar gof a chadw)
- Grammar   (Gramadeg)
- The unit soap   (Yr opera sebon)
- Ask a question   (Gofyn cwestiwn)
- Real speakers on video   (Cymry ar fideo)
- More reading practice   (Ymarfer darllen)

Each unit was uniformly formatted and structured, but individual learners had some degree of control and autonomy over how they progressed through them. Each page was headed with a series of graphical icons corresponding to each of the ten sections listed above, enabling learners to access any part of the unit that they chose. This allowed learners to navigate from one page to another in the non-linear way that is so characteristic of texts on the web (Gorard and Selwyn, 2001).

The 'Vocabulary', 'Patterns', 'Grammar' and 'Reading practice' sections were all concerned with the more 'technical' aspects of the Welsh language and presented in traditional text format. There was a key difference from traditional textbooks, however, in that users could click on individual words for a sound-clip detailing pronunciation. The 'Ask a question' section was not as promising as it initially sounds, in terms of providing an interactive learning experience. Rather than providing a context in which individual learners have the opportunity for interactive discussion this section simply presented (once more) written instructions on how to ask questions relevant to each topic. The section heading 'Visual memory aids' was similarly somewhat misleading. Instead of using visual media to teach students, this section detailed memory aids in written form, encouraging learners to build up mental images and use mnemonics to memorize particular Welsh phrases covered in each unit. This facility is also limited to a few key words in each section. The 'Unit soap' was a topic-related 'soap opera' in script form, consisting of approximately a page of dialogue. Here once more, users were able to click on specific sentences to hear the correct pronunciation. 'Real speakers on video' was the section of the web-site which comes closest to meeting Acen's promise of using multimedia learning aids and capitalizing upon the innovative techniques offered by the information and communications technology. By clicking on a choice of thumbnail images, users were able to watch a short video clip (no longer than ten seconds) of Welsh-speakers interacting. At the time of writing, this innovative technique was hampered by technological constraints – the video clips were very small (approximately two inches square), slow to load and rather short.

(iii) Other facilities to aid learning

These individual units constituted the main body of the 'On-line for Welsh Learners' course, but the site contained other facilities to aid learning. They were:

- Discussion forum (Fforwm trafod)
- Assessment (Asesu)
- Notice-board (Hysbysfwrdd)
- Live web-casts (Gweledu byw)
- Account details (Eich cyfrif)
- Advice and guidance (Cyngor ac arweiniad)
- Study methods and on-line tutors (Dulliau astudio a thiwtoriaid ar-lein)

The discussion forum, potentially an especially useful facility for the practice of language learning, was not operational at the time of writing. Similarly, there was no facility available for contacting on-line tutors, despite a message stating that a full assessment system would be available from 1 January 2000. As with several pages described above, the name 'Advice and guidance' was slightly misleading as it suggested that on-line guidance is available. Instead, these pages contained a written document on the importance for individuals recognizing their 'learning type' and managing their learning accordingly. The 'Study methods' page merely duplicated this document.

The addition of a 'live web-cast' facility on-line was encouraging and again had enormous potential. However, once more, the content was very limited and at the time of writing consisted solely of a recording of a National Assembly Member's speech at the official opening of the web-site in October 1999. Finally, the notice-board was more established than the other sections of the web-site and contained various documents from vocabulary lists to details of residential courses (which were often out of date, however). The notice-board also contained links to other sites ranging from the Welsh Language Board to an on-line Welsh bookshop.

Although the web-site was professionally presented, with icon-based and conventional text 'hyper-links' to different sections of the site, a striking gold-on-blue colour scheme and coherent site 'identity', it remained rooted in a rather linear, text-orientated paradigm consistent with more 'traditional' learning materials. Although concessions appeared to have been made to more interactive, multimedia options, such sections are either non-operational or very brief. In terms of user autonomy the site felt very much as a 'readerly' text; offering little flexibility and creative use beyond the structure of the site. Nevertheless, the more 'innovative' options such as the discussion forum or on-line tutors offered the potential for a more interactive 'multimedia experience'.

WEB-SITE USAGE ANALYSIS

(i) Who is using the 'On-line for Welsh Learners' web-site?

Having examined the content of the web-site it is now possible to investigate its usage – first by exploring the patterns of site activity and second by examining the characteristics of registered learners.

Table 10.1 Use of the 'On-line for Welsh Learners' web-site by geographical region

Region	Mean no. of accesses	Standard deviation
Unspecified	491.46	271.06
General UK web addresses	600.07	539.27
Specific Welsh web addresses	200.12	203.51
Europe	27.27	36.00
North America	11.07	14.37
Rest of the world	23.09	64.02

Data are mean number of accesses per week made from each region.

Although users of the site came from countries as widespread as New Zealand, Singapore, Belgium and Canada, the vast majority of site usage originated from within the UK (see table 10.1). Most UK users' geographical location was not readily apparent from their web addresses, but a further 23 per cent of accesses to the web-site were made from identifiable Welsh locations (such as *RuralWales.Net*, Welsh educational and government institutions etc.). Although this predominance of Welsh and UK users for a Welsh-language learning web-site may not appear surprising, it does mark a shift from previous demographic analyses of web-site usage. There does not seem to be, for example, the predominance of North American users, as has been reported by earlier studies of Internet sites dealing with Welsh culture and language (Mackay and Powell, 1996).

(ii) When is the 'On-line for Welsh Learners' web-site being used?

As figure 10.1 shows, after the 'launch' of the web-site at the end of August 1999 there was a rapid increase in visits made to the site, which then gradually decreased to a level of between 100 and 150 accesses per week. Such 'peaking' of site traffic during the initial launch of a web-site followed by a tailing-off of activity with an eventual steady state of users can be considered as typical of the web in general (McLaughlin et al., 1999). Also of interest is the dip and 'steadying-off' in activity from the beginning of April 2000 – coinciding with the end of the free trial period and the introduction of subscription fees for learners.

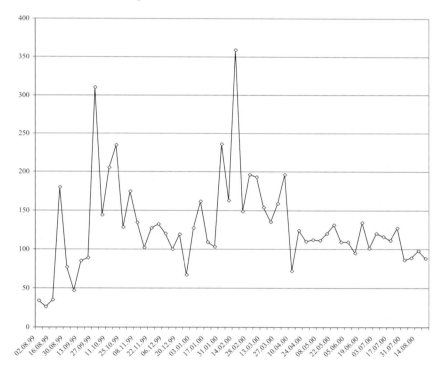

Figure 10.1
Number of visits to the 'On-line for Welsh Learners' homepage (August 1999–August 2000)
Data are number of recorded visits to the homepage per week. NB: a visit to the homepage can be treated as a 'session', with each visit potentially entailing more than one access.

Within these weekly data it is possible to identify more specific patterns of usage by day and even by hour. This level of analysis can be useful in identifying whether the site is attracting users on a 'flexible' learning basis. As can be seen in figure 10.2, the majority of site activity took place during weekdays, with weekend activity accounting for only 18 per cent of the overall volume of accesses made. Moreover, although the majority of visits were made during daytime (08.00–17.00 hrs., user's local time) as opposed to night-time (17.00–08.00 hrs.), 'after-work hours' access remained significant in the evening until a tailing-off around midnight. As figure 10.3 shows, the hours between 17.00 and 00.00 hrs. accounted for 34 per cent of the visits made to the site. Moreover, both these daily and weekly access trends appear to remain fairly consistent over the twelve-month period of study. Thus, although studies of web-site activity in the USA would suggest that weekday/weekend access is perhaps more equitable (e.g. McLaughlin et al., 1999) the 'On-line for Welsh Learners' web-site nevertheless would appear to be attracting a significant level of activity outside 'work hours' and at times contiguous with flexible modes of learning.

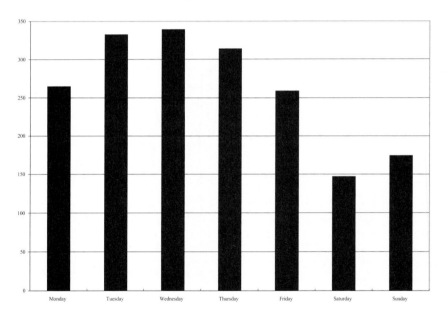

Figure 10.2
Activity on the 'On-line for Welsh Learners' web-site by day of the week
(August 1999–August 2000)
Data are mean number of accesses to pages.

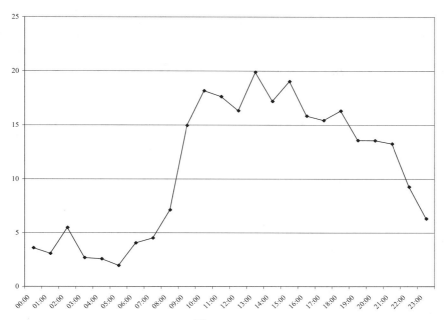

Figure 10.3
Activity on the 'On-line for Welsh Learners' web-site by hour of the day
(August 1999–August 2000)
Data are mean number of accesses to pages.

(iii) What is the 'On-line for Welsh Learners' web-site being used for?

The final level of site usage data allows some analysis of which elements of the web-site are being used, albeit at the level of general sections of the site. Thus, although data are not available on how the specific aspects of each section are being used (e.g. how often the video clips are used in the learning units), it is possible to identify the areas of the site attracting most and least usage.

As table 10.2 shows, the sections of the site attracting most usage were, in first place, the units of work and, in third place, the section dealing with vocabulary. It would, therefore, be reasonable to extrapolate that the site was primarily being used for some level of learning activity. However, issues of payment for learning and registering as a recognized user then take up the bulk of the remaining activity. Some of the more 'innovative' options such as the user notice-board and discussion forum, live web-casts and on-line guidance for learning remained relatively untouched – in part reflecting the undeveloped nature of these options.

Table 10.2 Use of the 'Online for Welsh Learners' web-site by activity

Section of site	Description	Mean no. of weekly accesses	Standard deviation
Uned	Units of work	187.61	268.90
Cyfrif	Information about user's account	160.84	84.77
Geirfa	Word/vocabulary List	96.34	146.61
Mewn/Mynededfa	Logging on a registered user	57.27	46.82
Cwrs	Payment agreement	18.45	71.32
Cyswllt	Links to external pages	15.63	5.87
Hysbys	Notice-board	7.05	10.55
Cyngor	Guidance and support with learning	6.68	8.42
Gramadeg	Grammar pool	6.45	9.30
Cynnwys	Contents	5.20	16.35
Gweledu	Live web-casts	2.34	4.71
Fforwm	Discussion forum	1.89	3.73

Data are mean number of accesses (including standard deviations) made per week to each section of the site.

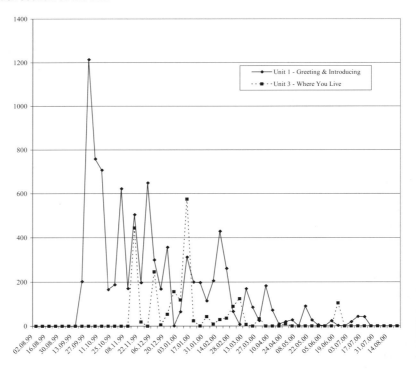

Figure 10.4
Activity on the 'On-line for Welsh Learners' web-site on units 1 and 3 of work (August 1999–August 2000)
Data are mean number of accesses to each unit.

At the time of the study the 'On-line for Welsh Learners' web-site offered six main units of study, although only the first four were operational. These four units were:

Unit 1 – Cyfarch a chyflwyno'ch hun/ Greeting and introducing yourself
Unit 2 – Trafod gwaith a'r gweithle/ Discussing where you work
Unit 3 – Trafod ble dych chi'n byw/ Discussing where you live
Unit 4 – Trafod mynd i rywle/ Discussing going places

As figure 10.4 shows, using the example of learning units 1 and 3, once the early 'surge' of overall site activity had subsided and other units had been introduced, the demand for the units fluctuated more or less in unison – suggesting that learners were progressing through the schemes of work, or at least making use of all the available units of work. Use of learning units dramatically tailed away from April 2000 – again coinciding with the introduction of subscription fees.

(iv) User analysis

Having examined the content and usage of the site it is finally pertinent to examine the study's third question: *who* was accessing the 'On-line for Welsh Learners' site and how do patterns of participation reflect the Wales Digital College's overall goals of extending participation beyond those social groups already engaged in 'conventional' learning? Although the previous site activity data provided an indication of users' countries of origin, these questions can be more accurately answered by examining the characteristics of those users registering as 'official' learners on the Acen web-site. In this way it is possible to examine the geographical location, age and gender of on-line learners, the percentage taking advantage of the reduced rates for those on low incomes and, most interestingly, the reasons expressed by learners for participating in the programme.

As table 10.3 shows, there was little or no indication from our (admittedly very limited) achieved questionnaire sample of the 'On-line for Welsh Learners' web-site attracting learners with the characteristics most commonly associated with non-participation in education; i.e. the unemployed and others on low incomes, the unskilled and unqualified, ex-offenders, part-time or temporary workers, 'blue-collar' as opposed to 'white-collar' workers, those with learning difficulties or low levels of basic skills, and some ethnic groups. Although the ages of learners ranged from twenty-four to sixty-nine with a mean age of forty-five, all the respondents had educational qualifications at NVQ Level Three or higher – suggesting hitherto successful learning 'trajectories' prior to enrolling on

Table 10.3 Summary of registered user data collected from email survey

Male	11
Female	7
Age	Age range: 24 years to 69 years
	Mean = 45.53 years, s.d. = 14.32 years

Place of access to the Acen web-site

Home computer	12
Work computer	8

Highest level of educational qualification

NVQ Level 3 +	17
NVQ Level 2	
NVQ Level 1	

Current Status

Full-time working	10
Part-time working	3
Unemployed	0
Retired	4
Full-time student	1

Current or usual occupations
- **IT** (i.e. *ILT development officer, IT operations director, electronic design engineer, computer technician, computer scientist*)
- **Education** (i.e. *head of dept in secondary school, Ph.D. student, college instructor*)
- **Other professional/ managerial** (i.e. *managing director, charity worker, architect, RGNurse, sales manager, accountant, public sector manager*)

Locations
Cardiff, Swansea, Penarth, North Powys, Gwynedd, Wrexham, Chester, Wigan, Cheltenham, Stoke-on-Trent, Sweden, USA

(n=18)

Table 10.4 Access to ICT in Wales, 1999 (percentages)

	At home	At work
Telephone	91	41
Computer	33	26
Internet	13	19
None of these	7	53

Table 10.5 Differential access to computers in Wales, 1999 (percentages)

	all	male	age 17–19	class AB	ftce 21+	degree	current
Home	33	38	49	60	61	58	57
Work	26	31	44	51	51	54	54

class AB: usual occupation is professional or managerial.
ftce21: continued in full-time continuous education until at least age 21.
degree: qualified to at least NVQ Level 4 equivalent.
current: currently involved in formal education or training.

Table 10.6 Differential access to computers in Wales, 1999 (percentages)

	all	age 55–64	age 65–74	class E	ftce 16	unqualified	non-particip.
Home	33	28	7	12	24	13	17
Work	26	14	1	12	15	7	7

class E: usual occupation is manual unskilled.
ftce16: did not continue in full-time education past minimum legal age.
non-particip.: currently not involved in formal education or training.

the 'On-line for Welsh Learners' web-site. Similarly, the range of current or usual occupations of learners was largely restricted to professional and managerial occupations. These findings must be tempered with the caveat that people with higher levels of educational qualification and from professional social groups may be more likely to respond to unsolicited survey instruments (A. N. Oppenheim, 1992; Gorard, 2001b). It is also the case that the nature of the website (devoted to Welsh language learning) is particularly attractive to these same social groups (see Giggs and Pattie, 1994). Nevertheless, this small sample provided no evidence of the 'Online for Welsh Learners' web-site attracting and retaining learners who are unemployed or with few previous educational qualifications. In other words, as with many other forms of lifelong learning, the survey suggests that the Acen website was being used solely by the 'usual suspects' (Fryer, 1999).

This finding is confirmed, if confirmation were necessary, by the much larger household study we analysed for NIACE Dysgu Cymru (table 10.4). In 1999, when the WDC started its pilot operations, we estimate that only 13 per cent of the population of Wales had access to the Internet at home, and only 19 per cent had access to the Internet at work. The majority of people in Wales do not have a computer, and a substantial proportion do not even have access to a shared public payphone at their place of residence. Leaving aside for a moment the notion of distributed centres for access to ICT which we discuss in the next chapter, this means that courses like 'On-line for Welsh Learners' are currently only available to the few.

If we move to a consideration of who it is that has access to the various technologies a similar picture emerges for each. Access to computers, for example, is considerably greater than average among the younger, educated, qualified males currently involved in formal education or training (table 10.5). It is correspondingly less among older age groups, unskilled or unemployed, with no post-compulsory education and no qualifications (table 10.6). It is, of course, these last that the notion of widening participation via ICT is intended to attract. The question, therefore, must be – how? Perhaps the answer lies not so much in on-line learning at home (if the client base does not have a telephone let alone a computer) or at work (if the client base does not have suitable, or indeed any, work). Perhaps the answer lies in providing access to computers at specialist centres.

(v) User reactions to the 'On-line for Welsh Learners' course

The final part of this particular element of our study was to gauge some reaction from those learners who had actually used the 'On-line for Welsh Learners' web-site. During our subsequent telephone interviews, some of the learners described initial barriers that they had encountered which had curtailed their use of the site – even after they had paid for the service:

> I approached it with enthusiasm, but I had a lot of trouble getting from the initial web page. The web pages contained too much information. The instructions were much too complicated. I actually forgot the password I was given and found great difficulty in finding out what my forgotten password was. The person at the end of the telephone line I contacted was not at all helpful! I know they had to be aware of security, but in the end I gave up – even after paying my subscription! (Male 69 – retired teacher, Wales)

For other learners, the limited nature of the learning content and other services which the site purported to offer also discouraged any sustained participation:

> [Female]: It clearly wasn't finished . . . we actually couldn't get the word spoken, if you clicked on the Welsh word, you were supposed to hear the sound of the word as it's pronounced and that wasn't working. And the video clips weren't working; they wouldn't play at all.
> [Interviewer]: *Right.*

[Male]: And we thought we were assigned a tutor when we were first signed on and registered. We emailed our tutor a few times but we were never given a response.

[Interviewer]: *Really?*

[Male]: But after that we didn't bother because we were doing night classes as well.

[Female]: We were going to use it as a sort of back up, but what we found was that the site was so unfinished that we found that we had already learned whatever the site had to offer in the first two lessons of our evening class. (Married couple 55, 52 – retired, Wales)

If you want people to learn a language then the last thing you want to do is supply them with a system which is not working properly because, I mean, it just puts people off. (Male 24 – electronic engineer, England)

Similarly, for some interviewees who already had experience of information technology, the technical quality of some of the site's more innovative features was cited as a problem. As this interviewee describes, her professional experience with web design left her dissatisfied with the audio and visual elements of the 'On-line for Welsh Learners' learning package. Indeed, this ultimately ended in a decision to stop using the course rather than 'go through the pain barrier' of downloading unwieldy video and sound clips:

The video clips and the actual excerpts . . . were very poor.

[Interviewer]: *In what way?*

Sound quality and picture quality. To a certain extent you think why are they bothering to do a video? . . . I think it really did detract, you know I think there would have been a lot cleverer ways of doing it. I mean a bit interactively when you click on the words or as you're hearing the video the words are just popping up you know, there are much simpler ways of doing something like that, which you could do in flash or something, as opposed to a clunky not very nice sounding click. I mean it's hard enough trying to understand the Welsh as it is never mind trying to understand the other noises they've added. So I think that from a kind of technical point of view . . . there are better ways to do it, so I wasn't necessarily that unprepared to sort of go through the pain barrier. (Female 30 – IT operations director, Wales)

Nevertheless, it was clear that the learners were initially attracted to the web-site because of its attempts at innovative use of the worldwide web. For example, the same interviewee also described her satisfaction in the more 'interactive' elements of the site, such as the 'test-yourself' sections:

[Interviewer]: *Were there any aspects of it that you think were useful ways of learning?*

Yeah, definitely the bits where you basically have to copy the answers across, you're actually having to type it out. And then you click on it to hear it and it was fantastic because you were interacting with it, you were hearing it, you were instantly rewarded by a kind of 'Yes, that's right', kind of thing and I think that really encouraged you to go along with it, so I found that quite useful. (Female 30 – IT operations director, Wales)

Some learners were attracted to the prospect of being in contact with an on-line tutor – even though the reality of a 'disembodied' tutor proved unnerving for others:

[Female]: Well I mean it's the idea of the site we liked.
[Male]: Yeah well it's the whole idea of working at home, if you go to night school you've got a tutor you can talk to a tutor and get help. If you've got trouble on the machine at home, providing the machine can talk to you . . .
[Female]: It's very important, especially in Welsh because the pronunciation isn't very easy at all especially for English people, and I think it's very important to be able to hear the word being spoken to you and played over again and the site's got to do with that. (Married couple 55, 52 – retired, Wales)

[Interviewer]: *Have you got an on-line tutor with Acen?*
Initially I did have but I haven't ever used her but I think probably I would be afraid to actually answer any of the questions, ha ha.
[Interviewer]: *So you think it would be intimidating?*
I don't know. I mean never having met them or seen them can be kind of pretty daunting.
[Interviewer]: *So would you be happy with a face-to-face tutor?*
I don't know, it depends really, I mean even if you had a picture of the person for the on-line tutor it wouldn't be so daunting.
[Interviewer]: *Yeah, a bit less anonymous.*
Yeah, of course. (Male 24 – electronic engineer, England)

In practice the meshing of the on-line course with the human element of the on-line tutor was not always smooth, as this interviewee described with regard to her firm subscribing to the course which then unexpectedly led to demands for a 'one-off' consultation with their human support:

The on-line tutor just never worked … We did have a snotty woman that phoned us up saying – I need to come in and do a lecture with you or a training session with you in the Welsh language – and I said – well I can't possibly take six people out of the office in day's notice – and she said – well you have to because I'm going back to school next week. (Female 30 – IT operations director, Wales)

It was clear from all of the interviews that, despite their varying specific experiences of the 'On-line for Welsh Learners' site, the current users were enthusiastic and broadly supportive of on-line learning in general. In this way they could be seen as classic examples of 'early adopters', with many describing other on-line learning courses which they were also 'experimenting' with. As this interviewee argued, in his opinion the flexible use of ICT 'could only help' with the provision of education in the future:

Ah, definitely I think that different people pick up things in different ways and with all the different media that you provide them with should be able to do that and it can only help really with making it more available and making it more approachable for people. Some people like classrooms and some people like learning from books, then some people like learning from the TV or something. So I think that providing that for everybody, plus in the first place, making it more accessible, making it more open to people, I think it makes it a bit easier. I think that a lot of people would like to do these kinds of learning experiences later on in life, but obviously by that time, it makes it a bit more difficult to get involved in these things.

[Interviewer]: *And the idea of formal learning can be ...*

I think TV is kind of a lot less intimidating I suppose and you're not being forced to be . . . with the times and having to do the lessons every week and so on.

[Interviewer]: *So you can dip in when you want to kind of thing.*

And come back to it like if you get bored or something then you can leave it and come back to it a bit later kind of thing. (Male 24 – electronic engineer, England)

For lots of the learners, the 'On-line for Welsh Learners' web-site was just one of a variety of ICT- *and* non-ICT-based sources they used to learn to speak Welsh. Many of the interviewees spoke about the need to learn to speak a language with other learners and the associated benefits of learning in a traditional class situation. For many learners, the Internet provided a useful but not essential 'support resource' for their studies; a supplement rather than replacement to 'conventional' methods of learning. Nevertheless, as this first interviewee argued, 'learning a language anyway is better than not learning it at all':

Well, I think as far as learning a language goes, I think when you have the opportunity I think it's better to learn in a classroom because you can converse with other students and you can practise things that when you're working by yourself you can't do. I've tried and I can't get my husband interested in learning this with me, so you know I can say things and practise with me but it's more that if he could ask me words or even quiz me on my vocab but he can't really help me with my pronunciation.

[Interviewer]: *Yeah, right.*

So that I think that as far as a language goes when you can I think it's better to learn in a classroom but when you don't have that opportunity then I think that learning it anyway is better than not learning it at all. (Female 32 – college instructor, USA)

[Female]: I would like to do it with people as well. I only regard [the web-site] as a support resource; I wouldn't regard it as a replacement for an evening class or a class I should say.

[Male]: The thing is, in many parts I mean we're in rural Wales and there's always pressure with night school classes with numbers. And there's not always plenty of places, I mean we weren't sure whether we were going to get on the Level 2 Course this year but the advantage of the Internet thing is that providing you've got the kit at home to do it then you haven't got the number problem.

[Female]: I would still think presumably that if the night school didn't go ahead then we would be looking for lots of different ways and we would certainly use the web-site regularly then. I mean we don't just learn Welsh by the one medium because we find that it is better if you grab the learning experience over different methods. But I mean we've got some neighbours that speak Welsh and they help us now and again over the garden fence. (Married couple 55, 52 – retired, Wales)

CONCLUSIONS

The 'On-line for Welsh Learners' web-site provides a 'first glimpse' into the realities of Internet-based lifelong learning. Although focused around the Welsh language, there is little to suggest that our findings are necessarily unique to Welsh-language adult education. Basic Welsh-language learning is a popular element of adult education in Wales (and has always been so, see chapter 5), and in its conventional form attracts substantial numbers and a wide range of learners. In theory, therefore, Internet-based Welsh-language learning should be seen as a potentially attractive proposition. So what conclusions can be drawn from the 'On-line for Welsh Learners' web-site in terms of attracting adults to learning via the Internet?

Although the web-site was obviously restricted in terms of process and content of Internet-based adult learning, this would perhaps be tempered if there was evidence that these programmes were reaching those individuals previously disengaged from learning and, therefore, truly widening participation in lifelong learning. Certainly the usage data for the web-site would suggest that some sustained level of activity, and even learning, was taking place. However, the level of between 100 and 150 visits to the web-site per week only represents a modicum of use in a medium where the

Church of England web-site, for example, receives around 350,000 visits per week (BBC, 2000). Usage of the 'On-line for Welsh Learners' web-site can only be assumed, at this stage, to be by a minority of learners. Furthermore, the apparent decline in site usage after the implementation of the £14.95 monthly subscription fee would suggest that this minority coverage will persist, or even worsen, in the short to medium term. Whilst this small scale of use is understandable at the beginning of the programme, it cannot continue if the Internet is indeed to be used to provide 'education for all' as the policy-makers would have us believe.

11

Voices of 'Technological' Participants in Education

With Sara Williams

The previous chapter described some of the experiences of early participants in virtual learning and learning via information technology. As we have seen, the nature of ICT-based learning is, at best, variable. Yet in setting out to gauge the effectiveness of such initiatives we need a more detailed picture of those learners currently taking part. What kind of people are they? Are they, as suggested by the on-line survey, already educated to a high level and already participating in lifelong learning episodes? Or has the use of ICT already managed to overcome the barriers of time, space and personal motivation to such an extent that virtual learners in Wales now include previous non-participants?

In this chapter we expand on these questions in the light of information relevant to the learning trajectories of individuals taking part in a variety of schemes. Building on the picture of participants of the 'On-line for Welsh Learners' programme, we now broaden our study to also include those learners accessing ICT-based learning in different learning centres. In this way we interviewed thirty-six such technological participants, and we encountered them in the following contexts:

- Our on-line survey of learners taking the WDC 'On-line for Welsh Learners' web-based course – attracting remote learners from Wales, the rest of the UK, Scandinavia and the United States.
- An elementary 'Introduction to IT' course, lasting four days full-time, and taking place in the 'Enterprise Centre' attached to a job centre in Wales. The student:teacher ratio was 1:7. Each day took the form of semi-structured exercises using a piece of application-free software, followed by unstructured investigation.
- A drop-in centre located in a community centre in a small town in one of the coalfield valleys north of Cardiff. This community-run centre offers a range of leisure and adult-learning opportunities for local residents, including two computer suites where the Internet and graphic design is taught. One of the local FE colleges also uses the centre as a location for 'outreach' education provision teaching basic IT skills and the RSA CLAIT qualification.

- An Information Technology and Enterprise Centre (ITEC) in south Wales. Originally set up by the Conservative government in the 1980s as one of the first IT-based drives in adult education and training, this is one of four remaining ITEC centres in Wales offering a range of IT-based training for individuals and businesses. Significantly, this ITEC centre had also been appointed as a local 'learndirect' centre.

Whilst the first group were taking part in a web-based language course, the others were all taking courses learning about IT by using IT in distributed learning centres. Local interviews were conducted face to face, and overseas interviews were telephone-based. A few of these were conducted with pairs of respondents at one time. It is noteworthy that our initial representative household sample of 1,104 people and the follow-up interviews with a 10 per cent sub-sample (see chapter 8) revealed very few people learning via the use of ICT. The household survey found fewer than twenty people who were classified as non-participants who reported using a computer for leisure purposes (see Gorard et al., 1999d), which primarily entailed games consoles and other machines unlikely to be Internet-capable. Where respondents (two in total) described learning experiences via the Internet or software packages, they were both already classified as lifelong learners for their other more traditional learning experiences, and they were professionals (a lawyer and a midwife). We have therefore had to 'sample' deliberately by seeking existing participants. As is shown below, these participants are still not representative of the larger population.

LEARNING CAREERS

By and large the individual participants in ICT-based learning we encountered fall into three discernible groups. First, there are those who are clearly already lifelong learners for whom the use of ICT is simply a further medium to add to book, radio, television, and face-to-face tuition. These formed the majority of those actually engaged in a web-based course. Second, there are young people who have recently left initial education, and see IT-based learning and IT courses as vocational training in a non-school setting. These form the majority of learners in a training company or drop-in centre. Finally, there are those for whom ICT-based learning is a revelation. These few were encountered only on a four-day course at the Enterprise Centre attached to a local job centre. Using the nomenclature from chapter 8 these are discussed under the subheading of lifelong, transitional and delayed learners. There were, by definition, no non-participants since all were involved in a course at the time. More significantly, very few (much fewer than the 31 per cent in the general population) would be classified as non-participants even if their present ICT-based learning activity is ignored.

Lifelong learners

A clear majority of IT users/learners, proportionately much higher than in the general population, were already on lifelong learning trajectories. For example, in the ITEC centre, there was a very youthful, almost school-type, culture since nearly all of the participants were within a few years of school-leaving age. Jerome was an exception. Aged fifty he had been sent along to the classes from his local job centre, and his attendance and travel were paid for by the Training for Work scheme. There he was taking an NVQ Level One qualification in IT which he felt was necessary to find a post in his normal work in warehousing (to which he switched after suffering skin problems as a painter and decorator). As he said, 'You can't get a job in a warehouse without computer literacy nowadays.' Jerome left school at the earliest opportunity, aged fifteen, found the present course boring 'sitting in front of a computer', had no previous experience of IT and was having problems with typing. At first sight therefore he was a non-participant in lifelong learning forced by economic changes to take training in order to continue in his line of work. He was on this course with teenagers because no other places are available, having pursued advertisements for training with computer-aided design but being told that these were not up and running yet.

However, Jerome described his days at school with enthusiasm and affection, remembering his English teacher as an excellent motivator. He left school chiefly because of the financial need of his family following the state execution of his father. He described himself as always an 'avid reader', particularly of biographies, and a fairly regular attendee at evening classes, discussing his O level in British Constitution, and an RSA qualification. To a large extent these educational interests were related to seeking a posthumous pardon for his father (granted in 1997), rather than stemming from personal development or vocational motives. As part of the same 'mission', Jerome had assisted in the creation of a family web-site by providing oral histories for some family members. This, therefore, is the story of a delayed or possibly a lifelong learner in terms of the typology developed in chapter 8. Neither the technology nor the provision of this specific class have persuaded Jerome to participate in significant later learning. As far as it is possible to glean from this brief biography Jerome was already a self-motivated adult learner – albeit for unusually tragic reasons.

Similarly, Carol, who was at the end of her first week studying Advanced Software at ITEC via learndirect when we interviewed her, already had a history of participation in a variety of post-compulsory courses. She had already been studying an RSA course at ITEC where we contacted her, so it is also clear in this instance that the learndirect telephone brokering service had made no difference. Carol had stayed at school until eighteen, and moved to day-release courses, licenceship of the Royal Society of Chemistry, 'a little bit on archaeology and a little bit on geology'. At the age of forty she is qualified with A levels, a Higher National Certificate with distinction in Business Administration, an Advanced National Certificate, and a degree with the Open University. She has passed Life Insurance Association examinations, taken correspondence courses, and is a member of Royal Society of Chemistry. She has moved around a lot, worked in a variety of jobs – including life insurance sales and working in an architect's office – and had an Internet-capable computer at home. 'I have always liked reading and have always been interested in books and I suppose I liked school and I suppose I am in a minority there.' 'I am quite happy to go along and learn things on my own and I have got the motivation.'

Even at the Enterprise Centre several of the interviewees would have already been classified as lifelong learners. Simon was forty-four years old. He is most clearly not a non-participant in later learning who has been enticed into learning by the IT revolution. He ended his initial education with a degree from Cardiff University, and has subsequently received training at work relating to sales along with 'minimal computer training'. He has always worked with computers, and was clearly the most proficient in the room in using the keyboard. He owned a computer at home, with printer and scanner, ostensibly bought for his three children, and learned his skills on 'a needs-must basis'. He had been a building society manager until made redundant, and was signed up for the course by his wife who had previously attended the same course. He had qualified as a financial adviser following a distance learning course in accountancy, and completed a 'night school' course in navigation. He was studying at home using materials on CD for the Royal Yachting Association examination, with the intention of buying a boat. In a fortnight he was starting a new job in financial services requiring regular use of a laptop computer.

John was fifty-two and had never used a computer before, and did not have one at home. He had left school at sixteen with some qualifications (four O levels), and then completed a couple of apprenticeships:

> Well the problem was when you left school in that day, at that time, like I was working down the Steel Works doing electrical and mechanical. Got fed up at

that and you could finish work at 12 o'clock and by one o'clock you'd have another job . . . You could just say to your boss I don't like the colour of your suit, I'm finishing and going down the road to work for the next bloke, and the next bloke would be there waiting for you.

He moved to a college of food and technology to take more O levels, and started A levels but gave these up as they clashed with his work. He started a course with the Open University in the 1970s but gave it up during the miners' strikes. 'There were no videos available then, and transmissions at antisocial hours, and then the three-day week. After six months of that, writing essays by candlelight I just gave up.' He has been working as a bus driver (having received training in that) but has had a stroke. He now has two part-time jobs and is attending a local FE college one day per week for an Association of Welfare Studies certificate, and doing an ITEC course as preparation. He intends to use his Individual Learning Account to help pay for his course. He was going to university to do sociology until 'I found out that grants are not what grants used to be. And you've got to pay everything back'. John is also an enthusiastic informal learner, watching nature programmes, anthropology and cable TV. He prefers actual college to on-line learning as 'you get motivation off people'. His sister has a Ph.D. and is a child psychologist consultant. For John 'it's just accumulating the qualifications and experience'.

At the community drop-in centre we encountered people who were less clearly motivated and certainly less qualified than this, and yet still described numerous previous non-ICT-based formal learning episodes. Robert left school at sixteen, and went on to 'schemes and was in hospital'. He came to the course as 'it is somewhere to go as we don't have anything up the Valleys and it is something to do'. He has a computer at home but no Internet access. Was he a non-participant included by a combination of community learning and ICT? No, for he had completed several paper-based courses at home, at a local college and by correspondence in the last four years. He received an award for scholarship in writing, and now plans to get a job with a local newspaper.

Also at the Valleys community drop-in centre, Fiona is now nearly fifty. She has a computer at home with Internet access, but only her son uses it regularly. She left school at sixteen since she was deemed a failure. 'I went to a secondary modern school . . . If you failed the eleven-plus then your life had gone.' However, she moved directly to a secretarial course at Pontypridd College, and thence to employment. She had then found work in a bank, and while there completed numerous training courses (not involving computers). However, she was made redundant three years ago. As she was a typist, 'I could see that the computer actually made me redundant. At the end of the day they didn't want typists and secretaries because the clerks could produce their own documents.' She also took a course in integrated business technology at Pontypridd College. Since redundancy Fiona has tried numerous courses, but wanted to attend local classes in informal settings with small numbers of people, as she found going back into learning 'terrible'. 'I did do, not last year but the year before, I went down to Pontypridd College and did GCSE IT, which was a bit horrendous in a class full of seventeen-year-old boys and girls that did not want to be there.'

She thought that she had found the solution in satellite courses, but has discovered that despite the outreach work carried out by another local FE college, various e-learning schemes, and even learndirect, that in the end she had to attend the institution. 'That is what the people over there [i.e. learndirect] were saying that we're trying to encourage people to learn, and it was going along quite nicely and they do this.' She was doing a course at the Bell Centre with ten weekly sessions per year and a test at the end (at her nearest university). She moved to the present course, in the drop-in centre, as she wanted to know about the Internet, and 'all of a sudden last week they pulled the plug on the course'. 'And what I can't understand is that they don't want to run these courses in the community; they want people to go to the University of Glamorgan, which I don't want to.' 'I'm not the only one.' She has come down here to try as it is so close to home – 'I have nowhere else to go now.' 'Once you get a bit advanced it has to be at the University.' She believes that younger school-leavers don't want the community courses, so it 'is all people of forty plus like me', but that when they get interested they will not go down and do a degree. She has complained but they 'pass the buck . . . So I am a bit disillusioned really.' 'I spent time through the project nearly crying as you had to do the coursework and I had never done anything like that . . . I am just clutching at straws now . . . There is nothing I can do.'

The only totally virtual course that we involved in our study was based on the 'On-line for Welsh Learners' web-site via the Wales Digital College, as discussed in chapter 10. At least six of the 'students' we interviewed were professional web-site developers needing to work on Welsh translations for their own web-sites. One worked in computer systems at the University of Wales College of Medicine. All have degrees, and they all described further training, marketing diplomas, training in writing business plans and in health and safety.

Another student was already a university graduate, with a master's degree in engineering, and some work-based training, and some 'on-line lectures and courses relating to my job I suppose . . . Electronic and all that kind of stuff. They've got this thing called Tech On-Line University which has courses.' He had already studied Welsh (the subject of the on-line course) until the age of thirteen at school, and has always wanted to continue, since leaving Cardiff to go to Birmingham University. He had already registered for and followed a course at the University of Lampeter, and another in the US, and used books, tapes and records. He 'stumbled across the course'. He is only an occasional user of his PC at home since he also uses a PC at work all day.

Another was a teacher and lecturer in Celtic studies in the US, educated to degree level, for whom Welsh is 'my area of scholarship'. She had already taken an on-line literature course in Welsh heroic poetry, and 'well I'm currently sitting in on a German class . . . but other than that I haven't done any courses since I got my last degree'. 'I'm going to be teaching a course myself on the Internet next semester . . . an English composition class.' She has tried to learn 'with just books and tapes and stuff', and has also discovered and tried the on-line course at Lampeter.

We interviewed one older married couple who did their on-line learning together. Originally from Liverpool, both passed their eleven-plus going to the local grammar school, and both have degrees (in mathematics and physics respectively). Both worked in the Liverpool University Computing Service. One reported, 'I was a registered trainer . . . with the Ceramics and Minerals Products Industrial Training Board and also with the Hotel Industry Training Board.' 'We've also been to the summer schools.' 'We've been computer professionals for a very long time, so you know the IT side of it doesn't really put any sort of barrier up to us.' 'I actually run evening classes for computing for the terrified.' The female interviewee also read and taught herself craftwork. Her partner reported going on several work-related courses previously, had learnt to drive rally cars, and had gardening as a hobby. He agreed, 'So we were both in computers before you see.' They had moved to learning on-line once in rural Wales (where they moved on retirement): 'there's always pressure with night school classes with numbers.' 'We also go on Welsh guided walks, we're supposed to walk and talk Welsh at the same time.'

As can be glimpsed from these accounts, many of the participants in learning about IT are already qualified, motivated, and have already been involved in other forms of education or training. The participants in on-line learning are even more highly qualified. Because of the nature of the course they were also relatively privileged economically (given the correlation between Welsh language and economic advantage; see Gorard et al., 1997a). Several had moved from Wales and described themselves as becoming 'more patriotic' in doing so, while others had moved to Wales and found the minority local language intriguing.

Transitional learners

A reasonable number of our respondents on the various courses would instead be classified as transitional, or immature, learners rather than lifelong learners. For the most part this is simply because they are very young (all of these were aged fifteen to eighteen), and by moving from compulsory schooling to some form of training they are mostly lifelong learners in the making. Again, for this group of learners there is very little evidence in their accounts that the use of technology *per se* has broken down any barriers to participation for them.

Josh had left school at the earliest opportunity, and was now eighteen. He was taking an NVQ level One course in IT as he was unable to find a suitable job, and his attendance and travel were paid for by ITEC and via Careers Newport. Was Josh the typical non-participant drawn into learning through IT? Apparently not. Josh comes from a family in which both of his parents are professionals. His sister is taking a degree course at the University of Wales. Neither of these are characteristics of the typical non-participant. Josh already had NVQ2 in IT but was doing the more elementary NVQ1 subsequently because nothing else was available and he did not want to do nothing. He enjoyed the social-life aspects of the course, found it easy and wanted to help others who were finding it more difficult. He would, of course, have preferred to move on to NVQ Level Three, but he described this as being dependent on a job placement. Josh does not appear to be non-participant drawn into learning by the opportunities available. He is a keen learner, who feels that his impetuous decision to leave school may have been a mistake, and that he is actually being held back from advancement in his chosen area of IT due to a lack of suitable job opportunities.

Patrick was only eighteen at the time of the interview, and had been referred to a one-week ITEC course on using IT by the job centre. He was already able to use a computer, with a 'games' computer at home, but was new to the Internet. 'I always liked computers, always fiddling around with computers.' 'The last four days I've been here I've really enjoyed the course.' He had left school at sixteen with GCSEs in maths, English, and keyboard applications, subsequently working in a fruit shop, and then as a cleaner in a hotel. Both of his parents were unemployed.

All of the following interviews were with students on the ITEC course. We will not report the relatively brief accounts of these teenagers in detail here. Jenny was fifteen, taking an NVQ1 in business administration at ITEC, as she had been bullied at school. She reported being unlikely to return to education in case it was like school. Rhiannon (sixteen) was on the same course for the same reason (bullying at school). Amir was aged sixteen, and had a brother with 'a good job working with computers'. He had not done well at school in Wales, but aged fourteen he went to Bangladesh and was transformed in outlook by the one-to-one tuition he had received there. Having returned, it is now too late to enrol for GCSEs this year. The NVQ1 course he was currently taking was described as a 'holding operation'. Suzanne stopped going to school at age fourteen as they could not handle her epilepsy. Now aged sixteen, she wanted 'what she should have got before', and not to end up 'looking after babies at home' like her two sisters.

Alison was aged sixteen with no qualifications. She had worked as a receptionist, and was encouraged to attend an IT course by her firm, but promptly resigned and changed her course to child-care. In doing so, she was cut off from her peer group: 'as soon as I started coming here they don't want to know me because I've got out of the crowd.' David agreed with this view of his friends: 'most of them says they want to go to college but I don't think they will.' He was also sixteen with no qualifications, and wanted to gain some now. After being unemployed for a few months he contacted Career Paths, and eventually found this course (NVQ1 IT). Tracy was seventeen and had left school at sixteen with no qualifications. She then described her life as hanging around the city centre, and getting into trouble with the police. 'Suddenly reality hits you and you realize that you should do something.' Despite her epiphany, she saw the specific course she was on – learning to use IT – as 'a bit of a waste of time'. David, now eighteen, had left school before taking any GCSEs, took a job and left it as he was being paid more on the current training scheme in NVQ1 Retail. He was now studying as 'I don't want to be low-life scum', but he agreed with Tracy about the irrelevance of learning about IT – 'you don't hardly need it for normal life'. The final transitional learner with no existing qualifications was Mike. He was aged eighteen, and reported having considerable learning difficulties. He was unsure of which course he was taking.

Among the students with existing qualifications, Bernadette, aged seventeen, like Alison changed from an NVQ1 in IT to child-care. She has a range of GCSEs from school, and her own computer at home. She is attending the ITEC course as they 'pay you to learn' as well as giving travel expenses, and she found the idea of going to college in evenings off-putting as it was too expensive. Edward (seventeen) was funded by the local TEC (as it then was) and routed through Career Paths, to study for NVQ2 in IT at ITEC. He had never heard of learndirect. He had an Internet-capable computer at home, and had originally started an A level course (and was considered very bright) before leaving school. Similarly, Anna (seventeen), taking an NVQ1 in business administration, had gone to college for a year after obtaining GCSEs but had then dropped out.

Delayed learners

So far the learners encountered in ICT-based courses do not appear to fulfil the category of traditional non-participants (although for some of the younger ones it may be too early to tell). Indeed, for many if not all, their present ICT-based learning followed on from a history of learning. What evidence then was there for ICT-based learning attracting people back to education?

Other than in the course run in the Enterprise Centre, the only example of someone with more than a year's break in participation after leaving school at an early age was in an ITEC group. He had contacted them via learndirect, and had heard of learndirect via a newspaper advertisement. Anthony had missed a lot of school, and did not like the idea of more. He left officially at age sixteen with no qualifications, and worked in warehouses, as a panel beater, and an upholsterer. In each of these jobs he trained 'by doing'. He also undertook a correspondence course for eight years in electronic repair. Anthony has the same profile as many non-participants, aged twenty-eight, having always lived in Splott in Cardiff, with an unqualified mother and siblings who now all work as cleaners. However, like many of the unrecognized informal learners he enjoys reading. He clearly likes the use of IT in learning because 'you don't have to keep up with the class, you know some people in some cases there are people who are slower or find it too fast', but he had already become a delayed learner anyway through work-based episodes of training, and a prolonged period of voluntary study, neither involving IT in the delivery.

All of the participants in the New Deal introduction to IT course run in the Enterprise Centre were adults. Susan was thirty-two years old and finding it hard to concentrate on the course. She was not sure whether to finish this one-week course. She left school aged sixteen with no qualifications, moved to YTS aged seventeen and has not worked since. She reported no subsequent episodes of learning, and was not concerned with gaining any qualifications. When asked whether she read much, she answered, 'No, I used to smoke.' She was taking this course because it was one of the few available while her children were at school. Now that all of the children are old enough for school she was considering trying get a job as a 'dinner lady'. She enjoyed the social contact on the course as she 'would normally be doing housework', but had now 'realized there is more'. Susan was clearly less proficient and less confident in the use of a computer than the others in the room, despite having a '[Windows] 3.1 at home' and a partner who has organized to get access to the Internet through the cable TV. Of all the participants in any of the schemes Susan appeared closest to someone whose life might have been transformed by the course. In the typology from chapter 8 she would already have been a transitional learner, but showed some signs of becoming a lifelong learner. However, it appeared to be neither the organization of the course, nor the technology involved that was assisting the change to her lifestyle. The barriers she faced were family-based, her children and, above all, her partner. Her intrinsic motivation to look beyond her home appeared, in this instance, to be being fostered by the relatively inspirational nature of the face-to-face teacher in the introductory class.

Gordon was fifty-one years old, formerly a BT telephone engineer, and now unemployed. He had left school at sixteen with O level qualifications, and then trained on the job with BT mostly by 'sitting next to Nellie'. He explained that he could have taken relevant qualifications at the time but like many contemporaries did not bother as he could do the job of wiring-in exchanges perfectly well, and assumed that 'it was for life'. On being made redundant fifteen years ago he worked as a groundsman. Now he would like to take some qualifications, but explained that he knew little about them. He was attracted to the IT course as 'everyone is going on all the time about the worldwide web'. He was currently searching the Internet for the themes of the universe and space and was reading a paper entitled *What is Life?* In terms of the typology in chapter 8 Gordon would, like Susan, have been classified as a transitional learner before attending this course. Unlike Susan, Gordon presented more evidence of patterns of informal learning prior to attending.

John (thirty-six) is, in his own description, the closest respondent so far to the classification of a non-participant in lifelong learning other than the present course. He left school at sixteen and his only qualifications are 'silly ones'. He walked straight into a job and has worked as a shop assistant, bus driver, taxi driver and road digger. In these jobs, especially bus driving, he received work-based training and, despite his downplaying of it, is therefore also close to a lifelong learner. As with his peers, he had been enthused by the teacher. '[Teacher] downstairs was saying yesterday now, there's another course hopefully starting at the end of this month . . . and if you're interested I'll be sending out letters. [I said] Don't bother sending out letters. I'll be there!' He has also heard of a local scheme renting computers to those unemployed for £5 per week, and is investigating how to take part.

Finally, we report meeting a respondent, Jenny, who claimed to have undertaken no education or training since leaving school at age sixteen. 'I was never there.' She has worked in a shop, factories and bars (apparently without any retraining). This is her first experience since school, and she has this to say about computers. 'Well they're just interesting aren't they? It's been really interesting. I've only been late once . . . none of us wants to go home, none of us has a dinner break now.' 'It's brilliant because it's your choice isn't' it? When you're in school you had to do it, but now you want to do it.' 'Like the spreadsheets yesterday. I said oh I'm not doing maths, I hate maths. And he said no, you watch and it was really . . . Once he showed us how to do it and we didn't have to *add* nothing.' 'We've been to Australia this morning, haven't we?'

QUALITY OF TECHNOLOGICAL PROVISION

To a large extent, the quality of individual experience and the potential transformatory effect of each episode on an individual's trajectory was linked to the quality of the technology. This was obvious in their reflections on the nature and value of each course, but must also be considered in terms of their prior learning histories (above).

Many of the fourteen to eighteen-year-olds at the ITEC Centre, including Bernadette, Edward, Anna, Rhiannon, Jenny, Mike, David, Suzanne, Amir, Daniel, Alison and Josh, liked working with computer packages. The exercises allowed them to work at their own pace, and made the experience 'not like school'. They particularly liked not having to wear uniforms, or call the staff 'sir'. In addition, they mostly expressed interest in working with computers, and believed the courses to have vocational relevance. They had previous experience of working with computers at school, but, unlike school, they felt that here there was always someone in class to help. Again the human/social contact is a key factor. Despite this relative ease with the technology, all stated that they would be *unlikely* to use the Internet for learning in the future.

Three respondents were not so keen on their course. Tracy said she was unlikely to finish, and Jerome was bothered by not being able to operate the keyboard. Anthony complained about having to go to the same computer every time, otherwise the teaching software did not remember where they got to last time. This means that 'some days you can't get anything at all, it don't work at all and some days it takes a long time to work sort of thing'.

The Enterprise short course produced similarly positive comments from Jenny, John, Patrick, Gordon and Simon, especially about the tutor. 'If we do get stuck we just, well he helps us all the time.' 'Yeah. He's brilliant, isn't he . . .? If we're stuck like, we just shout oi, over here and he's here.' Susan mostly enjoyed the social contact that the course provided. John felt that there were severe limitations in learning via computer, and had experienced the isolation of trying to learn at home:

If you're on a campus course, you're there with people working. But if you're at home you'll have the distraction of being at home. A knock on the door – can you take me down the shop? . . . The temptation would be, I imagine, oh I'll leave that 'til tomorrow . . . There's so many distractions . . . The other thing I think with the course over the computer system if you fully understand it then that's all right. But if you bump into troubles – oh I don't know how to do this – there's no one there to show you . . . I think also with the college you get motivation off other people.

Fiona felt that the policy of drop-in centres and distributed access learning was a sham. It was being used by colleges to attract traditional paying students, rather than as a valid learning experience in its own right. Her progression course had been cancelled, and she was very angry:

Well, I rang up and complained and spoke to three different people, and what I can't understand is that they don't want to run these courses in the community, they want people to go to the University . . . So I am stuck now.

She does not feel able to travel to the local university, a problem that learning via ICT was supposed to overcome, and she is only one of several in the same situation. Anyway she prefers to learn in the local community centre, not just because it is closer but because it is not full of youths who 'did not want to be there':

No, I just think these universities put these modules on . . . they seem to make these modules up and send them out to the community. But there doesn't seem to be anything in between . . . if you want to do a bit more like this then they say that it is a bit too advanced, we had better not have that in the community we had better have it taught down in the university. This is the feedback I am getting from the people I have spoken to.

The themes of lack of human contact and problems of technology are most clear in the on-line learning episodes. Carol had been using a learndirect course, and, like John above, finds that using the same computer every time is not possible in a true drop-in situation:

I have been here now this morning and I still haven't actually logged on. I cannot get into where I left off yesterday which is really a pain . . . If you stay with the same computer stations and it remembers where you were in the process and when you log on again it will automatically go back for that, you can save a stage. If you access from another computer then you can still get into the system but it doesn't remember where you go to.

The problem is coming in and actually connecting into learndirect, and I am told that the problem comes because there are too many people logging onto the system at a time which seems ridiculous to me because they know how many people are registered with them . . . At the moment as they are having so many problems we are guinea pigs really.

She has no on-line tutor, because none have been assigned yet due to technical difficulties. She cannot get access to the system report, and is unable to print any text which appears on screen with pictures. This is causing serious delays for her course assessment.

CONCLUSION

As already stated, we did not find enough people to interview about learning and IT from our representative sample of 1,104 households. We therefore sampled again purposively in a variety of less formal learning contexts, all involving ICT. Of the thirty-six achieved interviews only one of the respondents (Jenny) could be classified as a former non-participant (discounting the present episode). The other individuals for whom the course about which they were interviewed was their only post-compulsory episode would be classified as 'immature', having experienced less than a year in total not in full-time continuous education or training. The only impressive transformation appeared in a week-long face-to-face course on the use of IT, and was attributed, by the participants at least, to the nature of the teacher and teaching.

The rush to the Internet, prompted in part by political pressure on the providers, means that much of what makes ICT-based learning special does not actually work. Teething troubles will, of course, be sorted out in time through testing and the use of the first cohorts as 'guinea pigs'. But if the history of IT development has taught us anything, it is that by the time existing software systems are relatively bug-free the technology itself, and the software it supports, will have advanced again.

As always, absence of evidence cannot be treated as identical to evidence of absence, and of course e-learning was still in its relative infancy in Wales in 2000 when the supplementary fieldwork was conducted. Nevertheless, it would be fair to conclude that there is no reason here to believe that ICT is significantly overcoming the barriers to lifelong participation in Wales, and it would be unreasonable on this evidence to conclude otherwise.

12

The Future for Wales in an Information Age

To recapitulate our thesis so far: advances in the use of technology can solve some of the problems faced by Wales in an information age, but they cannot solve all, and they will, almost inevitably, introduce new ones. These problems are geographical, cultural, political, economic and educational. We have used education, in the form of lifelong learning, as an extended case study of ICT solutions to public-policy problems. We do so for two main reasons. Education, as currently presented, has a role to play in several other areas, especially to do with social justice, culture, and the economy. Secondly, UK government initiatives based on ICT, such as the University for Industry and National Grid for Learning, are more advanced in education than in many other areas.

We find, first of all, that some of the problems in lifelong learning in Wales have been misconstrued. It is not initial continuous education that has the greatest need, although it still receives the most political and media attention. Participation in later episodes of adult learning is, however, declining despite an apparently pressing need for greater learning throughout the life-course. Participation is also becoming more systematically structured in terms of participants' backgrounds. The intention of the virtual education movement both to extend and to widen participation in adult learning is therefore both timely and appropriate. It is also possible to test the success of this aim empirically. As far as we can tell, and despite the best intentions of all involved, ICT-based solutions in Wales are so far 'failing' that test. The difficulties of over-optimistic political claims, lack of individual motivation, poor access to equipment in remote areas, technical troubles, legal wrangles and what we have termed 'surf' wars between education providers have all combined to give the movement a weak start. Where on-line provision is available it is not only continuing to attract and recruit the 'usual suspects', but perhaps an even more privileged and better-educated sub-set of these. With this in mind, what conclusions can we draw for both lifelong learning *and* Wales in an information age?

THE ENDURING NATURE OF INFORMATION AGE 'SOLUTIONS' AND 'PROBLEMS'

It is important to note at the outset that, despite the 'snapshot' nature of our study, the issues that we raise are of long-term relevance. The policy approaches described and examined in this book are forming the basis of long-term information age agendas for politicians and educationalists alike. We can, therefore, be certain that the virtual education approach is here to stay, if for no other reason than that ICT-based education is now proving to be big business around the world. In the USA alone, it is predicted that over two million students are taking on-line courses as part of a worldwide on-line learning marketplace expected to be worth US\$50 billion by 2005 (Dumort, 2000). With multinational corporations such as Microsoft beginning to become actively involved in such programmes, virtual education does not look set to fade away quietly just because it may not be fulfilling its societally inclusive aims.

In addition, too much time, effort and resourcing has probably already been invested in ICT-based lifelong learning for future governments of any political persuasion to deviate substantially from the approaches described throughout the book. Whilst the New Labour government regularly proclaims its new ICT policies to be 'breaking new ground' (Blair, 2000), the political predilection for using ICT as primary means of establishing a learning society was already set. This continuity in both theoretical approach and intended outcome can be seen in the latest raft of lifelong policies in 2001. For example, while the aim of the new Learning Skills Council is to 'overcome the false divisions between our foundation learning and the post-compulsory system' (National Skills Agenda, 2001: 5), the logic remains firmly that of simple human-capital theory. Apparently 'higher skills lead to higher earnings' (p.5), 'matching people's aspirations to the skills employers need will be a key priority' (p.6), and we need 'to strengthen the link between learning and employment' (p.6). Yet the same plan argues that ICT-based developments such as the UfI 'will offer flexible, accessible opportunities to learn online to a wide audience including some of our most disadvantaged communities' (p.7). 'ICT can play a key role in breaking down the barriers to learning that people face, offering new opportunities to access learning for the most disadvantaged and those who have not traditionally taken up learning opportunities' (New Opportunities Fund, 2000b: 5). ICT-based programmes therefore continue apace with initiatives such as the Learning and Work Bank offering Internet access to the Employment Service Job Bank as well as 'Worktrain', linked to the Employment Service vacancy list, offering on-line details of half a million training courses and details of the qualifications needed for 'any job' (Johnston, 2001a).

On the other hand, we can be fairly confident that, as they stand, these initiatives face more or less the same enduring problems and the limited success in widening participation as the examples examined in this book. We know that participation in adult learning has not improved over the past few years, despite considerable political activity intended to promote lifelong learning (NIACE, 2000). More than half of the respondents in the most recent NIACE survey of lifelong learning stated that they were not likely to take part in any formal learning in the future, and the systematic differences between these non-participants and the likely participants is growing in terms of occupational class, employment and prior education. Thus, as we have illustrated, ICT-based or not, the problems of establishing an inclusive learning society in the information age are deep-rooted and stretch far beyond issues of accessibility, time and distance. How can we explain this apparent lack of positive effect on the part of ICT and what can be done to improve the impact of such policies as a whole in Wales?

TECHNOLOGICAL CONCERNS

The most immediately obvious area of contention could be that of the technology itself. Indeed, many people would point towards technological issues as a primary cause of discrepancy between the rhetoric and reality of the information age. This was reflected in our interviews with the key actors, who generally saw technical issues as constituting the overriding problems faced by virtual educational provision in Wales. From a practical perspective even the most enthusiastic commentator would have to admit that there is weight to this argument. Although on paper the concept of providing 'virtual education for all' sounds attractive, in practice the realities of implementing such a concept entail often insurmountable technical challenges. The sheer technical scope of establishing and operating an ICT centre in the south Wales Valleys, having to rely on sporadically reliable network connections and not always perfect software belies the rhetoric of the seamless 'network society' and the provision of twenty-four-hour on-line learning 'any time, any place, any pace'. As always, ICT is not perfect and, despite inevitable improvements, these will lead to further teething troubles.

The impact of technical shortcomings was amply illustrated in our interviews with those learners already using ICT-based provision. Faced with the considerable limitations of a real-life web-site via a real-life Internet connection on a real-life computer, the promises of constantly streamed video footage of Welsh-speakers and interactive access to on-line tutors suddenly appeared rather naïve. Similarly, the technical problems faced by those learners in distributed learning centres (such as the learndirect centre where the same learner had to use the same computer every day in order for the system to work), although appearing trivial on paper, often led to dissatisfaction with and disengagement from the learning process. From this perspective technology can be seen to be part of the problem as well as part of the solution.

Our study also pointed to the limitations of allowing ICT-based learning initiatives to be too focused on specific technological developments. For example, the Wales Digital College's faith in digital television as the vehicle through which to reach the masses is fraught with potential difficulty. Digital television (DTV) is widely seen by the telecommunications community as the technology which will overcome the existing élite of professional Internet users and bring the worldwide web 'into the living room', thereby making it a 'true consumer medium' (Withey, 1998). As such, DTV is being heavily signposted by broadcasters before most people will use it. To what extent the key role that DTV is seen as playing in the Wales Digital College is commercial 'wishful thinking' on the part of S4C remains to be seen. In Wales, as in the rest of Europe, audience demand for DTV has remained low throughout the 1990s and into the first years of the twenty-first century; replicating the previous failure of satellite and cable television to establish more than a minority hold in the UK marketplace. Thus, as Corcoran (1999: 67) observes: 'on the face of it, DTV would seem to be a technology for which consumer demand is weak at best. As a production, delivery and display innovation, its deployment is more obviously driven by a technological rather than audience imperative.'

Whether or not the government and telecommunications companies engineer a 'coerced' implementation of DTV during the next decade as they currently plan (with the Labour government proposing to give away DTV equipment to those who do not convert of their own accord) remains to be seen. But the centring of the WDC around such a technology is speculative. The trend on the part of providers to be looking continuously for the next 'perfect' learning technology rather than the one currently being 'imperfectly' used is also evident in the most recent ICT-based learning initiatives which are being sold around access to learning via third-generation mobile telephones; a technology which, at the time of writing this book, has barely moved beyond the prototype stage of development. Our suggestion is that once the technical difficulties of learning and providing learning via DTV are apparent, virtual education providers will simply move their attention and efforts on to the 'next big technology' – always chasing a moving target.

This illustrates a weakness of relying wholly on technology as a solution. Golding (2000) reasons that there are two types of technology: 'type I' technologies such as the Internet, which have the capability to do things that we could already do before but more quickly and more efficiently; and 'type II' technologies such as the telegraph and bio-technologies which have the capability to transform radically our ability to do things which were previously impossible. Because of the success of type II innovations we are in danger of putting too much faith in 'type I' technologies such as the Internet, digital television and mobile telephony which will only offer to streamline rather than fundamentally transform activities such as education and training. Illustrating this argument, Toulouse (1998) observes that so-called 'interactive' services via the Internet and DTV can only ever be at best participative. Visions of ICT providing the currently excluded an individual responsive 'hotline' to educators, governments or businesses therefore grossly misrepresent the present-day technology. At best, ICT can offer an 'improved means' to 'unimproved ends': '[ICT] has not brought about any obvious improvement in the information provided to citizens. Sure, it has brought virtuoso technologies, but these – to para- phrase Thoreau – have led to improved means for unimproved ends' (Webster, 2000: 86).

MOVING BEYOND THE TECHNOLOGICAL

Nevertheless, to point solely towards the shortcomings of technology is, of course, to overlook the real issues faced by information age policy-making. As we have repeated throughout our analysis, the crucial issues of the information age are not just technological: they are social, economic, cultural and political. The 'cyber-guru' Nicholas Negroponte could not have been more wrong in asserting that in the information age 'all that is solid melts into bits'. The problems of the information age are firmly rooted in the reality of real-life Wales rather than the rhetoric of 'Cyber Cymru'. Although still in its infancy, it is clear that providers of technology-based lifelong learning cannot assume that ICT on its own will necessarily lead to 'better' forms of learning and education attended by many more indi- viduals unfettered by previous impediments to participation. For a host of technological *and* non-technological reasons, many adults remain un- willing or unmotivated to participate in lifelong learning programmes.

CONCERNS OF ACCESS AND USE OF ICT

The continued importance of non-technological factors to apparently information age issues is amply illustrated by the issue of access to ICT.

Access to technology remains a recurrent problem for virtual education providers in our study. Of greatest concern here was the apparent complacency of Welsh politicians, educationalists and industry figures in our key actor interviews with regard to the ease with which inequalities in access to ICT would soon be overcome, either by the 'promises' made by the Westminster government to achieve 'universal access' by 2005 or by the introduction of 'less socially divisive' technologies such as digital television.

There is little or no evidence to support their complacency. As already mentioned, behind New Labour's promise of achieving 'universal access' is the optimistic figure of up to 70 per cent of the population making regular and effective use of ICT (Booz, Allen and Hamilton, 2000); with the remaining 30 per cent therefore not making effective use. This figure of 30 per cent non-participation in ICT-based activity is alarming when seen in relation to the recurring inequalities surrounding educational participation in evidence in Wales. Significantly, the data within the National Assembly's (2001) *Cymru Ar-lein* document show clearly that areas of Wales with low rates of qualification among the population, also have low rates of training and reported learning, *and* low use of and access to computers. Areas of disadvantage that stand out from comparison across several of these maps are Blaenau Gwent and Neath Port Talbot (two of the three sites for our initial household survey), with perhaps Gwynedd and Pembrokeshire as well. It is important for the authors of *Cymru Ar-lein*, and the relevant Assembly Members, to realize that simply altering one of these problems will not lead to amelioration of the other. The causal model, if indeed there is one here, is far from clear, but the results we have presented in the latter part of this book do make one thing clear. Simply increasing the availability of computers (and other digital media) will not lead to changes in training and qualification among current non-participants. What these maps actually show is that ICT is replicating and thereby reinforcing the existing barriers to inclusion in Wales. Similar maps can be presented for initial education, housing, crime and health. The same areas come up again and again as problematic. The root problem is actually poverty, and rather than trying to ameliorate access to each public-policy service separately, real joined-up government might devote resources to solving the poverty and then watching the other indicators, including ownership of computers, improve as well. Indeed, to imagine a digital world free from the inequalities of the off-line world is again indicative of technological naïvety rather than foresight. As Luke argues:

> Clearly one can access [cyberspace] remotely and interoperate amidst some connections from many places with the right equipment and adequate

resources, but these pre-requisites are exceptional in most real-life situations. Moreover, making the world digital in access or equal in capability is destined simply to generate digitised inequalities, uncapabilities and inaccessabilities. (Luke, 1997: 135)

Even apart from these insubstantial notions of cause and effect, the prevailing political notion of 'access to ICT' can also be seen as fundamentally flawed. Firstly, access to ICT goes far beyond a dichotomous notion of 'haves' and 'have-nots'. As Toulouse (1997) observes, there are two distinct types of access: whether groups have access at all and the hierarchy of access amongst those that do. Thus, beyond the simple issue of 'access/ no access' to ICT come more complex questions of levels of connectivity in terms of the capability and distribution of the access concerned. On a practical level, for example, access to a personal computer does not guarantee a connection to the Internet, any more than 'access' to the Internet is a guarantee of effectively accessing every available web-site and on-line resource. In addition, it has been estimated that the cost of purchasing a personal computer and relevant software is only 16 per cent of the total cost of running a system (G. Cole, 2000). Computers have been likened to a 'puppy dog sale', attractive and cheap to buy but costly to keep if used as intended. The divide is not really about purchasing power and physical access (Passey, 2000). It is more to do with infrastructure (needing high-bandwidth connections), access technology, content, curriculum use, and learning outcomes. The current policy focus is only on the second of these, but educational inclusion needs more than a simple model of access.

Similarly, disparities in the *context* of ICT access are also an important consideration. Will accessing on-line information and resources from a home-based computer or digital television set be equitable to accessing the same materials via an open-access work station in a public library or other community-based ICT centre? The danger is that by focusing solely on issues of basic access politicians and educationalists are overlooking the quality of that access and, it follows, the quality of access to information and services once experienced on-line. This simplification is further compounded by what Golding (2000: 174) terms 'the fallacy of universal abundance'. As Golding reasons, the skewed distribution of access to new technologies towards the more affluent can only continue to be consolidated, given the fact that ICT goods require recurrent investment for updating, replacing or reinforcing with peripheral 'add-ons'. Thus, unlike terrestrial television (a technology often cited in support of the universal access argument) modern-day ICTs can never be ubiquitously available.

In these respects, the Cardiff and Westminster governments are not alone in their oversimplification of the issue of ICT access. From Newt Gingrich's off-hand comment that it may be worthwhile 'giving every poor person a laptop' (Resnick, 1997) to other countries' pledges to achieve 'universal access' to ICT, worldwide political thinking about achieving equitable participation in on-line services has yet to move beyond the 'have/have-not' dichotomy. This is most evident with regard to the question of *what* such access to ICT can actually be used for. Indeed, within the UK policy drive, the area of providing public services via ICT is perhaps where the rhetoric most outweighs the reality. The vague concept of ICT being used for interactive participation with public services, as the Westminster government is claiming, shows little sign of being borne out by the services on offer. Indeed, the majority of on-line learning provision available to date can be characterized by a linear and largely one-way, 'top-down' delivery of general material; far from the notion of ICT turning public services 'the right way up' for the socially excluded (Cabinet Office, 1999b).

Given this background, there is a very real danger that the government's ICT policy drive as it currently stands will only redefine a 'digital divide' rather than overcome it. For many commentators, governments are simply not in a position to challenge inequalities in ICT use, given the market-driven nature of technological access. Looking beyond the fallacy of universal access there is, therefore, the danger that under the government's present framework of provision those presently seen as 'have-nots' will, at best, be elevated to a 'second-class' status of ICT use unless they also choose to 'take individual responsibility for the economics of getting on-line' (Haywood, 1998: 23). Indeed, Calabrese and Borchet (1996) contend that the inherent economic nature of information and communications technology will most likely lead to two distinct models of use: (i) a civic model of adequately resourced and skilled élite users able to demand and experience interactive, empowering forms of network use; as opposed to (ii) a lower stratum of users – experiencing qualitatively and quantitatively different one-way, 'top-down' passive consumption of information. Thus, with government intervention or not, there may always be a division between the 'information used' as opposed to the 'information users' (Dordick et al., 1988).

Kanter's (1995) broader view of an informational divide between 'cosmopolitans' and 'localists' nevertheless reinforces this scenario, arguing that the 'three Cs' of competence, concepts and connections will underpin an ability to thrive in the global economy – with a relatively excluded class of localists curtailed by their embeddedness at fixed sites, 'connections limited to a small circle in the neighbourhood and opportunities confined to their own communities' (Kanter, 1995: 23). Although deliberately polemic, both these scenarios suggest a host of non-technological factors as underpinning 'digital divisions' – which conceptualizing the 'digital divide' as existing merely in terms of access to a computer terminal or digital TV set goes nowhere near addressing (Haddon, 2000). New technologies 'may deepen the divide between educational haves and have-nots' because, although they shatter barriers of space and time, they create new ones of differential availability (Gladieux and Swail, 1999: 5). Thus, leaving aside technical concerns, the distributed community-site model does not and cannot equate to inequality of access to ICT as its supporters would claim.

RECOGNIZING THE 'EDUCATIONAL' BASIS OF VIRTUAL EDUCATION

Developing our discussion of the non-technological issues, we can also identify a host of educational reasons underlying the effectiveness of ICT-based learning: primarily that many of these 'new' approaches to learning are faced by established 'old' problems. For example, during our case study, the content of the 'Welsh on-line' language course could not be described as a genuinely 'new' form of education provision, but more as a 'pseudo-new' form of adult learning (Kenway et al., 1994). As an on-line presentation of largely pre-existing Welsh learning materials, previously released on videotape, the web-site could be seen as an additional means of delivering distance education, but little more. Certainly, the 'innovative' uses of ICT to develop critical thinking, reflection or even social, collaborative and conversational experiences so often celebrated by techno-logical enthusiasts were not in evidence during our empirical research. In this respect, the nature of much of the ICT-based learning that is currently taking place is perhaps indicative of the gulf that persists in technology-based lifelong learning between the rhetoric and reality of on-line learning provision, a tension also highlighted in our learner interviews.

There were, for example, very few features of the on-line Welsh-language course that could be classed as genuinely 'transformative' or 'revolutionary'. Moreover, those features that could potentially offer interaction with tutors and other learners, or provide access to interactive, multimedia resources, were, more often than not, conspicuous by their absence in practice. Of course, the term 'virtual education' is 'widely and indiscriminately used around the world' (Jurich, 1999: 35) and should perhaps be seen as nothing more than a contemporary reference to most forms of computer-based distance learning. As Mayes (2000) argues, for reasons of cost alone the interactive pedagogical opportunities offered by information *and communications* technology are often overlooked by lifelong learning providers, leaving ICT-based pedagogy rooted in more 'old-fashioned' linear and restricted models:

There are really two pedagogies associated with ICT. One is the delivery of information – this is predominantly the pedagogy of the lecture or book, and emphasizes the 'IT' – the other is based on the tutorial dialogue and involves conversations between tutors and students, and mainly emphasizes the 'C'. Of course, successful teaching is underpinned by both – and the rapid interplay of the two is ideal – but in the context of lifelong learning policy the real problem is that 'IT' is cost-effective and the 'C' is not. Unfortunately, in terms of pedagogic effectiveness the second is better than the first. (Mayes, 2000: 3)

This point was highlighted by the comments of our on-line learners, bemoaning the lack of human and social contact when participating in ICT-based provision. Learners through the Internet may feel isolated when presented with the unstructured nature of the data and the sheer quantity. This could be the biggest barrier for on-line learning (Doring, 1999) for 'education is a fundamentally conversational business'. It is, or should be, critical and emancipatory rather than about the transfer of information and determinate skills. Yet it is the latter which dominates current on-line provision. As Holmes (1997: 3) contends, 'the expanding use of the Internet as an imagined means of total knowledge in a globalised world empties out the identity of its participants and, therefore, the "social" context in which the pursuit of knowledge can be thought of as a shared goal.' ICT should not necessarily be seen as providing *better* educational contexts, but *different* contexts for learning (Selwyn, 1999a, 1999e). When discussing the educational application of ICTs we have to weigh up the benefits of increased access to information and artefacts at the cost of the *nature* of this access. As Zuboff (1988: 376) reasons, 'Information technology . . . produces a voice that symbolically renders events, objects and processes so that they become visible, knowable and sharable in a new way.' However, should this 'new way' of experiencing events, objects and processes always be treated as an adequate substitute for face-to-face experiences?

There are at least two distinct forms of pedagogy using ICT (Scottish Forum on Lifelong Learning, 2000). The delivery-of-information model is cheaper, and the myth of teaching by telling underpins many current initiatives. The second model of tutorial dialogue is better, but simply not in evidence on-line. The evidence from the past is clear. New technology does not in itself lead to changes in education. Innovations like the Open University have been made possible by the technology, but their success is actually based on organizational change.

The effectiveness of the 'new' forms of lifelong learning in our study was also noticeably reliant on mostly pre-existing structures of education. Despite the high-profile positioning of distributed learning centres in a few innovative locations such as football stadia and pubs, the fact remains that the vast majority of community access to ICT will be provided through learning centres such as the ones in our study, housed in existing educational and community institutions including schools, colleges and libraries. Moreover, the majority of commissioned on-line content and learning resources will be supplied by existing and established educational providers. Whereas this fashioning of the 'new' system of lifelong learning around 'old' structures will ensure an initial stability, it may not go far in overcoming many of the existing problems regarding participation in lifelong learning. There is considerable evidence to suggest that merely providing additional access to ICT in colleges will not necessarily overcome the existing institutional, situational and motivational barriers to learning that prevented many individuals from choosing to learn there previously (Gorard et al., 2000b). Even providing education via the Internet does not in itself necessarily constitute an individually empowering 'new form' of education. Although the Internet may seem to challenge traditional notions of power, it is only a microcosm of real-life social relations; reproducing and reinforcing hegemonic relations (Kitchen, 1998). For example, an 'official' web-site from the 'University' for Industry or Digital 'College' may still provide a significant deterrent to some current non-participants in learning.

Moreover, at a macro level, perhaps the most significant 'educational' factor in the long-term effectiveness of this 'new' agenda of lifelong learning was the resulting 'surf wars' from the positioning of initiatives such as UfI and WDC around pre-existing structures of education. In doing so, it was naïve for virtual education providers to believe that they could truly complement existing forms of adult education without being seen as a competitive threat by the very institutions that they were paradoxically relying on for partnership. One of the very real barriers faced by virtual education turns out to be the pre-existing micro-politics that characterize the education sector, and particularly the FE/adult education sector, in Wales.

It could also be argued that the Wales Digital College's current reliance on digital television and Welsh-language provision are highly politically, as well as economically, motivated decisions. With the Digital College themselves admitting that their 'digital' title and focus was decided by S4C even before the initial feasibility study in 1994, to what extent is the Wales Digital College merely an attempt by the Welsh-language broadcasters to boost the numbers of Welsh-speakers and permeation of DTV into their marketplace? At present the Wales Digital College is not being constructed in a way to widen participation in lifelong learning. The reliance of the Wales Digital College on technologies, such as digital television and the Internet, which are themselves primarily reliant on private rather than public control in their distribution and spread, is a major area of concern in terms of its inclusive mission, as is its Welsh-dominated learning provision.

There is, further,

> a wholly contradictory double focus on, on the one hand, the need to protect
> and foster a presumed [Welsh] culture and, on the other hand, the need to
> enhance [Welsh] industrial and economic focus in the ICT sector. In the UK it is
> plainly the latter which prevails, as the emergence of the information society is
> embodied in the imposition of commercial need and corporate strategy onto
> the remnants of cultural and social policy in the communications field.
> (Golding, 2000: 170)

None of the employers, and less than one-fifth of 1 per cent of the
employees, in the Future Skills Wales Survey (1998) responded in Welsh.
And, apart from product-specific training, Welsh language was the least
important skill required by the Welsh economy. The Welsh language faces
considerable difficulties in the information age, in the face of English as an
ICT lingua franca, although, as our study shows, ICT is also allowing the
creation of more global 'community' of interest involving expatriates and
those in the US seeking an ancestral culture. In Wales, Welsh-speakers are
not, by and large, those excluded from lifelong learning, coming as they
tend to do from families with higher levels of education, qualification and
occupational prestige. They are also almost entirely bilingual. Expenditure
on Welsh educational broadcasts is therefore likewise largely a political
decision – and, like the economic imperative, it works against inclusion to
some extent since it allocates already scarce funds to a disproportionately
small and currently disproportionately privileged sub-population of
Wales. The immediate language demands for Wales as a prospective
learning society are rather for 'compensatory' schemes in basic literacy in
English, and English-language teaching for those for whom their first and
only language is not English (or Welsh).

OVERCOMING THE 'ECONOMIC IMPERATIVE'

Our discussion so far of the enduring nature of the socially mediated
nature of participation in education, inequalities in basic access to ICT and
participation in education via ICT brings us to the core of the whole
'information society' and 'learning society' debates. What exactly are the
underlying aims of such initiatives, programmes and policy agendas? As
we saw in chapter 6, from both the Cardiff and Westminster governments'
perspective, policies such as UfI, IT for All and UK Online are intended to
be both socially inclusive and economically focused. ICT-based learning, it
is repeatedly claimed, aims both to widen participation in education *and* to

increase economic competitiveness via the technological 'upskilling' of the British workforce. Yet, as we have seen from our study, there is little evidence that the first, socially focused, aim is being achieved or even addressed by the raft of ICT-based policies and initiatives such as UfI and WDC. This may lead us to ask the question: if we had concentrated on the second, economically focused aim, would we have found any signs of success? Can ICT-based learning really be seen as capable of achieving either of these dual goals?

From our evidence we would argue that a fundamental dichotomy that runs throughout current lifelong learning policy-making is the role of technology-based education as a means of increasing *social inclusion* and as a means of increasing *economic competitiveness*. On the one hand, there is a powerful rhetoric regarding the use of technology-based learning to reskill and upskill the workforce and increase the country's economic competitiveness. On the other hand, there are the exhortations from politicians and educationalists to use technology as a means of overcoming the exclusion of various social groups from both renewed educational opportunities and the wider opportunities of the information age. Yet beyond broad statements regarding a 'digital divide', it is clear that the present lifelong learning agenda is almost exclusively economically focused in practice, and that any concern with the socially excluded can be more accurately seen as a concern with the economically excluded (Bynner, 1998; Tight, 1998b).

The 'clash' between the economic and the non-economic is perhaps best encapsulated in the emphasis throughout all the current initiatives on the use of technology-based lifelong learning for developing work-based, predominantly technological skills, as opposed to the use of technology for general learning or liberal education. Very little is said about the types of learning that ICT-based education will be suitable for. To date, the majority of UfI pilot projects and learning centre activities have been predominantly focused on using ICT to deliver ICT-skills education. It was significant, for example, that all but a few of our learning centre interviewees were learning how to use ICT. Whereas, it can be argued that developing technological skills is a prerequisite to using ICT for more diverse learning outcomes, what form this learning will then take appears to have been given very little consideration above and beyond workplace-orientated 'key skills'. Indeed, as Newman and Johnson (1999) assert, to assume that all aspects of learning can be delivered via ICT exhibits a 'naïve empiricism' towards the diverse nature of lifelong education. Using the gadgets themselves should not be a lifelong learning issue, and the fact that so much time and effort *is* being devoted to just that is an indictment of the technology. The gadgets themselves need to be easier to use for the general population (Thimbleby, 1999).

There is also a tension throughout all the initiatives between merely *increasing* levels of participation in education and *widening* levels of participation in education. As we have already stated, we know a lot about the nature and attitudes of those who do not currently participate in formal education and training after compulsory schooling, i.e. individuals who are unemployed, female, older, socio-economically disadvantaged, less qualified and with less favourable attitudes towards institutional learning. Thus, if the rhetorical claims of reducing social exclusion from learning are to be believed, such individuals form the key target group for the government's lifelong learning agenda. Nevertheless, the present emphasis of the UfI on 'helping people reskill throughout their working lives' and the fact that ICT continues to be more attractive to those individuals who are most likely to be already engaged in learning casts significant doubt over this aim.

This prioritizing of the economic over the social characterizes current government policy-making in general. For example, it has been argued strongly that the UK government's ICT drive merely mirrors the 'employability'-dominated nature of their overall social exclusion strategy (Levitas, 1996; Byrne, 1997; Preece, 2000). A 1999 budget announced that vocational tax relief was to be phased out and with it public support for non-vocational courses. Learners therefore receive no help from the Treasury unless their learning is apparently of immediate economic benefit (Tuckett, 1999). As Barry (1998: 9) observes, social exclusion would appear to be 'culturally defined, economically driven and politically motivated', and, as such, initiatives such as the UfI merely reflect the wider 'new work ethic' that is underpinning the current New Labour policy agenda. As Holden (1999: 529) starkly concludes, 'increasing participation in the labour market is at the heart of the current government's social policy'.

Yet, as many authors have argued, such a narrow conception of 'exclusion' in terms of deficiency of the skills demanded by the information age/knowledge economy, and subsequent exclusion from paid employment is deeply problematic. As Byrne (1997: 31) reasons, 'It has to be said that there is something almost perverse about [. . .] the thematic of social exclusion as constituted through separation from work where there is abundant evidence of the real immiseration of employed workers.'

Similarly, it has been strongly argued that the conventional wisdom that governments should prepare 'all' citizens for highly skilled employment in a 'high-tech' economy ignores the actual lack of 'high-skill' jobs (Apple, 1997; Robins and Webster, 1999). It is useful to distinguish between high-tech *industries* and high-tech *occupations*. As Apple (1997) points out, the majority of jobs in high-tech industries do not themselves require a substantial knowledge of technology, with only the relatively few individuals in high-tech occupations needing technological skills. Furthermore, a counter-trend in technological deskilling is possible, as ICTs become more sophisticated and the need for knowledge to use them declines. As Neill (1995) contends, buttressing social-policy reform by pointing to the presumed high-skill information economy ignores the fact that most workers will require little more than a 'McDonald's level' of familiarity with technology, primarily consisting of lower-order data-entry and limited problem-solving skills. Unfortunately, as Winner (1994) concludes, for many citizens the 'high-tech' economy may promise little more than low-skilled employment and a state of increasing bewilderment.

It is of concern with regard to Welsh policy-making that the need for high skills continues to dominate the policy agenda. So one of the key recommendations of this book could be that the economic demands of the information age are approached in a more realistic light. This will be by no means an easy task. Despite acknowledgement of the relevance of lifelong learning to issues of social inclusion and relative disadvantage, recent Welsh Office, Assembly and New Labour policy in this area remains rooted in what has been termed the 'economic imperative' (Gorard, 2000c). This is a view based on human-capital theory that investment in education and training leads to a 'return' for the individual and for society, and in policy terms it has been shown to be antagonistic to the inclusive strand of arguments for greater adult participation. It is tied up with somewhat confused notions of contingent labour, trainability, careership, and the value of human resources in a global economy. Such notions have been expressed in a variety of policy and discussion documents in Wales, including LIFE, BEST, Pathways to Prosperity, Institute for Welsh Affairs proposals for the National Assembly, and most recently in ETAG (1998) and 'the Learning Country' strategy (National Assembly for Wales, 2001b).

To give an example of the fallacies induced by the economic imperative and the fact that evidence for the whole notion of human capital is lacking, we can look to one of the economic success stories of the 1990s in England and Wales, that of attracting and retaining inward investment. When Siemens and Samsung opened plants in north-east England, or LG invested in south Wales, they chose areas of the UK which had three characteristics in common – high unemployment/cheap labour, relatively low qualifications in terms of UK population, and substantial incentives in the form of regional grants. When Siemens pulled out of north-east England, and LG threatened to pull out of south Wales, they did not do so because their workforce was not educated enough, and they did not move their investment to an area with greater human capital. So for a community it is doubtful whether a highly qualified (and perhaps highly paid) workforce is actually attractive to all investors. For an individual, once the impact of prior family background is taken into account, there is little evidence that education or training 'pays off' in an economic sense (Green-halgh and Stewart, 1987; Roberts et al., 1991; McNabb and Whitfield, 1994). On the other hand it can be argued that the current economic focus of adult learning detracts from its potentially transformative nature for the individual, and for society, regardless of later financial reward. In a sense, lifelong learning is reduced to the simple claim that education and training are good because they earn you money, rather than the more complex and perhaps more realistic: education and training are good because they are fulfilling (and they could earn you money).

FOCUSING ON THE SOCIAL: ALTERNATIVE PATHS TO A BARRIERLESS LEARNING SOCIETY

In summary, we know that occupation, mode of employment, status, class, industry, organization, qualifications, gender, and age are currently the major determinants of later training in the UK by creating relatively stable lifelong learner identities. These results have important implications for policy development. Hence, non-participation is largely a product of the fact that individuals do not see education and training as appropriate for them, and these views, in turn, are structured by factors which occur relatively early in life. This suggests that policies which simply make it easier for people to participate in the kinds of education and training which are already available (for example, removing 'barriers' to participation, such as costs, and lack of time and child-care) will have only limited impacts, especially when delivered via ICT. Despite the apparent ineffectiveness of the ICT-based lifelong learning agenda in addressing widening participation in education and training, is there any way that barriers to participation can be overcome using ICT?

Participation in lifelong learning would be made more attractive to the excluded one-third of the population of Wales by introducing something similar to the Education Maintenance Allowance pilot scheme in England, which has proved successful in retaining students at age sixteen, and increasing completion rates (Piatt, 2001). If this was extended to older age groups it could be very effective. However, this is another example of an initiative that is for England only. The National Assembly for Wales has until now been rather lethargic in this regard. In many respects devolution has simply meant that Wales is now excluded from a larger number of educational events, programmes, and schemes already implemented in England (Educational Action Zones, Excellence in Cities, phases I and II of the Teaching and Learning Programme, Literacy and Numeracy Hours, and so on). We have known for some time what the factors are that would genuinely encourage wider participation (e.g. McGivney, 1992). There is, perhaps surprisingly for educational research fields, almost unanimity on these. As has been illustrated in our own research, individuals do not wish to engage in activities that are not perceived as normal within their peer and reference groups. Therefore we need to target outreach work, provide counselling support, encourage group formation to overcome feelings of isolation, and help to establish a work routine. These would be valid whatever the nature of course delivery, ICT or otherwise. Most of the other apparent barriers could be overcome technically but, in itself, this would be insufficient. Time, cost, distance and so on are only barriers if there is motivation, and ironically our historical analysis suggests that where there is motivation the role of barriers is less.

Thus, as the Scottish Forum on Lifelong Learning (2000: 20) recently concluded: 'For non-traditional students, developments in ICT would not make any difference in encouraging participating in learning. What we should be concentrating on are questions about what motivates and encourages people to take the first steps to learning.'

We have presented evidence that non-participants in formal educational episodes are not particularly deterred by traditional barriers such as time, cost, travel and lack of initial qualification. This evidence comes partly from the role of long-term socio-economic background characteristics, especially the influence of family, in creating a learner identity which does not view current opportunities as appropriate, interesting or useful (Gorard et al., 1999b). Evidence also comes from a model of two separate sets of determinants for extended initial and later learning respectively (Gorard et al., 1999a), and from the accounts of widespread informal learning for which barriers are, by their very nature, less relevant (Gorard et al., 1999d).

These doubts have been confirmed to some extent by our results from the 1999 NIACE survey. When asked why they did not take part, or plan to take part, in learning, the non-participants replied as summarized in table 12.1. Despite differences in detail, the consistency of the total for the overall survey and for Wales is remarkable. Nearly two-thirds of these respondents reported no actual barrier to their participation, suggesting that their patterns of behaviour would remain unaffected by any initiatives to ease their entry back into formal episodes. Of course, it is always possible to doubt the realism/accuracy of these responses, and to suggest that virtual colleges or community programmes could whet their appetites again. However, such a suggestion (i.e. doubting the accuracy of responses) can be a two-edged sword and not one likely to find favour with the survey designers. In summary, this recent survey confirms the prediction of

Titmus (1994) that there is a substantial subset of the population who are 'beyond all attempts to reach them' (see also Harrison, 1993; McGivney, 1993).

Table 12.1 Barriers to participation (percentages)

	No barrier	No interest	Too old	Other	Total
UK	17	27	15	4	63
Wales	9	22	15	17	63

Other: includes 'don't know', 'I already know all I need', and 'haven't got round to it'.

To some extent this rather depressing conclusion can be tempered by consideration of the nature of the opportunities on offer in Wales (Gorard et al., 1998d), and the policy of National Lifetime and Training Targets (which are unaffected by informal learning, however substantive in nature). Much lifelong learning policy is prescriptive (Tight, 1998). Non-participants are often blamed for their situation, and threatened with further exclusion, since the alternative of admitting the existence of socio-economic determinants for non-participation might require a totally different, and rather more expensive, government programme. The prevailing view is that people *ought* to participate since it is good for them, but this shows a form of historical amnesia. The current emphasis on formal vocational education and training, and on learning as a positional good (Keep, 1997), thus ignores the emancipatory, individual and radical nature of the original proposals for lifelong learning, on whose rhetoric current policy is justified. A compulsion to train and retrain for a flexible 'career-ship', or to prevent the damage caused by social exclusion may benefit those in power and meet the requirements of the productive system (Furter, 1977; Johnson, 1993), but if nearly a third of the population do not wish to take part after formal schooling it is just possible that the problem lies in the provision and not in the non-participants. As well as leading to economic competitiveness (perhaps) and social mobility (probably), education is nearly always a genuinely transformative experience for an individual (Lewis, 1993), and one that impacts on the local community. Learning should not therefore be viewed as an escape route *from* anything, but a normal part of an accomplished life in a democratic society (Rees, 1997). Viewed in this way, it is not clear that the experiences offered by the virtual education movement, which is of necessity based on a model of information transmission, can be genuinely educational, or that they *can* lead to better reasoning skills, creativity and the ability to value divergent cultures claimed by Roll (1995, see above). Given these severe limitations, it may therefore be seen as completely rational for an individual to decline to participate. Unfortunately, at least partly because progress is measured in terms of the qualification targets used to attract inward investors, such a conclusion is not generally favoured by policy-makers in Wales.

RECOGNIZING THE IMPORTANCE OF INFORMAL LEARNING

Eraut (1997) suggests that significant learning goes on in work which is virtually unnoticed by researchers, and even by employers. This oversight has simply been replicated by ICT initiatives according to Bob Fryer (McGavin, 2000a). The emphasis of the Learning and Skills Council is still too much on the supply of courses, and provision for the young, with little consideration of the role of motivation, according to the director general of British Chamber of Commerce and chair of the Skills Task Force (McGavin, 2000b). Informal learning may be vitally necessary to the organizations people work for (and perhaps also to the fulfilment of the individuals concerned), but it is not acquired in any formal manner. But Eraut's approach is ahistorical and does not take into account the way in which the degree of importance attached to informal learning as opposed to formal learning has changed. If increased formalization had occurred because it is more effective in transmitting necessary knowledge and competencies then Eraut's thesis would be weakened. While no definitive answer to the question of whether people were more likely to acquire necessary knowledge and competencies in a formal way is provided here, our study has produced evidence which would tend to suggest that this is not so (also cf. Stasz, 1997). Perhaps largely as a consequence of credentialism, increased formality has also increased the proportion of unnecessary learning which is undertaken while more necessary learning continues in informal and uncertificated settings. As has been noted elsewhere:

> the individuals who make a career of 'informal' learning may do it because learning is part of their wider identities (wider than work, that is): they learn at work because they like to learn everywhere, and what they learn is the necessary knowledge and skills they need to actually achieve something, whether this be a practical achievement or self-transformation. (Fevre et al., 2000: 164)

If informal and leisure learning is a characteristic of later-life learners, surely it is a characteristic that creators of a learning society should seek to enhance? But this self-reliance may be negated by 'the audit society' (Ecclestone, 1998). Informal learners learn at home in their spare time, not seeking certification and not linking learning to their work, and they may be disappearing in association with the growth in formal participation. Although south Wales is associated with relatively low levels of training and qualification, there is a tradition of 'autodidacts' and hobbyists outside work who are not yet included in the supposedly 'inclusive' learning society of today (although they may have been picked up to some extent by the findings of the National Adult Learning Survey 1997 that while the frequency of vocational learning in Wales was very low compared with regions of England, the frequency of non-vocational learning was high; Beinhart and Smith, 1998) . Do such learners have to certify their activities, or start to pay an external provider simply to gain recognition?

An inclusive learning society cannot be encouraged simply by more pressure to conform to the existing set-up (Gorard et al., 1998d). It may be necessary to overcome real barriers to participation, to make people more aware of opportunities available (widen their subjective opportunity structures), but three other changes are also, and perhaps more clearly, needed. Changes are needed in the nature of opportunities available, since even in a system of rationality which is seen as heavily bounded by socio-economic constraints, it seems that there many people do not want to take part in the courses that *are* available to them. Progress is necessary towards economic and societal justice other than through increased education. We would also argue that it is possible to recognize wider existing skills cheaply. Greater inclusion in a learning society may come more easily from greater recognition of tacit knowledge than more participation. Unfortunately this recognition of the value of informal learning and of individual autonomy (Strain, 1998), with its tradition of self-reliance, does not link up with the economic imperative and its human-capital approach to systems of education and training. It is therefore less than surprising that some recent Green Papers on lifelong learning do not address any of these issues (DfEE, 1998; Welsh Office, 1998), any more than they address the decline in substantive training financed by employers. They do not start from the premise that informal learners are involved in a lifelong process. Their simple answer is to leave society as it is, and to encourage learning chiefly through publicly or individually financed episodes of certified formal learning.

WIDER IMPLICATIONS FOR WALES IN AN INFORMATION AGE

We hope that the above discussion provides some answers to our initial question of how to approach lifelong learning in an information age effectively. That said, our educational case study throws up wider issues for Wales which are also worthy of consideration, especially with regard to the place of small countries and regions in an information age. It is to this wider picture that we now turn.

Countries like Wales are undoubtedly facing substantial challenges at the beginning of the twenty-first century as larger 'competitors', richer in economic and technocultural capital, appear to be relentlessly forging a trail into the technological sunset. Indeed, in the areas of technology, social inclusion and learning, the policy agendas of countries such as the USA would, at first glance, appear to dwarf the efforts being made in smaller countries. At this juncture there is a strong temptation for those on the periphery of the information age to adopt a 'heads-down' approach, either choosing to ignore global developments or stridently adopting an isola-tionist attitude to policy-making – both options rooted in the perspective of battling against the inherent disadvantages of being a small country.

As we have seen throughout this book, there are certainly significant disadvantages that countries and regions such as Wales face in developing and implementing technology-based policy agendas. These disadvantages stem primarily from economies of scale – particularly in terms of resources and power. As we have seen from our extended study of educational policy-making and implementation in Wales, countries are often hampered by lack of investment in an adequate ICT infrastructure, they often lack the stimulating presence of a large, multinational IT industry base to move policy and practice along and, especially in Wales's case, they often lack sufficient political power to forge a coherent, effective policy agenda purely on their own. Coupled with a physically inhospitable terrain, the temptation to approach information age policy-making in Wales from a defensive, or even defeatist, perspective is understandably strong.

In learning from the progress we have observed so far in Wales, it is possible to begin to construct an alternative scenario, based upon the advantages rather than disadvantages of being a small country. Thus, it is possible to contrast the material advantages of large countries gained from their relative technological and economic superiority with the 'be-havioural' advantages of small countries. As Rothwell and Dodgson (1993) reason, such behavioural advantages could be seen to include a certain dynamism, internal flexibility and responsiveness to changing circum-stances that characterize smaller organizations and, it should follow, smaller countries.

From an economic and industrial perspective, writers have therefore begun to explore the potential for small countries to begin to develop distinctive 'techno-nationalist' approaches to creating sustainable national innovation strategies (e.g. Lundvall, 1992). Here the emphasis is less on creating national ICT policy agendas *per se* (as in the national information infrastructure mould of policy-making presented in chapter 3), but on stimulating the technological capabilities of a small nation's firms and citizens. Although the human-capital leanings of this approach are questionable from a social and educational perspective, this model can at least suggest a range of areas where small countries *are* in a position to create strategic advantages in formulating policies for the information age. In particular we can highlight the following areas as potential 'small country advantages' in the information age:

Organization of government/economy	Generally simple and focused. Fewer layers of control (e.g. state and federal). Fewer institutions.
Management of economy	Less bureaucracy than for a large country; more consultation coverage, rapid economic decision-making; less formal style; possibly risk-taking.
Networks/communication	Potentially rapid and effective *internal* country communication; extensive informal networks. Affords a fast response to internal national problem-solving; provides ability to reorganize rapidly to adapt to change in the external international environment. May have extensive *external* networks and linkages through international relations.
Learning ability	Should be capable of 'fast learning' and adapting government/economic routines and strategies.
International schemes	Some schemes to support less developed nations, e.g. EU collaborative programmes can favour smaller EU countries.
Inter-governmental joint ventures and strategic alliances	Can prove attractive partner if technological leader internationally. Can be a useful test market. Can play a role in international relations.

(Adapted from Davenport and Bibby (1999), Rothwell and Dodgson (1994))

If we relate these areas back to the specific case of Wales as a small country, the key recurring concern that comes to the fore is that of Wales's autonomy, power and control over its policy-making, both economic and social. Welsh government at the moment could not easily be described as 'simple and focused', 'less bureaucratic' and 'more risk-taking', 'fast-responding' and 'fast-learning'. Yet it is clear from the above analysis that only if these issues are addressed can Wales draw upon the other 'small-country' advantages listed above. So before we conclude this chapter with a brief set of suggestions for action the overriding key question to be tackled is how the governance and politics of Wales can be adjusted best to fit the role of a small country in an information age.

REDEFINING POWER AND POLITICS OF A DEVOLVED WALES IN AN INFORMATION AGE

A principal question posited at the beginning of the book was to what extent Wales, as a 'stateless' nation, could possibly be expected to make its own way in the information age. At first glance Wales at a political level would seem to be inexorably linked with its partners in the United Kingdom. Indeed, the New Labour government's explicit intention to focus on ICT as one of its key public-policy areas would seem to have fundamentally shaped the ability of the Welsh government substantially to influence the implementation of ICT in Wales, above and beyond mediating UK policies in a Welsh context. Certainly from our key actor interviews there was a sense that the party-political dimension of New Labour's UK-wide ICT drive was dictating the responses to initiatives such as the UfI from Crickhowell House and the Labour-led Welsh government.

There is little doubt that on a UK-wide level New Labour are strongly steering their overall ICT agenda from the centre, in particular in public-policy areas such as education and health. As a high-profile sector of their first-term policy agenda, New Labour's early efforts to transform the public sector technologically, via ICT, suffered a series of setbacks, including the much-publicized failure of efforts to computerize the Passports and Benefits Agencies (Campbell, 1999; Watt, 1999; E. Bell, 1999). In the case of policies such as UfI, the Westminster government is keen to avoid replicating these earlier controversies. ICT policy-making is now part of the rational central rule model of governance, with the Westminster government as key actor operating effective co-ordination with other subservient actors, including the National Assembly for Wales (Kickert et al., 1997).

In attempting to account for this picture of the ICT policy process and its implications for Wales it is perhaps appropriate to look towards wider, macro-level explanations for the current Labour government's determination to take a central role in the formation and implementation of such policies. Beyond its immediate party-political utility, the emergence of an ICT agenda in the guise of UfI and UK Online can be seen as indicative of New Labour's underlying philosophy of *new paternalism*, using the state to enforce rather than merely encourage conformity to generally non-controversial but important values for national success in the global economy (Teles, 1998). New Labour's tight central control could be argued to reflect their recognition of the need to tackle the dilemmas of the 'information society' on behalf of their citizens rather than leave matters to the vagaries of choices and the market. For supposedly centre-left administrations, such as that currently in the UK, this is seen to entail the construction of policies based on forms of state-directed 'benevolent capitalism' (Malina, 1999). It could be argued that, using initiatives such as UfI, New Labour has taken an active role in equipping citizens and constituent countries within the UK to 'deal with the associated risks and uncertainties' of the 'free-market thrust of globalisation' (Thompson, 1998: 5). In taking a firm grip on the formation of the NGfL, New Labour can be seen to be 'responding to the pre-established priorities' and 'acquiescing to the powerful imperatives of global economics' (Robins and Webster, 1999: 75–6). In closely adhering to Reich's (1991) vision of an information economy and the seeming inevitability of globalization, 'coping' policies such as the NGfL are, in many ways, as much as nation-states can attempt to provide by way of a response to supranational economic trends:

> There will no longer be national economies, at least as we have come to understand that concept. All that will remain rooted within national borders are the people who comprise a nation. Each nation's primary assets will be its citizens' skills and insights. Each nation's primary political task will be to cope with the centrifugal forces of the global economy. (Reich, 1991: 3)

Given this rather bleak and challenging global perspective, how bad can this be for the Welsh implementation of ICT and the fortunes of Wales in the global information economy? On the one hand in attempting to fight for Wales and the rest of the UK in a global context, does it make any difference whether such policies come from the Westminster government as long as the eventual benefits are felt in Wales? It could be argued that the combined weight of the UK, as opposed to the separate influence of Wales, Scotland, Northern Ireland and England, would be far more beneficial for the Welsh cause – especially in the light of Wales's consistently poor showing in UK regional comparisons of ICT take-up and use. On the other hand, the need for the National Assembly to take more of the initiative in ICT policy-making in Wales can be seen in the light of the UK government's approach to ICT as a 'market maker' responsible for co-ordinating and accelerating the nascent markets for ICT-based education by franchising the supply of approved courseware (Harris, 2000).

In attempting to establish the UfI, for example, the UK government were clearly looking to create a viable and sustainable commercial marketplace for educational ICT, with the state acting as regulator and evaluator. In doing so, the UK government appear to have distanced themselves from the model of ICT policy-making adopted in Europe, America and Japan, which firmly positions the role of the state as one of facilitator and the private sector as the generator of change. Instead, the UK government appear to be a driving force in generating the 'change' of the UfI and NGfL and attempting to guide the actions of other public and private bodies, at least throughout the early stages of the initiatives. Thus, in terms of the UfI, the option of leaving ICT-based adult learning to the push and pull of market forces was seen as undesirable right from the outset. As Hillman (1996) argued in the initial framing policy document:

> The objective is [. . .] to provide a framework for people to choose. Learning will be provided 'on demand', in response to the combinations of skills identified by learners themselves, at times and places convenient to them. The alternative, laissez-faire approach would be to treat education and training as goods like any other, allowing the market to develop at its own pace. The risk of this approach is that provision remains piecemeal and haphazard. Certain groups of learners would continue to be excluded, particularly since there would be no subsidies.

Yet, in practice, as we saw from our empirical study, imposing a framework of ICT-based learning from Westminster was resulting in significant problems on the ground in Wales – including a fair degree of hostility towards an initiative seen not to have been formulated with the needs or demands of Welsh education and Welsh learners in mind. Thus, whatever the *global* intentions of UK technological policy-making, the *local* context cannot be overlooked if such initiatives are to be implemented effectively. It is here therefore that the National Assembly can be seen to have a vital role to play – instead of simply mediating Westminster ICT policies, they could be wholly reconstructing them from a Welsh perspective, to fit in with the needs of the Welsh people, Welsh businesses and Welsh social needs.

CONSTRUCTING A WELSH AGENDA FOR AN INFORMATION AGE

It is at the level of the local that Wales may be able to shape and recon-struct, at least partially, its fortunes in an information age. This conclusion may, at first glance, go against the grain of political thinking in these globalized times. As Lovering (2000: 14) argues, 'One of the ironies of "Actually Existing Devolution" [in Wales] is that it has come at a time when the intellectual arguments for autonomous economic policies at the small country level have sunk to their lowest level.'

Indeed, despite the many compelling reasons that can be presented for greater economic autonomy from the UK such a scenario is unlikely to come about in the short to medium term. But the National Assembly *can* make a discernible difference in terms of social policy and the opportunity exists therefore for Welsh government to alter the social impacts of technology. Nevertheless, as we have seen throughout this book, this is by no means an easy task.

So what could this social and local agenda for information age policy-making entail? There is a need for a 'bottom-up' approach to building technology-based opportunities and services in Wales. Whatever its early failings 'on the ground', the success of the Wales Digital College concept in gaining acceptance and support from education providers in Wales, especially in relation to the hostile reception afforded to UfI, could act as a model for further public-sector ICT activity in Wales. The ability of Welsh organizations, in both the public and private sectors, to develop and implement Welsh ICT-based programmes should be seen as a fruitful way of shaping the information age at the local level, regardless of wider political concerns.

This point highlights the need for the establishment of strategic and joint information age alliances, both within and outside Wales. As we have seen from our case study, there are many organizations ostensibly progressing towards the same information age goals, yet working in nothing but the loosest partnerships within Wales. As demonstrated in the 'surf wars' that have come to the surface during the establishment of the implementation of virtual learning in Wales, such lack of genuine collaboration can prove to be a significant barrier to real progress on the ground. There is, therefore, a need for substantial partnership between Welsh organizations – both public and private – to ensure the effective development and implementation of policies. Similarly, with regard to Wales's neighbours and competitors, the scope for strategic alliances and, more importantly, joint action between small countries and regions is an obvious starting-point. Such links are beginning to be made at the EU level, via initiatives such as the European Development Fund INTERREG community programme, but the opportunity for the newly devolved Wales to forge other strategic links with 'peripheral' countries such as Ireland and the Scandinavian countries as well as the increasingly powerful multinational corporations should be seized.

There are also pressing practical issues that Welsh government must address in order to make the most of its small-country advantages in an information age. On a practical level the development of a rapid and effective nationwide information technology infrastructure would seem paramount to ensuring social inclusiveness. Wales is not the only country with inhospitable terrain and disadvantaged rural and urban regions currently ill-provided for in terms of ICT. Socially focused solutions can be engineered to address many of these deficiencies and must be implemented quickly and effectively. This will involve a heightened impetus from the Cardiff and Westminster governments as well as a heightened social consciousness on the part of usually profit-hungry private telecommunications companies. But the need to establish an adequate telecommunications infrastructure across all of Wales and to provide corresponding facilities in community sites where people will want to, and have a need to, use them is paramount.

Of course, it would be unrealistic to argue for the National Assembly to formulate a 'National Information Infrastructure' (NII) policy agenda for Wales when Wales is so strongly subject to the Westminster government's UK-wide ICT agenda. Were subsequent Westminster governments less proactive and focused with regard to ICT, then the Assembly would conceivably have more of a role to play, but this would be unlikely in the short to medium term. Whilst Westminster continues to be directing ICT implementation and establishing a form of 'NII' in Wales, the very least that the National Assembly can be attempting to do is to act as effective local 'reconstructors' of that NII. To be fair, initial attempts are beginning to be made by the Assembly in this direction, such as the £16 million 'ICT for Learning' initiative launched in 2001 and the overall thrust of the *Cymru Ar-lein* strategy, although its effectiveness in moving beyond the overall UK ICT framework remains to be seen (Johnston, 2001b). The fact remains that recontextualizing policies such as UfI and NGfL, and augmenting spending and resourcing plans to fit in with Wales and the Welsh, needs to be done far more effectively. Above all, the key watchwords for Wales – as with any small country or region – in an information age should be simplicity, speed and lack of bureaucracy and boundary-building in terms of both policy formulation and implementation. Unfortunately, as we have witnessed in our extended study, such qualities are not easily achieved.

CONCLUSION

We do not contest that the Westminster government and various other organizations in Wales are making a serious effort to address the issue of ICT. As the main focus of our book has indicated, the present range of ICT-based education policies certainly marks an unprecedented commitment to integrating new technologies into lifelong education. For this alone, all involved are to be commended. Yet throughout this book we have striven to look beyond the self-congratulatory and overly optimistic tone of many other commentators on technology and the information age, and attempted to look at the realities of the present rather than the rhetoric of the future. That we have uncovered more problems than solutions when doing so is to be expected. Yet recognizing the inconsistencies of the information age is surely the next step to effectively implementing ICT in public policy.

If we cannot move beyond the 'hype' of ICT then we cannot hope to assist any lasting or effective social change to occur for the better.

Indeed, it may be largely the hype of ICT that threatens to undermine the genuine efforts of many of those involved. That the current 'buzz theories' of social policy-makers and commentators, such as social exclusion and lifelong learning, have been so readily married to that other 'buzz area' of ICT should be no real cause for surprise. That ICT alone has often been seen as beyond criticism should also not be much of a surprise. Indeed, such lack of criticism can be seen as the defining feature of the hype of the information age. When approaching the future of small countries and regions in an information age, we would do well always to bear in mind the limitations of ICT as well as the potential opportunities. Moreover, to view the role of technology in public policy as some sort of panacea for existing societal shortcomings is, at best, short-sighted and potentially damaging to the long-term effectiveness of such programmes. As Postman (1992: 119) argues, to maintain a blind faith in a technical fix for education is to lose sight of wider societal barriers to learning: 'Our most serious problems are not technical, nor do they arise from inadequate information . . . Where education is impotent it does not happen because of inadequate information.'

Technology will undoubtedly remain an attractive option to educators and policy-makers alike, adhering to the societal tendency to view the future merely as a more desirable and glamorous version of the present (Marvin, 1988). However, throughout this book we have attempted to argue that we would perhaps do better to see the future of Wales in an information age as an equally flawed and unglamorous version of the present-day Wales. As Neill (1995: 184) concludes, 'the savage inequalities of the past will extend into the wired savagery of the future. There is neither empirical nor theoretical reason to believe this scenario will change for the better.' Thus, it is not enough for advocates of virtual education to 'speak in the name of abstract equality and empowerment amidst concrete conditions of severe inequality and disempowerment' (Luke, 1997: 133). Above all, we cannot afford to lose sight of fundamental issues of inequality and disempowerment which technology may not be capable of addressing.

Appendix

Further Details of Research Methods

In chapter 7 we presented an outline of the methods of data collection and analysis drawn upon in the second half of the book. As is inevitable with a complex study, more detailed and technical information relating to the research methods employed has been omitted from the main body of the text for reasons of clarity, brevity and relevance to the general reader. However, we feel that it is important that the interested reader is able to find out something more about our approaches and the methods used, and so enrich their understanding of our subsequent analysis and discussion. To this end the appendix presents details of further references, and more detailed descriptions and rationales for the research methods employed. The complex sampling and analysis of the three waves of our household survey are described in more detail in Gorard et al. (1997d, 1999a), and especially in Gorard and Rees (2002). This represents our work on a much larger project forming part of the ESRC's Learning Society Programme from 1996 to 1999. We replicate a small section of that here, but the focus of this appendix is on our methods for investigating specifically ICT-related learning episodes.

THE HOUSEHOLD SURVEY

The questionnaire was designed to collect data of four principal kinds: the social/demographic characteristics of individual respondents; detailed histories of respondents' educational and training careers; simplified histories of respondents' employment careers; and simplified histories of the educational and training careers of respondents' family members (in this way we gathered learning histories for 2,482 individuals). Information on individual histories was collected on a modified 'sequential start-to-finish date-of-event basis' (Gallie, 1994: 340). Whilst careful pre-piloting and a pilot study provided the basis for question design, there remain problems with this approach arising from the fallibility of respondents' recall. However, the alternatives of longitudinal panel designs and cross-sectional designs also face major problems (Gorard, 2001b).

The task of describing the ensuing trajectories as the result of either choices or determinants is a difficult one. Training (and educational) placements are usually the result of negotiation between several people, not a simple choice by one person (Greenhalgh and Stewart, 1987), and there is interaction with other 'stakeholders' in the decision (Hodkinson et al., 1996). To a large extent, the characteristics of those who participate or do not participate in education and training are cross-sectional, rather than clearly causal. What is needed is knowledge of how the trajectory of each individual interacts with their personal history and general economic historical events (cf. Gershuny and Marsh, 1994). In this study it was achieved by collecting retrospective life histories of the respondents, tied to secondary histories of the specific areas in which they lived and learned. In addition, all analyses were performed in several stages, in historical order and using only that information knowable about each individual at that time. Even this careful analysis may exhibit misplaced trust in forward-looking causal models, since there is evidence that people can use future expectations as a constraint in present choice (Gambetta, 1987). People may take into account not only their real options but the expected probability of the success of each (e.g. working-class individuals may be traditionally more cautious about staying on at school).

Our logistic regression analysis permits the identification of those characteristics of individuals (independent variables) which provide good predictions of which 'lifetime learning trajectories' they follow (dependent variable). This method of analysis is especially fruitful, as independent variables may be added into the regression function in the order in which they occur in real life: that is, the statistical procedure models exactly the social phenomenon it is analysing ('trajectories'). At birth these variables include gender, year, place, and parental occupational and educational background. By the end of initial schooling these variables include details of siblings, type of schools attended, examination entry and performance, and so on. In this way, the variables entered at each step can only be used to explain the variance left unexplained by previous steps. We believe that this innovative method of analysis constitutes a significant advance over previous approaches in this field. In summary, the survey described the actual patterns of participation as experienced by residents. The survey also enabled a preliminary consideration of why people did and did not participate in particular ways, with a considerable emphasis on the long-term socio-economic determinants of behaviour.

Our comparison of patterns of trajectories within families was based on the established genre of work which relates occupational categories across generations in the same family (e.g. Blau and Duncan, 1967; Goldthorpe et al., 1987). Using standard forms of odds calculations, it is possible to measure changes over class from one generation to the next in a form that takes into account the changes over time in the frequency of occupational classes (Marshall et al., 1997). A similar approach is used here, but replacing the analysis of occupational class with pattern of lifelong participation.

ANALYSIS OF ON-LINE LEARNING ACTIVITY

Analysis of Internet usage can only ever claim to be *transitory*, since any study purporting to measure Internet activity is invariably outdated as soon as it is completed. As Mitra and Cohen (1999: 180) argue, 'given the dynamic of worldwide web (WWW) use, with its rapid changes and the on-going addition of innumerable users, any analysis of WWW yields conflicting results.' Nevertheless, in providing a 'snapshot' or even a longitudinal indication of learners' use of the 'On-line for Welsh Learners' web-site we felt able to go some way to identifying emerging patterns and trends. Moreover, in the case of 'mapping' educational use of the Internet we felt confident in beginning to examine whether or not the Internet is being used in ways consistent with the claims and hopes of virtual educators.

As Mitra and Cohen (1999) point out, there are two broad approaches to analysing the worldwide web. First there are the increasingly popular methods of examining the *people* who are using the web. Thus there are a burgeoning number of 'rating' studies attempting to analyse empirically levels of use and, to a lesser extent, the behaviour of users once on-line (e.g. Patrick and Black, 1997). Second, there is also an emerging literature focusing on the *content* of the web (e.g. Stern, 1999; Chandler and Roberts-Young, 2000). This approach is rooted in a textual or content-analysis tradition and focuses more on the web as text rather than as human activity. Together both these approaches begin to form a more coherent picture of how the Internet is being used in society. Our analysis of the 'On-line for Welsh Learners' web-site adopted both a user-based and content-based approach.

Content-based methodology

In analysing the content of the worldwide web we were interested in the *text* of the Internet, referring to both the written word and the many other visual and aural multimedia features that the Internet offers. In doing so, we were therefore concerned with both the content of the text and how the text presents information. However, as Mitra and Cohen (1999: 198) reason, on-line content analysis poses additional challenges:

The WWW text poses a unique analytical challenge because of its characteristics. An analyst is confronted with a textual form that has many elements of
the traditional text and is thus open to analysis with time-tested tools . . .
However, independent of the critical approach used, there is a set of fundamental concerns about the uniqueness of the text that needs to be addressed.
These are issues related to the specificity of the text – its inherent intertextuality, its lack of centre, its volume, its multimedianess, its international
scope, and the resulting altered sense of authorship.

As this quotation suggests, any analysis of on-line text therefore requires
consideration of its many features. To this end, Mitra and Cohen (1999)
suggest a three-layered approach focusing on:

- the formal aspects of the text, such as its semiotics and structure, thus
  uncovering the way it is constructed;
- the text's interconnectedness, thus recognizing the intertextuality of hypertext;
- the role of the reader(s) in giving the text meaning, thus recognizing the non-
  linearity of hypertext and the role of the reader as writer.

User-based methodology

In attempting to measure the 'popularity' of a site, most studies offer
analyses of the number of visits or 'hits' to sites as a surrogate method of
citation. Although, indicative of web-site activity, such data are, at best,
ambiguous, given the non-equability of hits or visits with different users.
In other words, it is not possible to assess whether a large number of visits
to a site are the result of numerous accesses from a small group of users or
single accesses from a large group of users. Thus, although useful data, it
can be misleading to equate the number of visits or hits with individual
users. Nevertheless, it is possible to complement 'hit' data with other forms
of cross-referential statistics. First, many educational sites require regular
users to register officially with sites in order to gain passwords and full
access to the site. The nature of such registration data varies, but may
include location, status, age, gender and motivation for using the site. A
third proxy measure of the popularity of a web-site is the number of 'links'
to and from a site; thus how well 'connected' the site is within the worldwide web. As Mitra and Cohen (1999: 193) reason, 'WWW pages gain their
meaning and purpose from the interconnectedness designated by the[ir]
links.' Thus mapping out the connections between the pages of a web-site,
both internally and externally, can provide another means of assessing the
status of a web-site.

From this background, the following methods of inquiry were used for
the user-based analysis of the 'On-line for Welsh Learners' web-site:

(a) A cumulative log file record for the 'On-line for Welsh Learners' web-site covering a thirteen-month period from 1 August 1999 to 31 August 2000. Such logs, maintained by the Wales Digital College themselves, cover who was visiting the site (via individual Internet addresses); when they came (in terms of month/week/day/hour/minute/second-level data); where they came from; what aspects of the site were being used and what software (and often hardware) they were using.

(b) An email-based survey of registered users of the 'On-line for Welsh Learners' web-site covering users' location, occupation, age and motivations for using the site. As has been argued by a range of social science researchers (Selwyn and Robson, 1998; Mann and Stewart, 2000), the use of email-based questionnaires and interviews is most valid when dealing with on-line populations. Given the necessity for computer access to use the 'On-line for Welsh Learners' web-site, an email survey was felt to be an appropriate method of data collection. Therefore, email questionnaires constructed by the researchers (see below) were sent via the Wales Digital College to fifty-nine registered learners. Responses from eighteen registered learners had been received a month after mailing – yielding an overall response rate of 31 per cent. These responses were then used to provide tentative indications of the characteristics of registered learners.

(c) Finally, to gauge some reaction from those learners who had actually used the 'On-line for Welsh Learners' web-site, semi-structured telephone interviews were carried out with seven of the eighteen learners who had responded to the email questionnaires. These seven learners were a self-selecting sample who had indicated that they were willing to participate in follow-up interviews.

Questionnaire on background to web-based participation

<u>INFORMATION ABOUT YOUR LEARNING</u>

1. How often do you use the on-line   At least once per week
    Welsh for Learners web-site?   Less than once per week
                                              No longer use it

2. Where do you access the Internet from?   Home
                                              Work
                                              Elsewhere*
    if 'elsewhere' please specify   . . ..

3. Are you still in full-time education?   Yes
                                              No*
    if 'no', how old were you when you left . . ..
    full-time education?

4. Which of the following levels best   Level three: 2+ A levels (or
    describes your highest qualification?   equivalent), GNVQ Advanced,
                                              NVQ3, OND etc.

                                              Level two: 5+ GCSEs grade A*–C
                                              (or equivalent), 5 O levels, 5 CSE
    grade 1 etc.

                                              Level one: less than 5 GCSEs
                                              grade A*–C (or equivalent)

<u>INFORMATION ABOUT YOURSELF</u>

5. Sex   Male
                                              Female

6. Date of birth   . . ..

7. Postcode (or area name)   . . ..

8. Are you currently employed?   Yes
                                              No

9. What is your current or usual occupation?   . . ..

References

Acen (2000). Welsh Learners Website, *http://www.acen.co.uk/*

Ainley, P. (1998). 'Towards a learning or a certified society? Contradictions in the New Labour modernisation of lifelong learning', *Journal of Education Policy* 13 (4), 559–73.

Antikainen A., J. Houtsonen, J. Kaupilla and H. Huotelin (1996). *Living in a Learning Society: Life Histories, Identities and Education*, London, Falmer Press.

Apple, M. (1997). 'The new technology: is it part of the solution or part of the problem in education?', in G. E. Hawisher and C. Selfe (eds.), *Literacy, Technology and Society: Confronting the Issues*, Englewood Cliffs, Prentice Hall.

Armour, R. and A. Fuhrmann (1993). 'Confirming the centrality of liberal learning', in L. Curry, J. Wergin and Associates (eds.), *Educating Professionals*, San Francisco, Jossey-Bass.

Arthur, C. (1995). 'And the net total is . . .', *New Scientist*, 146, 1977.

Ashley, R. and S. Walkley (1996). *Education for employability*, Occasional Paper, London, Coutts Career Consultants.

Ashton, D. and F. Green (1996). *Education, Training and the Global Economy*, Cheltenham, Edward Elgar.

Atkinson, K. and T. Powell (1996). 'Welsh language ban in Wales', *Planet* 116, 81–4.

Balnaves, M., P. Caputi and K. Williamson (1991). 'The development of a methodology for assessing telecommunication needs: preliminary steps towards an index of information and communication poverty', *Australian Journal of Communication* 18 (3), 99–118.

Banks, M., I. Bates, G. Breakwell, J. Bynner and N. Emler (1992). *Careers and Identities*, Milton Keynes, Open University Press.

Barry, M. (1998). Introduction, in M. Barry and C. Hallett (eds.), *Social Exclusion and Social Work*, Dorchester, Russell House Publishing.

BBC (2000). *The Message*, BBC Radio Four, 12 May.

Becker, G. (1975). *Human Capital: A Theoretical and Empirical Analysis*, Chicago, University of Chicago Press.

BECTA (2001). *The Digital Divide: A Discussion Paper*, Coventry, British Educational Communications and Technology Agency.

Beinhart, S. and P. Smith (1998). *National Adult Learning Survey 1997*, Sudbury, DfEE Publications.

Bell, D. (1973). *The Coming of Post-Industrial Society*, New York, Basic Books.

Bell, D. (1980). 'The social framework of the information society', in Tom Forester (ed.), *The Microelectronics Revolution*, Oxford, Blackwell.

Bell, E. (1999). 'Government too close for comfort with ICT', *The Observer*, 16 May, p.B2.

Bentley, T. (1998). *Learning Beyond the Classroom*, London, Routledge.

Berghman, J. (1995). 'Social exclusion in Europe: policy context and analytical framework', in G. Room (ed.), *Beyond the Threshold: The Measurement and Analysis of Social Exclusion*, Bristol, The Policy Press.

Besser, H. (1995). 'From Internet to information superhighway', in J. Brook and I. A. Boal (eds.), *Resisting the Virtual Life: The Culture and Politics of Information*, San Francisco, City Lights.

Beynon, A. (1996). 'Creative chaos', *Planet* 116, 45–9.

Blair, A. (2000). Speech at the Knowledge 2000 Conference, 7 March *http://www.number-10.gov.uk*

Blau, P. and O. Duncan (1967). *The American Occupational Structure*, New York, John Wiley and Sons.

Blunkett, D. (1997). 'On the starting grid', *Educational Computing and Technology*, December, 11–12.

Blunkett, D. (1999). 'Blunkett's vision of the learning age', *Times Educational Supplement*, 2 July, p.41.

BMRB International (1999). *Is IT for All?* London, Department for Trade and Industry.

Booz, Allen and Hamilton (2000). *Achieving Universal Access*, London, Booz, Allen and Hamilton.

Bosworth D. (1992). 'The extent and intensity of skills shortages 1990', *International Journal of Manpower* 13 (9), 3–12.

Boyson, R. (1975). *Crisis in Education*, London, Woburn Press.

Breathnach, P. (1998). 'Exploring the Celtic tiger phenomenon: causes and consequences of Ireland's economic miracle', *European Urban and Regional Studies* 5 (4), 305–16.

Bromley, H. (1997). 'The social chicken and the technological egg: educational computing and the technology/society divide', *Educational Theory* 47 (1), 51–65.

Brown, M. (1998). 'The tyranny of the international horse race', in R. Slee, G. Weiner and S. Tomlinson (eds.), *School Effectiveness for Whom? Challenges to the School Effectiveness and School Improvement Movements*, London, Falmer Press.

Brown, P. (1987). *Schooling Ordinary Kids*, London, Tavistock.

Brown, P. and H. Lauder (1996). 'Education, globalization and economic development', *Journal of Education Policy* 11, 1–25.

Bryson, M. and S. de Castell (1998). 'New technologies and the cultural ecology of primary schooling: imagining teachers as luddites in/deed', *Educational Policy* 12 (5), 542–67.

Burchardt, R., J. Le Grand and D. Piachaud (1999). 'Social exclusion in Britain 1991–1995', *Social Policy and Administration* 33 (3), 227–44.

Burge, A., H. Francis, C. Trotman, G. Rees, R. Fevre and S. Gorard (1999). *In a Class of Their Own: Adult Learning and the South Wales Mining Community 1900–1939*, Cardiff, School of Education.

Burstall, E. (1996). 'Second chance stifled', *Times Educational Supplement*, 22 March, p.27.

Bynner, J. (1989). *Transition to Work: Results from a Longitudinal Study of Young*

People in Four British Labour Markets, ESRC 16–19 Initiative Occasional Papers 4, London, City University.

Bynner, J. (1998). 'Youth in the information society: problems, prospects and research directions', *Journal of Education Policy* 13 (3), 433–42.

Bynner, J. and S. Parsons (1997). *It Doesn't Get Any Better*, London, Basic Skills Agency.

Byrne, D. (1997). 'Social exclusion and capitalism: the reserve army across time and space', *Critical Social Policy* 17 (1), 27–51.

Bysshe, S. and D. Parsons (1999). *Evolution of Learndirect*, Research Report RR132, London, DfEE.

Cabinet Office (1999a). *Modernising Government*, White Paper, London, HMSO.

Cabinet Office (1999b). 'IT revolution will drive public service evolution', Cabinet Office press release 265/99, London, Cabinet Office.

Cabinet Office (2000a) 'Government to speed up introduction of on-line services', Cabinet Office press release 140/2000, London, Cabinet Office.

Cabinet Office (2000b). 'Switching on to banishing exclusion', Cabinet Office press release 28/00, London, Cabinet Office.

Calabrese, A. and M. Borchett (1996). 'Prospects for electronic democracy in the United States: rethinking communication and social policy', *Media, Culture and Society* 18 (2), 249–68.

Campbell, D. (1999). 'Computing that doesn't compute', *The Guardian*, 22 June, p.15.

Carr, A. A., D. H. Jonassen, M. E. Litzinger and R. M. Marra (1998). 'Good ideas to foment educational revolution: the role of systemic change in advancing situated learning, constructivism and feminist pedagogy', *Educational Technology* 38 (1), 5–15.

Castells, M. (1996). *The Information Age: Economy, Society and Culture*, vol. I: *The Rise of the Network Society*, Oxford, Blackwell.

Castells, M. (1997). *The Information Age: Economy, Society and Culture*, vol. II: *The Power of Identity*, Oxford, Blackwell.

Castells, M. (1998). *The Information Age: Economy, Society and Culture*, vol. III: *End of Millennium*, Oxford, Blackwell.

Castells, M. (1999). 'An introduction to the information age', in H. Mackay and T. O'Sullivan (eds.), *The Media Reader: Continuity and Transformation*, London, Sage.

CBI (1989). *Towards a Skill Revolution*, London, Confederation of British Industry.

Central Office of Information (COoI) (1998). *Our Information Age: The Government's Vision*, London, HMSO.

CERI (1975). *Recurrent Education: Trends and Issues*, Paris, OECD.

Chambers, P., S. Gorard, R. Fevre, G. Rees and J. Furlong (1998). *Changes in Training Opportunities in South Wales 1945–1998: The Views of Key Informants*, Working Paper 12, Cardiff, School of Education.

Chandler, D. and D. Roberts-Young (2000). 'The construction of identity in the personal home pages of adolescents in Wales', *Welsh Journal of Education* 9 (1), 78–90.

Clark, R. (2000). 'Crucial computer advance for language', *The Western Mail*, 13 October, p.7.

Cockrill, A., P. Scott and J. Fitz (1996). 'Training for multi-skilling: a comparison of British and German experience', paper presented at BERA conference, Lancaster.

Coe, N. (1999). 'Emulating the Celtic tiger? A comparison of the software industries of Singapore and Ireland', *Singapore Journal of Tropical Geography* 20 (1), 36–55.

Coffield, F. (1997a). 'Nine fallacies and their replacement by a national strategy for lifelong learning', in F. Coffield (ed.), *A National Strategy for Lifelong Learning*, Newcastle upon Tyne, Department of Education, University of Newcastle.

Coffield, F. (1997b). 'A tale of three little pigs: building the learning society with straw', *Evaluation and Research in Education* 11, 1–15.

Coffield, F. (1999). 'Breaking the consensus: lifelong learning as social control', *British Educational Research Journal* 25 (4), 479–99.

Cole, G. (2000). 'A dream that can turn into a living nightmare', *TES ONLINE* 14 April, pp.12–15.

Cole, M. (1998). 'Globalisation, modernisation and competitiveness: a critique of the New Labour project in education', *International Studies in Sociology of Education* 8 (3), 315–32.

Coles, L. (1972). 'Computers and society', *Science*, 10 November, p.561.

Compaine, B. and M. Weinraub (1997). 'Universal access to online services: an examination of the issue', *Telecommunications Policy* 21 (1), 15–33.

Connidis, I. (1983). 'Integrating qualitative and quantitative methods in survey research on ageing: an assessment', *Qualitative Sociology* 6 (4), 334–52.

Corcoran, F. (1999). 'Towards digital television in Europe: a race or a crawl?', *Javnost – The Public* (6), 3.

Courtney, I. and S. Gibson (1999). *Cymru.Com: Here's How*, Cardiff, Wales Media Forum.

Crequer, N. (1999). 'MPs seek to close the learning gap', *Times Educational Supplement*, FE Focus, 12 November, p.I.

Cutler, T. (1992). 'Vocational training and British economic performance: a further instalment of the "British labour problem"', *Work, Employment and Society* 6, 161–84.

Cymru Ar-Lein (2001). *On-line for Better Wales*, www.wales.gov.uk/cymruarlein/, last accessed 10 March 2001.

Daines, J., B. Elsey and M. Gibbs (1982). *Changes in Student Participation in Adult Education*, Nottingham University, Department of Adult Education.

Daniel, J. (1996). *Mega-Universities and Knowledge Media: Technology Strategies for Higher Education*, London, Kogan Page.

Daniel, J. (1997). 'The multi-media mega-university: the hope for the 21st century', keynote speech to the North of England Education Conference, Sheffield, January.

Davenport, S. and D. Bibby (1999) 'Rethinking a national innovation system: the small country as SME', *Technology Analysis and Strategic Management* 11 (3), 431–61.

Davies, P. (1998). 'Formalising learning: the role of accreditation', presentation at ESRC Learning Society informal learning seminar, Bristol.

DE (1988). *Employment for the 1990s*, London, HMSO.

DE (1994). *Competitiveness: Helping Business to Win*, London, HMSO.

Dearing, R. (1997). *Higher Education in the Learning Society. Report of the Committee under the Chairmanship of Sir Ron Dearing*, London, HMSO.

Delamont, S. and G. Rees (1996). 'The sociology of education in Wales: a future agenda', paper presented at British Educational Research Association annual conference, Lancaster.

Deloitte, Haskins and Sells (1989). *Training in Britain: A Study of Funding, Activity and Attitudes: Employers' Attitudes*, London, HMSO.

Denzin, N. K. (1978). *The Research Act: A Theoretical Introduction to Sociological Methods*, second edition, New York, McGraw-Hill.

DES (1991). *Education and Training for the 21st Century*, London, HMSO.

DfEE (1995). *Training Statistics 1995*, London, HMSO.

DfEE (1996a). *Skills and Enterprise Executive Issue 2/96*, Nottingham, Skills and Enterprise Network.

DfEE (1996b). *Participation in Education and Training by 16–18 Year Olds in England 1985 to 1995*, DfEE News 213/96.

DfEE (1997a). *Labour Market Quarterly Report*, Nottingham, Skills and Enterprise Network.

DfEE (1997b). *Meeting the Challenge of the 21st Century: A Summary of 'Labour Market and Skills Trends 1997/98'*, Nottingham, Skills and Enterprise Network.

DfEE (1997c). *Statistics of Education: Public Examinations. GCSE and GCE in England 1997*, London, HMSO.

DfEE (1998). *The Learning Age: A Renaissance for a New Britain*, London, HMSO.

DfEE (2000a). *ICT: Help Your Community to Get Ahead*, Nottingham, DfEE Publications.

DfEE (2000b). 'End the digital divide', DfEE press release 34/00, London, DfEE.

Dicken, P., M. Forsgren and A. Malmberg (1994). 'The local embeddedness of transnational corporations', in A. Amin and N. Thrift (eds.), *Globalisation, Institutions and Regional Development in Europe*, Oxford, Oxford University Press.

Dordick, H. S., H. G. Bradley and B. Nanus (1988). *The Emerging Network Marketplace*, Norwood, NJ, Ablex.

Doring, A. (1999). 'Information overload?', *Adults Learning*, June, pp.8–10.

Drabble, J. (1999). 'Lights, camera, interaction!', *Times Educational Supplement*, 7 May, p.19.

DTI (1998). *Our Competitive Future: Building the Knowledge Driven Economy*, White Paper, December, London, HMSO.

DTI (1999). *Competitive Advantage in the Digital Economy*, London, HMSO.

DTI (2000a). *International Benchmarking Study*, available on-line at:
  http://www.ukonlineforbusiness.gov.uk/Government/bench/International00.htm

DTI (2000b). *Closing the Digital Divide: Information and Communication Technologies in Deprived Areas*, London, Department of Trade and Industry.

Dumort, A. (2000). 'New media and distance education: an EU–US perspective', *Information, Communication and Society* 3 (4), 546–56.

Ecclestone, K. (1998). 'Care and control: defining learners' needs for lifelong learning', presentation at BERA annual conference, Belfast.

Edwards R., S. Sieminski and D. Zeldin (1993). *Adult Learners, Education and Training*, London, Routledge.

Edwards, R. and R. Usher (1998). 'Lo(o)s(en)ing the boundaries: from "education" to "lifelong learning"', *Studies in Continuing Education* 20 (1), 83–103.

Eraut, M. (1997). 'Perspectives on defining "the learning society"', *Journal of Education Policy* 12 (6), 551–8.

Eraut, M., J. Alderton, G. Cole and P. Senker (1998). *Development of Knowledge and Skills in Employment: Final Report of ESRC Project*, Brighton, University of Sussex.

ETAG (1998). *An Education and Training Action Plan for Wales*, Cardiff, The Education and Training Action Group for Wales, October.

European Union/Bangemann (1994). *Europe and the Global Information Society: Recommendations to the European Council*, Brussels.

Eurostat (1995). *Education across the European Union: Statistics and Indicators*, Brussels, Statistical Office of the European Communities.

Evans, C. (1979). *The Mighty Micro*, London, Coronet.

Felstead, A. (1996). 'Identifying gender inequalities in the distribution of vocational qualifications in the UK', *Gender, Work and Organization* 3 (1), 38–51.

FEU (1993). *Paying Their Way: The Experiences of Adult Learners in Vocational Education and Training in FE Colleges*, London, Further Education Unit.

Fevre, R., S. Gorard and G. Rees (2000). 'Necessary and unnecessary learning: the acquisition of knowledge and skills in and outside employment in south Wales in the twentieth century', in F. Coffield (ed.), *The Necessity of Informal Learning*, Bristol, Policy Press.

Fevre, R., G. Rees and S. Gorard (1999). 'Some sociological alternatives to human capital theory', *Journal of Education and Work* 12 (2), 117–40.

Field, J. (ed.) (1997). *Electronic Pathways: Adult Learning and the New Communication Technologies*, Leicester, NIACE.

Finch, P. (1998). 'WelshLit.Com', *Planet* 128, 13–17.

Fordham, P., G. Poulton and L. Randle (1983). 'Non-formal work: a new kind of provision', in M. Tight (ed.), *Education for Adults*, vol. II, London, Croom Helm.

Foreign and Commonwealth Office (1998). *Britain's Software Industry*, London, Foreign and Commonwealth Office.

Foster, D. (1996). 'Community and identity in the electronic village', in D. Porter (ed.), *Internet Culture*, London, Routledge.

Frazer, L. and K. Ward (1988). *Education for Everyday Living*, Leicester, NIACE.

Frow, E. and R. Frow (1990). 'The spark of independent working-class education: Lancashire 1909–1930', in B. Simon (ed.), *The Search for Enlightenment: The Working Class and Adult Education in the Twentieth Century*, London, Lawrence & Wishart.

Fryer, R. (1990). 'The challenge to working-class education', in B. Simon (ed.), *The Search for Enlightenment: The Working Class and Adult Education in the Twentieth Century*, London, Lawrence & Wishart.

Fryer, R. (1997). *Learning for the Twenty-First Century*, London, Department of Education and Employment.

Fryer, R. (1999). 'Practical implications of the learning age in Wales', speech given to the Wales Digital College Network Conference, Cardiff, January.

Furter, P. (1977). *The Planner and Lifelong Education*, Paris, UNESCO.

Future Skills Wales (1998). *Technical Report*, London, MORI.

Gallie, D. (1988). *Employment in Britain*, Oxford, Basil Blackwell.

Gallie, D. (1994). 'Methodological appendix: the social change and economic life initiative', in D. Gallie, C. Marsh and C. Vogler (eds.), *Social Change and the Experience of Unemployment*, Oxford, Oxford University Press.

Gambetta D. (1987). *Were They Pushed or Did They Jump? Individual Decision Mechanisms in Education*, Cambridge, Cambridge University Press.

Garfield, M. J. and R. T. Watson (1998). 'Differences in national information infrastructures: the reflection of national cultures', *Journal of Strategic Information Systems* 6, 313–37.

Garner L. and R. Imeson (1996). 'More bricks in the wall: The ending of the older students' allowance and the new "16 hour rule". Has the cost of higher education for mature students finally got too high?', *Journal of Access Studies* 11, 97–110.

Gates, W. (1995). *The Road Ahead*, Harmondworth, Penguin.

Gell, M. and P. Cochrane (1996). 'Learning and education in an information society', in W. Dutton (ed.), *Information and Communication Technologies: Visions and Realities*, Oxford, Oxford University Press.

Gershuny, J. and C. Marsh (1994). 'Unemployment in work histories', in D. Gallie, C. Marsh and C. Vogler (eds.), *Social Change and the Experience of Unemployment*, Oxford, Oxford University Press.

Giddens, A. (1998). *The Third Way: The Renewal of Social Democracy*, Cambridge, Polity Press.

Giggs, J. and C. Pattie (1994). 'Wales as a plural society', *Contemporary Wales* 5, 25–40.

Girod, R. (1990). *Problems of Sociology in Education*, Paris, UNESCO.

Gladieux, L. and W. Swail, W. (1999). *The Virtual University and Educational Opportunity*, Washington, DC, The College Board.

Golding, P. (2000). 'Forthcoming features: information and communications technologies and the sociology of the future', *Sociology* 34 (1), 165–84.

Goldthorpe, J., C. Llewellyn and C. Payne (1987). *Social Mobility and Class Structure in Modern Britain*, Oxford, Clarendon Press.

Gorard, S. (1997a). 'Paying for a little England: school choice and the Welsh language', *Welsh Journal of Education* 6 (1), 19–32.

Gorard, S. (1997b) *The Region of Study: Patterns of Participation in Adult Education and Training*, Working paper 1, Cardiff, School of Education.

Gorard, S. (1997c). *Initial Educational Trajectories: Patterns of Participation in Adult Education and Training*, Working paper 8, Cardiff, School of Education.

Gorard, S. (1998a). 'Four errors . . . and a conspiracy? The effectiveness of schools in Wales', *Oxford Review of Education* 24 (4), 459–72.

Gorard, S. (1998b). 'Schooled to fail? Revisiting the Welsh school-effect', *Journal of Education Policy* 13 (1), 115–24.

Gorard, S. (2000a). *Education and Social Justice*, Cardiff, University of Wales Press.

Gorard, S. (2000b). ' "Underachievement" is still an ugly word: reconsidering the relative effectiveness of schools in England and Wales', *Journal of Education Policy* 15 (5), 559–73.

Gorard, S. (2000c). 'Adult participation in learning and the economic imperative: a critique of policy in Wales', *Studies in the Education of Adults* 32 (2), 181–94.

Gorard, S. (2001a). 'International comparisons of school effectiveness', *Comparative Education* 37 (3), 279–96.

Gorard, S. (2001b). *Quantitative Methods in Educational Research: The Role of Numbers Made Easy*, London, Continuum.

Gorard, S. and G. Rees (2001). *Creating a Learning Society? Learning Trajectories and Their Relevance for Policies of Lifelong learning*, Bristol: Policy Press.

Gorard, S. and N. Selwyn (2001). *101 Key Ideas in Information Technology*, London, Hodder & Stoughton.

Gorard, S. and C. Taylor (2001). *Student Funding and Hardship in Wales: A Statistical Summary*, Cardiff: National Assembly for Wales.

Gorard, S., R. Fevre, G. Rees and J. Furlong (1997a). *Space, Mobility and the Education of Minority Groups in Wales: The Survey Results. Patterns of Participation in Adult Education and Training*, Working paper 10, Cardiff, School of Education.

Gorard, S., G. Rees, R. Fevre and J. Furlong (1997b). *Patterns of Participation in Adult Education and Training*, Working paper 4: *A Brief History of Education and Training in Wales 1900–1996*, Cardiff, School of Education.

Gorard, S., J. Furlong, R. Fevre and G. Rees (1997c). *Patterns of Participation in Adult Education and Training*, Working paper 5: *The Learning Society*, Cardiff, School of Education.

Gorard, S., G. Rees, J. Furlong and R. Fevre (1997d). *Patterns of Participation in Adult Education and Training*, Working paper 2: *Outline Methodology of the Study*, Cardiff, School of Education.

Gorard, S., G. Rees, R. Fevre and J. Furlong (1998a). 'Learning trajectories: travelling towards a learning society?', *International Journal of Lifelong Education* 17 (6), 400–10.

Gorard, S., G. Rees, R. Fevre and J. Furlong (1998b). 'The two components of a new learning society', *Journal of Vocational Education and Training* 50 (1), 5–19.

Gorard, S., G. Rees, R. Fevre, E. Renold and J. Furlong (1998c). 'A gendered appraisal of the transition to a learning society in the UK', in R. Benn (ed.), *Research, Teaching and Learning: Making Connections in the Education of Adults*, Leeds, Standing Conference on University Teaching and Research in the Education of Adults.

Gorard, S., G. Rees, R. Fevre and J. Furlong (1998d). 'Society is not built by education alone: alternative routes to a learning society', *Research in Post-Compulsory Education* 3 (1), 25–37.

Gorard, S., G. Rees and R. Fevre (1999a). 'Two dimensions of time: the changing social context of lifelong learning', *Studies in the Education of Adults* 31 (1), 35–48.

Gorard, S., G. Rees and R. Fevre (1999b). 'Patterns of participation in lifelong learning: do families make a difference?', *British Educational Research Journal* 25 (4), 517–32.

Gorard, S., G. Rees and N. Selwyn (1999c). *Lifetime Learning Targets in Wales: a Research Summary*, Cardiff, National Assembly for Wales.

Gorard, S., R. Fevre, and G. Rees (1999d). 'The apparent decline of informal learning', *Oxford Review of Education* 25 (4), 437–54.

Gorard, S., N. Selwyn and G. Rees (2000a). 'Meeting targets?', *Adults Learning* 11 (8), 18–20.

Gorard, S., N. Selwyn and S. Williams (2000b). 'Could try harder! Problems facing technological solutions to non-participation in adult learning', *British Educational Research Journal* 26 (4), 507–21.

Gorard, S., G. Rees, R. Fevre and T. Welland (2001). 'Lifelong learning trajectories: some voices of those in transit', *International Journal of Lifelong Education* 20 (3), 169–87.

Graham, P. (2000). 'Hypercapitalism: a political economy of informational idealism', *New Media and Society* 2 (2), 131–56.

Green, F. and D. Ashton (1992). *Educational Provision, Educational Attainment and the Needs of Industry*, Report Series no.5, London, National Institute of Economic and Social Research.

Greenhalgh, C. and G. Mavrotas (1994). 'Workforce training in the Thatcher era: market forces and market failures', in R. McNabb and K. Whitfield (eds.), *The Market for Training*, Aldershot, Avebury.

Greenhalgh, C. and M. Stewart (1987). The effects and determinants of training', *Oxford Bulletin of Economics and Statistics* 49 (2), 171–90.

Griffiths, D. (1999). 'The Welsh Office and Welsh autonomy', *Public Administration* 77, 793–807.

Haddon, L. (2000). 'Social exclusion and information and communication technologies', *New Media and Society* 2 (4), 387–406.

Hand, A., J. Gambles and E. Cooper (1994). *Individual Commitment to Learning: Individuals' Decision-Making about Lifetime Learning*, London, Employment Department.

Hanson, J. (1968). *Profile of a Welsh Town*, Swansea, J. I. Hanson.

Harris, M. (2000). 'Virtual learning and the network society', *Information, Communication and Society* 3 (4), 580–96.

Harrison R. (1993). 'Disaffection and access', in J. Calder (ed.), *Disaffection and Diversity: Overcoming Barriers to Adult Learning*, London, Falmer Press.

Hartley, D. (1994). 'Mixed messages in education policy: sign of the times?', *British Journal of Educational Studies* 42 (3), 230–45.

Haskel, J. and C. Martin (1993). 'The causes of skill shortage in Britain', *Oxford Economic Papers*, 45, pp.171–90.

Haywood, T. (1998). 'Global networks and the myth of equality' in B. D. Loader (ed.), *Cyberspace Divide: Equality, Agency and Policy in the Information Society*, London, Routledge.

HEFCW (2001). *E-University: Invitation to Express Interest in Pilots to Develop E-Learning Programmes*, HEFCW circular W01/28HE, Cardiff, Higher Education Funding Council for Wales.

Hesketh, A. (1998). *Graduate Employment and Training in the New Millennium*, Cambridge, Hobsons.

Hillman, J. (1996). *University for Industry: Creating a National Learning Network*, London, IPPR.

Hodkinson, P., A. Sparkes and H. Hodkinson (1996). *Triumph and Tears: Young People, Markets and the Transition from School to Work*, London, David Fulton.

Holden, C. (1999). 'Globalisation, social exclusion and Labour's new work ethic', *Critical Social Policy* 19 (4), 529–38.

Holderness, M. (1993). 'Down and out in the global village', *New Scientist*, 8 May.

Holderness, M. (1998). 'Who are the world's information poor?', in D. Loader (ed.), *Cyberspace Divide: Equality, Agency and Policy in the Information Society*, London, Routledge.

Holmes, D. (1997). *Virtual Politics: Identity and Community in Cyberspace*, London, Sage.

Hopper, E. and M. Osborn (1975). *Adult Students: Education, Selection and Social Control*, London, Francis Pinter.

Hornung, R. (2000). 'E-minister's vision of change', *Western Mail*, Forward Wales 2000 Supplement, p.25.

Hugill, B. and N. Narayan (1995). 'Must try harder . . .', *The Observer*, 5 November, pp.18–19.

Hunter-Carsch, M. (1996). 'The Eyres Monsell family reading groups project', paper presented at British Educational Research Association annual conference, Lancaster.

Husen, T., and T. N. Postlethwaite (1985). *The International Encyclopedia of Education*, Oxford, Pergamon Press.

IFF (1994). *Skill Needs in Britain*, London, Industrial Facts and Forecasting.

Information Infrastructure Task Force (1993). *The National Information Infrastructure: Agenda for Action*, Washington, DC, ITAF, *http://metalab.unc.edu/nii/NII-Executive-Summary.htm*.

Istance, D. and G. Rees (1994). 'Education and training in Wales: problems and paradoxes revisited', *Contemporary Wales* 7, 7–27.

Istance, D. and G. Rees (1995). *Lifelong Learning in Wales: A Programme for Prosperity*, NIACE Cymru policy discussion paper, Leicester, NIACE.

Jarvis, P. (1985). *The Sociology of Adult and Continuing Education*, London, Routledge.

Jarvis, P. (1993). *Adult Education and the State*, London, Routledge.

Johnson R. (1993). 'Really useful knowledge, 1790–1850', in M. Thorpe, R. Edwards and A. Hanson (eds.), *Culture and Processes of Adult Learning*, London, Routledge.

Johnston, C. (1999). 'Callers swamp learning line', *Times Educational Supplement*, 20 August, p.26.

Johnston, C. (2000a). 'College anger at university delays', *Times Educational Supplement*, FE Focus, 22 September, p.37.

Johnston, C. (2000b). 'Where learning is not so direct', *Times Educational Supplement* FE Focus, 23 June, p.I.

Johnston, C. (2000c). 'Ufl has to be "more honest" ', *Times Educational Supplement*, FE Focus, 7 April, p.I.

Johnston, C. (2000d). 'Contract worries delay set-up of Ufl hubs', *Times Educational Supplement*, FE Focus, 29 September, p.35.

Johnston, C. (2000e). 'Legal row hits Ufl launch', *Times Educational Supplement*, FE Focus, 6 October, p.33.

Johnston, C. (2001a). 'Job centre signs up to Internet', *Times Educational Supplement*, 9 March, p.29.

Johnston, C. (2001b). 'Outlining the way forward for Wales', *Times Educational Supplement*, Online Section, 11 May, p.6.

Jones, G. (1990). *Which Nation's Schools?*, Cardiff, University of Wales Press.

Jones, G. (1996). *Wales 2010 Three Years On*, Cardiff, Institute of Welsh Affairs.

Jones, S. G. (1997). *Virtual Culture: Identity and Communication in Cybersociety*, London, Sage.

Jurich, S. (1999). 'Virtual education: trends and potential uses', *TechKnowLogia* 1 (2), 35–8.

Jurich, S. (2000). 'The information revolution and the digital divide: a review of literature', *TechKnowLogia* 2 (1), 42–4.

Kanter, R. M. (1995). *World Class: Thriving Locally in the Global Economy*, New York, Simon & Schuster.

Kearsley, G. (1998). 'Educational technology: a critique', *Educational Technology* 38 (2), 47–51.

Keep, E. (1991). 'Missing presumed skilled: training policy in the UK', in R. Edwards, S. Sieminski and D. Zeldin (eds.), *Adult Learners, Education and Training*, London: Routledge.

Keep, E. (1997). 'There's no such thing as society . . . Some problems with an individual approach to creating a learning society', paper presented to second co-ordinating meeting, ESRC Learning Society Programme, Bristol.

Keep, E. (2000). *Learning Organisations, Lifelong Learning and the Mystery of the Vanishing Employers*, Global Internet Colloquium on Lifelong Learning, Open University.

Kelly, T. (1992). *A History of Adult Education in Great Britain*, Liverpool, Liverpool University Press.

Kennedy, H. (1997). *Learning Works: Widening Participation in Further Education*, Coventry, Further Education Funding Council.

Kenway, J. (1996). 'The information superhighway and post-modernity: the social promise and the social price', *Comparative Education* 32 (2), 217–31.

Kenway, J., C. Bigum, L. Fitzclarence, J. Collier and K. Tregenza (1994). 'New education in new times', *Journal of Education Policy* 9 (4), 317–33.

Kickert, W. J., E. Klijn and L. Koppenjan (1997). *Managing Complex Networks*, London, Sage.

Kitchen, R. (1998). *Cyberspace: The World in the Wires*, Chichester, Wiley.

Knowles, M. (1990). *The Adult Learner: A Neglected Species*, Houston, Gulf.

Labour Party (1995). *Communicating Britain's Future*, London, Labour Party.

Laffin, M., A. Thomas and A. Webb (2000). 'Intergovernmental relations after devolution: the National Assembly for Wales', *Political Quarterly* 71 (2), 223–33.

Langdale, J. (1997). 'International competitiveness in East Asia: broadband telecommunications and interactive multimedia', *Telecommunications Policy* 21 (3), 235–49.

Latzer, M. (1995). 'Japanese information infrastructure initiatives: a politico-economic approach', *Telecommunications Policy* 19 (7), 515–29.

Laurillard, D. (1995). 'The virtual university: value and feasibility', paper presented at the Higher Education for Capability Conference, 'Beyond Competence to Capability and the Learning Society', November, Manchester, UMIST.

Le Grand, J. and W. Bartlett (1993). *Quasi Markets and Social Policy*, London, Macmillan.

Leadbetter, C. (1999). *Living on Thin Air*, Harmondsworth, Penguin.

Lenoir, R. (1974). *Les Exclus: un Français sur dix*, Paris, Seuil.

Levitas, R. (1996). 'The concept of social exclusion and the new Durkheimian hegemony', *Critical Social Policy* 16 (1), 5–20.

Levitas, R. (1998). *The Inclusive Society? Social Exclusion and New Labour*, Basingstoke, Macmillan.

Lewis, R. (1993). *Leaders and Teachers: Adult Education and the Challenge of Labour in South Wales 1906–1940*, Cardiff, University of Wales Press.

LIC (1997). *New Library: The People's Network*, London, Library and Information Commission.

Livingstone, D. (1998). *The Education–Jobs Gap*, Toronto, Garamond Press.

Lloyd, D. (1996). 'Wales, Welsh-L and the Internet', *Planet* 116, 77–80.

Loader, B. D. (1998). *Cyberspace Divide: Equality, Agency and Policy in the Information Society*, London, Routledge.

Lovering, J. (2000). 'Economic strategy in a small country: adapting Wales to global capitalism or vice versa?', *Radical Wales* 2, 10–14.

Lowe, J. (1970). *Adult Education in England and Wales: A Critical Survey*, London, Michael Joseph.

Luke, T. (1997). 'The politics of digital inequality', in C. Toulouse and T. Luke (eds.), *The Politics of Cyberspace*, London, Routledge.

Lundvall, B. (1992). *National Systems of Innovation: Towards a Theory of Innovation and Interactive Learning*, London, Pinter.

Lundvall, B. and B. Johnson (1994). 'The learning economy', *Journal of Industrial Studies* 1 (2), 23–42.

Lyon, D. (1988). *The Information Society: Issues and Illusions*, Cambridge, Polity Press.

Lyon, D. (1996). 'The roots of the information society idea', in N. Heap (ed.), *Information Technology and Society*, London, Sage.

Mackay, H. and A. Powell (1996). 'Wales and its media: production, consumption and regulation', *Contemporary Wales* 9, 8–39.

Mackay, H. and A. Powell (1997) 'Connecting Wales: the Internet and national identity' in B. D. Loader (ed.), *'Cyberspace Divide: Equality, Agency and Policy in the Information Society*, London, Routledge.

McGavin, H. (1999). '£10 million to sell the UFI to industry', *Times Educational Supplement*, FE Focus, 8 October, p.2.

McGavin, H. (2000a). 'Lifelong learning drive is "insulting"', *Times Educational Supplement*, FE Focus, 29 September, p.35.

McGavin, H. (2000b). 'Executives should "sweat over skills"', *Times Educational Supplement*, E Focus, 7 April, p. I.

McGivney, V. (1990). *Education's for Other People: Access to Education for Non-participant Adults*, Leicester, NIACE.

McGivney, V. (1992). *Motivating Unemployed Adults to Undertake Education and Training*, Leicester, NIACE.

McGivney, V. (1993). 'Participation and non-participation: a review of the literature', in R. Edwards, S. Sieminski and D. Zeldin (eds.), *Adult Learners, Education and Training*, London, Routledge.

McKie, J. (1996). 'Is democracy at the heart of IT? Commercial perceptions of technology' *Sociological Research On-Line* 1 (4), *http://www.socresonline.org.uk/socresonline/1/4/1.html*.

McLaughlin, M., S. B. Goldberg, N. Ellison and J. Lucas (1999). 'Measuring Internet audience: patrons of an on-line art museum', in S. Jones (ed.), *Doing Internet Research*, London, Sage.

McLoughlin, C. and R. Oliver (1998). 'Maximising the language and learning link in computer learning environments', *British Journal of Educational Technology* 29 (2), 125–36.

McNabb, R. and K. Whitfield (1994). *The Market for Training*, Aldershot, Avebury.

Maddux, C. D. (1989). 'The harmful effects of excessive optimism in educational computing', *Educational Technology* 29 (4), 23–9.

Maguire, M., S. Maguire and A. Felstead (1993). *Factors Influencing Individual Commitment to Lifetime Learning: A Literature Review*, London, Employment Department.

Main, B. and M. Shelly (1990). 'The effectiveness of the Youth Training Scheme as a manpower policy', *Economica* 57, 495–514.

Malina, A. (1999). 'Third way transitions: building benevolent capitalism for the information society', *Communiciations* 24 (2), 167–87.

Mann, C. and F. Stewart (2000). *Internet Communication and Qualitative Research: A Handbook for Researching Online*, London, Sage.

Marginson, S. (1993). *Education and Public Policy in Australia*, Cambridge, Cambridge University Press.

Marsh, D. (1998). 'The development of the policy network approach', in D. Marsh (ed.), *Comparing Policy Networks*, Buckingham, Open University Press.

Marshall, G., A. Swift and S. Roberts (1997). *Against the Odds? Social Class and Social Justice in Industrial Societies*, Oxford, Oxford University Press.

Martin, C. (1996). 'The debate in France over "Social Exclusion"', *Social Policy and Administration* 30 (4), 382–92.

Martinez, L. (1997). 'Thinking about the information infrastructure', *Telecommunications Policy* 21 (1), 72–3.

Marvin, C. (1988). *When Old Technologies Were New: Thinking about Electronic Communication in the Late Nineteenth Century*, Oxford, Oxford University Press.

Marx, G. (1987). 'Does improved technology mean progress?', *Technology Review* (January), 31–41.

Mason, T. (2000). 'Welsh new media sector expanding at a rapid rate', *The Western Mail*, Dot.Com Wales Supplement, 30 August, p.2.

Masuda, Y. (1981). *The Information Society as Post-industrial Society*, Bethesda, MD, World Futures Society.

Mayes, T. (2000). 'Pedagogy, lifelong learning and ICT', in Scottish Forum on Lifelong Learning, *Role of ICT in Supporting Lifelong Learning*, Centre for Research in Lifelong Learning, University of Stirling.

Miles, I. (1996). 'The information society: competing perspectives on the social and economic implications of information and communications technologies', in W. Dutton (ed.), *Information and Communications Technologies: Visions and Realities*, Oxford, Oxford University Press.

Ministry of Education (1998). *Learning to Think, Thinking to Learn: Towards Thinking Schools, Learning Nations*, Malaysia, Ministry of Education,

Mitra, A. and E. Cohen (1999). 'Analysing the web: directions and challenges', in S. Jones (ed.), *Doing Internet Research*, London, Sage.

Moore, N. (1998). 'Confucius or capitalism? Policies for an information society', in B. D. Loader (ed.), *Cyberspace Divide: Equality, Agency and Policy in the Information Society*, London, Routledge.

Morgan, K. and G. Mungham (2000). *Redesigning Democracy*, Bridgend, Seren.

Morgan, R. (2001). 'We led the First Industrial Revolution and we can do it again', *OneWales*, September.

MORI (1999). *The British and Technology*, Basingstoke, Motorola.

Morrison, M., R. G. Burgess and S. Band (1998). *Evaluating Aspects of the University for Industry in the North East*, Sheffield, DfEE.

Murphy, A. (1997). *The Celtic Tiger: The Great Misnomer*, Dublin, MNI Stockbrokers.

Nash, I. (1996a). 'Labour launches post-16 cash study', *Times Educational Supplement*, 26 April.

Nash, I. (1996b). 'Thousands face the music on skill levels', *Times Educational Supplement*, 16 February, p.28.

Nash, I. (2000). 'Lecturers slow to exploit Internet', *Times Educational Supplement*, FE Focus, 31 March, p.III.

National Assembly for Wales (1999). *Official Record/Y Cofnod Swyddogol: 17th November 1999/17 Tachwedd 1999*, Cardiff, National Assembly of Wales.

National Assembly for Wales (2000). *www.betterwales.com*, Cardiff, National Assembly of Wales.

National Assembly for Wales (2001a). *Cymru Arlein – Online for a Better Wales*, Cardiff, National Assembly of Wales.

National Assembly for Wales (2001b). *The Learning Country: A Comprehensive Education and Lifelong Learning Programme to 2010 in Wales*, Cardiff, National Assembly for Wales.

National Skills Agenda (2001). *Opportunity and Skills in the Knowledge-Driven Economy*, Nottingham, DfEE Publications.

National Statistics (2000). *Internet Access: First Quarter 2000*, London, National Statistics.

National Statistics (2001). *Internet Access: Last Quarter 2000*, London, National Statistics.

Naylor, C. (1998). 'Another revolution, this time for real', *New Statesman*, 13 November, pp.xxii–xxiii.

Neill, M. (1995). 'Computers, thinking, and schools in the "new world economic order"', in J. Brook and I. Boal (eds.), *Resisting the Virtual Life: The Culture and Politics of Information*, San Francisco, City Lights.

New Opportunities Fund (2000a). *Lifelong Learning: Community Access to Lifelong Learning*, London, New Opportunities Fund.

New Opportunities Fund (2000b). *Lifelong Learning: Wales*, London, New Opportunities Fund.

Newman, R. and F. Johnson (1999). 'Sites for power and knowledge? Towards a critique of the virtual university', *British Journal of Sociology of Education* 20 (1), 79–88.

NIACE (1994). *Widening Participation: Routes to a Learning Society*, Leicester, NIACE Policy Discussion Paper.

NIACE (2000). *The Learning Divide Revisited*, Leicester, NIACE.

Nora, S. and A. Minc (1980). *The Computerisation of Society*, Cambridge, MA, MIT Press.

OECD (1996). *Education and Training: Learning and Work in a Society in Flux*, Paris, OECD.

Oftel (2000). *Consumers' Use of Digital Television: Results of Oftel Residential Survey*, London, Oftel.

OHMCI (1993). *Achievement and Under-achievement in Secondary Schools in Wales 1991–92*, Occasional Paper 1, Cardiff, Office of Her Majesty's Chief Inspector for Schools.

Oppenheim, A. N. (1992). *Questionnaire Design, Interviewing and Attitude Measurement*, London, Continuum.

Oppenheim, C. (1998). *An Inclusive Society: Strategies for Tackling Poverty*, London, Institute for Public Policy Research.

Osmond, J. (1999). *Wales Information Society*, Cardiff, Wales Information Society/Welsh Development Agency.

Park, A. (1994). *Individual Commitment to Lifelong Learning: Individuals, Attitudes. Report on the Quantitative Survey*, London Employment Department.

Parker, E. (2000). 'Closing the digital divide in rural America', *Telecommunications Policy* 24, 281–90.

Parkinson, M. (1998). *Combating Social Exclusion: Lessons from Area-Based Programmes in Europe*, York, Joseph Rowntree Foundation.

Parlette, M. and D. Hamilton (1972). *Evaluation as Illumination: A New Approach to the Study of Innovative Programs*, Occasional Paper 9, Centre for Research in the Educational Sciences, University of Edinburgh.

Parsons, W. (2000). 'From Beulah Land to Cyber Cymru', *Contemporary Wales* 13, 1–26.

Passey, D. (2000). 'ICT and social inclusion: what are the real issues?', *College Research* 3 (2), 37–8.

Patrick, A. S. and A. Black (1997). 'Who is going online? Results from the National Capital FreeNet', *Internet Research: Electronic Networking and Policy* 7 (4), 305–19.

Pettigrew A., C. Hendry and P. Sparrow (1989). *Training in Britain. A Study of Funding, Activity and Attitudes: Employers' Perspectives on Human Resources*, London: HMSO.

Phipps, L. (2000). 'New communications technologies: a conduit for social inclusion', *Information, Communication and Society* 3 (1), 39–68.

Piatt, W. (2001). 'Bribe students to study', *New Statesman*, 2 April, p.34.

Postman, N. (1993). *Technopoly: The Surrender of Culture to Technology*, New York, Vintage Books.

Prais, S. (1993). *Economic Performance and Education: The Nature of Britain's Deficiencies*, National Institute of Economic and Social Research, Discussion Paper no. 52.

Preece, J. (2000). 'Challenging the discourses of inclusion and exclusion with off limits curricula', in R. Edwards, J. Clarke and N. Miller (eds.), *Supporting Lifelong Learning: Working Papers*, Milton Keynes, Open University.

Pugh, A. (2000). 'Wiring Wales', *The Parliamentary Monitor – IT Briefing*, December, pp.20–2.

Pyke, N. (1996). 'Dearing champions the young no-hopers', *Times Educational Supplement*, 29 March, p.1.

Qvortrup, L. (1984). *The Social Significance of Telematics: An Essay on the Information Society*, tr. Philip Edmonds, Philadelphia, John Benjamins.

Rai, L. and K. Lal (2000). 'Indicators of the information revolution', *Technology in Society* 22, 221–35.

Rees, G. (1997). 'Making a learning society: education and work in industrial south Wales', *Welsh Journal of Education* 6, 2, pp.4–16.

Rees, G., R. Fevre, J. Furlong and S. Gorard (1997). 'History, place and the learning society: towards a sociology of lifetime learning', *Journal of Education Policy* 12 (6), 485–97.

Rees, G., S. Gorard and R. Fevre (1999). 'Industrial south Wales: learning society past, present or future?', *Contemporary Wales* 12, 18–36.

Rees, G., S. Gorard, R. Fevre and J. Furlong (2000). 'Participating in the learning society: history, place and biography', in F. Coffield (ed.), *Differing Visions of a Learning Society: Research Findings*, Vol. II, Bristol, Policy Press.

Rees, G. and T. Rees (1980). 'Educational inequality in Wales: some problems and paradoxes', in G. Rees and T. Rees (eds.), *Poverty and Social Inequality in Wales*, London, Croom Helm.

Rees, G., H. Williamson and V. Winckler (1989). 'The "new vocationalism": further education and local labour markets', *Journal of Education Policy* 4 (3), 227–44.

Reich, R. (1991). *The Work of Nations*, London, Simon & Schuster.

Resnick, D. (1997). 'Politics on the Internet: the normalisation of cyberspace', in C. Toulouse and T. Luke (eds.), *The Politics of Cyberspace*, London, Routledge.

Reynolds, D. (1990). 'The great Welsh education debate', *History of Education* 19 (3), 251.

Reynolds, D. (1995). 'Creating an educational system for Wales', *The Welsh Journal of Education* 4 (2), 4–21.

Rheingold, H. (1993). *The Virtual Community: Homesteading on the Electronic Frontier*, London, Minerva.

Rheingold, H. (1994). *The Virtual Community: Finding Connection in a Computerised World*, London, Secker & Warburg.

Roberts, C. (1983). 'The sociology of education and Wales', in G. Williams (ed.), *Crisis of Economy and Ideology: Essays on Welsh Society 1840–1980*, London, BSA Sociology of Wales Study Group.

Roberts, K., G. Parsell and M. Connolly (1991). 'Young people's transitions in the labour market', in M. Cross and G. Payne (eds.), *Work and the Enterprise Culture*, London, Falmer Press.

Robertson, D. (1998). 'The University for Industry: a flagship for demand-led training or another doomed supply-side intervention?', *Journal of Education and Work* 11 (1), 5–22.

Robins, K. and F. Webster (1989). *The Technical Fix: Education, Computers and Industry*, Basingstoke, Macmillan.

Robins, K. and F. Webster (1999). *Times of the Technoculture: From the Information Society to the Virtual Life*, London, Routledge.

Roll, R. (1995). Foreword, in J. Tiffin and L. Rajasingham (eds.), *In Search of the Virtual Class: Education in an Information Society*, London, Routledge.

Roszak, T. (1995). *The Cult of Information: A Neo-Luddite Treatise on High-Tech, Artificial Intelligence and the True Art of Thinking*, second edition, Berkeley, University of California Press.

Rothwell, R. and M. Dodgson (1993). 'Technology-based SMEs: their role in industrial and economic change', *International Journal of Technology Management*, Special Issue on Small Firms and Innovation, 8–22.

Rothwell, R. and M. Dodgson (1994). *Handbook of Industrial Innovation*, Cheltenham, Edward Elgar.

Rowe-Beddoe, D. (1999). Foreword, in J. Osmond, *Wales Information Society*, Cardiff, Wales Information Society/Welsh Development Agency.

Sainsbury, Lord (1999). 'Modernising learning: the role of the University for Industry', annual MacLaren Memorial Lecture, Aston University, Birmingham.

Sawhney, H. (1993). 'Circumventing the center: the realities of creating a telecommunications infrastructure in the USA', *Telecommunications Policy* 17 (7), 504–16.

Schiller, H. I. (1986). 'The erosion of national sovereignty by the world business system', in M. Traber (ed.), *The Myth of the Information Revolution*, London, Sage.

Schofield, J. W. (1995). *Computers and Classroom Culture*, Cambridge, Cambridge University Press.

Scottish Forum on Lifelong Learning (2000). *Role of Information and Communication Technology in Supporting Lifelong Learning*, Glasgow, Centre for Research in Lifelong Learning.

Seels, B. (1997). 'Taxonomic issues and the development of theory in instructional technology', *Educational Technology* 37 (1), 12–21.

Selwyn, N. (1998). 'A grid for learning or a grid for earning? The significance of the Learning Grid Initiative in UK education', *Journal of Education Policy* 13 (3), 423–31.

Selwyn, N. (1999a). 'Schooling the information society? The place of the information superhighway in education', *Information, Communication and Society* 2 (2), 156–73.

Selwyn, N. (1999b). 'Why the computer is not dominating schools: a failure of policy or a failure of practice?', *Cambridge Journal of Education* 29 (1), 77–91.

Selwyn, N. (1999c). 'A grid over troubled waters? The role of National Grid for Learning in UK schooling', *FORUM* 41 (3), 98–100.

Selwyn, N. (1999d). 'Educational superhighways – in the public or private interest?', *Internet Research: Electronic Networking Applications and Policy* 9 (3), 225–31.

Selwyn, N. (1999e). 'Virtual concerns: restrictions of the Internet as a learning environment', *British Journal of Educational Technology* 30 (1), 69–71.

Selwyn, N. (2000). 'The National Grid for Learning Initiative: connecting the learning society?', *School Leadership and Management* 20 (4), 407–14.

Selwyn, N. and P. Brown (2000). 'Education, nation states and the globalisation of information networks', *Journal of Education Policy* 15 (6), 661–82.

Selwyn, N. and J. Fitz (2001). 'The National Grid for Learning: a case study of New Labour education policy making', *Journal of Education Policy* 16 (2), 127–47.

Selwyn, N. and J. Fitz (2002). 'The politics of connectivity: the role of big business in UK education technology policy', *Policy Studies Journal* (forthcoming).

Selwyn, N. and S. Gorard (1999). 'Can technology really widen participation in lifelong learning?', *Adults Learning* 10 (6), 27–9.

Selwyn, N. and K. Robson (1998). 'Using email as a research tool', *Social Research Update* 21, 1–4.

Shackleton, J. and S. Walsh (1997). 'What determines who obtains National Vocational Qualifications?', *Education Economics* 5 (1), 41–53.

Simon, B. (1990). 'The struggle for hegemony 1920–1926', in B. Simon (ed.), *The Search for Enlightenment: The Working Class and Adult Education in the Twentieth Century*, London, Lawrence & Wishart.

Singh, P (1993). 'Institutional discourse and practice: a case study of the social construction of technological competence in the primary classroom', *British Journal of Sociology of Education* 14 (1), 39–58.

Skills Task Force (2000). *Tackling the Adult Skills Gap: Upskilling Adults and the Role of Workplace Learning*, Sudbury, DfEE.

Slack, J. D. (1984). 'The information revolution as ideology', *Media, Culture and Society* 6, 247–56.

Smith, C. (1999). 'New Labour, new libraries', *Times Educational Supplement*, 23 July, p.13.

Smithers, A. and P. Robinson (1991). *Beyond Compulsory Schooling: A Numerical Picture*, London, Council for Industry and Higher Education.

Smithers, R. (2000) 'The future of education', *Guardian Education*, 27 June.

Social Exclusion Unit (2000). *What Is Social Exclusion?* http://www.cabinet-office.gov.uk/seu/.

South Wales Echo (2000). 'Wales needs to get surfing', *South Wales Echo Quarterly Business Review*, 25 October, pp.11–14.

Spielhofer, T. (1996). 'Attitudes of local employers towards young people and their previous education', paper presented at British Educational Research Association annual conference, Lancaster.

Stasz, C. (1997). 'Do employers need the skills they want? Evidence from technical work', *Journal of Education and Work* 10 (3), 205–23.

Stern, S. R. (1999). 'Adolescent girls' expression on web home pages', *Convergence* 5 (4), 22–41.

Strain, M. (1998). Towards an economy of lifelong learning: reconceptualising relations between learning and life', *British Journal of Educational Studies* 46 (3), 264–77.

Streeck, W. (1992). *Social, Institutional and Economic Performance*, London, Sage.

Sussman, G. (1997). *Communication, Technology and Politics in the Information Age*, Thousand Oaks, CA, Sage.

Sutherland, P. (1997). 'The implications of research on approaches to learning for the teaching of adults', in P. Sutherland (ed.), *Adult Learning: A Reader*, London, Kogan Page.

Sweeting, C. and A. Rawstron (2001). 'Is Wales net-working?', *Big Issue Cymru*, 12 February, pp.20–2.

Tan, H. and C. Peterson (1992). 'Postschool training of British and American youth', in D. Finegold, L. McFarland and W. Richardson (1992) *Something Borrowed, Something Blue? A Study of the Thatcher Government's Appropriation of American Education and Training Policy, Part 1*, Wallingford, Triangle.

Tan, Z. (1995). 'China's information superhighway: what is it and who controls it?', *Telecommunications Policy* 19 (9), 721–31.

Taylor, J. (2000). *Towards the New Economy: The Scandinavian Experience and Wales*, Caerphilly, South East Wales Training and Enterprise Council.

Taylor, S. and L. Spencer (1994). *Individual Commitment to Lifelong Learning: Individuals' Attitudes. Report on the Qualitative Phase*, London Employment Department.

Teles, S. (1998). 'A blend of help and hassle', *New Statesman*, 6 March, pp.32–3.

Teo, T. and V. Lim (1998). 'Leveraging information technology to achieve the IT2000 vision: the case study of an intelligent island', *Behaviour and Information Technology* 17 (2), 113–23.

TES (1999). 'UfI pilot does not meet need', *Times Educational Supplement*, 26 February, p.29.

TES (2000). 'Learndirect accused of failing users', *Times Educational Supplement*, FE Focus, 24 November, p.36.

Tester, N. (2000). 'Storm warning', *Guardian Education*, 27 June, p.48.

Thimbelby, H. (1999). 'Smart to be simple', *Times Higher Education Supplement*, 12 February, p.15.

Thomas, R. S. (1972). *H'm*, Basingstoke, Macmillan.

Thompson, P. (1998). 'Strangers in a strange land', *Renewal* 6 (2), 1–5.

Thorpe, M. (2000). 'New technology and lifelong learning', in R. Edwards, J. Clarke and N. Millar (eds.), *Supporting Lifelong Learning: Working Papers*, Buckingham, Open University Press.

Thring, A. (1998). 'Training is for dogs', *Education Today* 48 (3), 54–8.

Tiffin, J and L. Rajasingham (1995). *In Search of the Virtual Class: Education in an Information Society*, London, Routledge.

Tight, M. (1996). *Key Concepts in Adult Education and Training*, London, Routledge.

Tight, M. (1998a). 'Education, education, education! The vision of lifelong learning in the Kennedy, Dearing and Fryer reports', *Oxford Review of Education* 24 (4), 473–86.

Tight, M. (1998b). 'Lifelong learning: opportunity or compulsion?', *British Journal of Educational Studies* 46 (3), 251–63.

Titmus C. (1994). 'The scope and characteristics of educational provision for adults', in J. Calder (ed.), *Disaffection and Diversity: Overcoming Barriers to Adult Learning*, London, Falmer.

Toffler, A. (1980). *The Third Wave*, London, Pan.

Toulouse, C. (1997). Introduction, in C. Toulouse and T. Luke (eds.), *The Politics of Cyberspace*, London, Routledge.

Touraine, A. (1969). *La Société post-industrielle. Naissance d'une société*, Paris, Denoël.

Trainingzone (2001). *Libraries to Build Stronger Links with University for Industry*, *www.trainingzone.co.uk/cgi-bin/item.cgi*, accessed 10 March.

Tuckett, A. (1997). 'An election shopping list for lifelong learning', *Times Educational Supplement*, 14 March, p.32.

Tuckett, A. (1999). 'Spring may be a difficult step', *Times Educational Supplement*, 2 April, p.24.

Tuckett, A. and N. Sargant (1999). *Marking Time: The NIACE Survey on Adult Participation in Learning 1999*, Leicester, NIACE.

US Department of Commerce (1998). *Falling Through the Net II: New Data on the Digital Divide*, Washington, DC, US Department of Commerce.

US Secretariat on Electronic Commerce (1998). *The Emerging Digital Economy*, Washington, DC, US Department of Commerce.

USA Today (2000). 'Digital divide closes – but schools aren't ready', *USA Today*, 26 April, p.16A.

Varanaya, G. (1995). 'Time we spoke their language', *Times Education Supplement*, 29 December, p.9.

Volti, R. (1992). *Society and Technological Change*, New York, St Martin's Press.

V-Wales (2001). *V-Wales Web-site http ://www.red4.co.uk/*.

Wales Digital College (1998). *The University for Industry and Wales: A Partnership Challenge*, Cardiff, Wales Digital College.

Wales Information Society (1998a). *Wales Information Society: Options Paper*, Cardiff, Welsh Development Agency.

Wales Information Society (1998b). *Wales Information Society: Strategy and Action Plans*, Cardiff, Welsh Development Agency.

Wales Information Society (1999). *Wales Information Society*, Cardiff, Welsh Development Agency.

Wales, C., A. Nadi and R. Stazer (1993). 'Emphasizing critical thinking and problem-solving', in L. Curry, J. Wergin and Associates (eds.), *Educating Professionals*, San Francisco, Jossey-Bass.

Walker, A. (1997), Introduction, in A. Walker and C. Walker (eds.), *Britain Divided: The Growth of Social Exclusion in the 1980s and 1990s*, London, Child Poverty Action Group.

Watt, N. (1999). 'Ministers drop £1.5 billion benefit swipe cards', *The Guardian*, 25 May, p.14.

Webster, F. (1995). *Theories of the Information Society*, London, Routledge.

Webster, F. (2000). 'Information, capitalism and uncertainity', *Information, Communication and Society* 3 (1), 69–90.

Weinberg, A. M. (1966). 'Can technology replace social engineering?', reprinted in G. E. Hawisher and C. L. Selfe (eds.), *Literacy, Technology and Society*, New York, Prentice Hall.

Weinholtz, D., B. Kacer and T. Rocklin (1995). 'Pearls, pith and provocation: salvaging quantitative research with qualitative data', *Qualitative Health Research* 5, 388–97.

Weizenbaum, J. (1972a). 'On the impact of the computer on society: how does one insult a machine?', *Science* 176 (12), 609–14.

Weizenbaum, J. (1972b). 'Computers and society', *Science*, 10 November, pp.562–3.

Welsh Development Agency (1995*). Wales: The Winning Location for Information Technology*, Cardiff, WDA.

Welsh Development Agency (1996). *Wales Information Society: A Partnership Approach to Developing a Regional Strategy*, Cardiff, WDA.

Welsh Language Board (2001). Welsh Language Board Web-site *http://www.bwrdd-yr-iaith.org.uk/*.

Welsh Office (1995a). *Arolwg Cymdeithasol Cymru 1992: Adroddiad ar y Gymraeg*, Cardiff, Welsh Office.

Welsh Office (1995b). *Further and Higher Education and Training Statistics in Wales, No. 3, 1995,* Cardiff, Welsh Office.

Welsh Office (1995c). *1994/95 Welsh Training and Education Survey,* Cardiff, Welsh Office.

Welsh Office (1996). *Digest of Welsh Local Area Statistics 1996,* Cardiff, HMSO.

Welsh Office (1998). *Learning Is for Everyone,* London, HMSO.

Whittaker, M. (2000). 'Lifeline for the lost learners', *Times Educational Supplement,* FE Focus, 7 July, p. IV.

Williams, K. (1996). 'All wired up and nowhere to go', *Planet* 115, 26–9.

Williams, K. (1997). 'Cardiff's silly burghers', *Planet* 121, 7–10.

Williams, R. and D. Edge (1996). 'The social shaping of technology', in W. Dutton (ed.), *Information and Communication Technologies: Visions and Realities,* Oxford, Oxford University Press.

Williamson, J. B., D. A. Karp and J. R. Dalphin (1977). *The Research Craft: An Introduction to Social Science Methods,* Toronto, Little, Brown.

Wills, M. (1999). 'Bridging the digital divide', *Adults Learning,* December, pp.10–11.

Wilson, B. G. (1997). 'Thoughts on theory in educational technology', *Educational Technology* 37 (1), 12–21.

Winner, L. (1980). 'Do artifacts have politics?', *Daedalus* 109, 121–36.

Winner, L. (1994). 'Three paradoxes of the information age', in G. Bender and T. Druckrey (eds.), *Culture on the Brink: Ideologies of Technology,* Seattle, Bay Press.

Wise, J. M. (1997). *Exploring Technology and Social Space,* Thousand Oaks, CA, Sage.

Withey, R. (1998). 'The web and the death of cultural imperialism', *ASLIB Proceedings* 50 (8), 203–7.

Wolf, A. (1998). 'The training illusion', *Prospect,* 33, 12–13.

Woolgar, S. (1996). 'Technologies as Cultural Artefacts' in W. H. Dutton (ed.), *Information and Communication Technologies,* Oxford, Oxford University Press.

World Bank Institute (2000). 'Measuring up access', *TechKnowLogia,* March, 12–14.

Wresch, W. (1996). *Disconnected: Haves and Have-Nots in the Information Age,* New Brunswick, Rutgers University Press.

Wright, A. (1999). 'A new way of learning?', *Adults Learning,* December, pp.15–17.

Wyn, E. (2001). 'Taking the e-road to knowledge' *The Western Mail,* 13 July, p.E2.

Yeomans D. (1996). *Constructing Vocational Education: From TVEI to GNVQ,* School of Education, University of Leeds.

Zuboff, S. (1988). *In the Age of the Smart Machine,* New York, Basic Books.

Index